Mercurial: The Definitive Guide

Mercurial: The Definitive Guide

Bryan O'Sullivan

O'REILLY®

Beijing · Cambridge · Farnham · Köln · Sebastopol · Taipei · Tokyo

Mercurial: The Definitive Guide
by Bryan O'Sullivan

Copyright © 2009 Bryan O'Sullivan. All rights reserved.
Printed in the United States of America.

Published by O'Reilly Media, Inc., 1005 Gravenstein Highway North, Sebastopol, CA 95472.

O'Reilly books may be purchased for educational, business, or sales promotional use. Online editions are also available for most titles (*http://my.safaribooksonline.com*). For more information, contact our corporate/institutional sales department: (800) 998-9938 or *corporate@oreilly.com*.

Editor: Mike Loukides	**Indexer:** Seth Maislin
Production Editor: Adam Witwer	**Cover Designer:** Karen Montgomery
Proofreader: Emily Quill	**Interior Designer:** David Futato
	Illustrator: Robert Romano

Printing History:

June 2009:	First Edition.

ISBN: 978-0-596-80067-3

[M]

1244820374

Table of Contents

Preface

Technical Storytelling

A few years ago, when I wanted to explain why I believed that distributed revision control was important, the field was so new that there was almost no published literature to refer people to.

Although at that time I was working on the internals of Mercurial itself, I switched to writing this book because that seemed like the most effective way to help the software to reach a wide audience, along with the idea that revision control ought to be distributed in nature. I am publishing this online under a liberal license for the same reason: to get the word out.

There's a familiar rhythm to a good software book that closely resembles telling a story: What is this thing? Why does it matter? How will it help me? How do I use it? In this book, I try to answer those questions for distributed revision control in general, and for Mercurial in particular.

Thank You for Supporting Mercurial

By purchasing a copy of this book, you are supporting the continued development and freedom of Mercurial in particular, and of open source and free software in general. O'Reilly Media and I are donating my royalties on the sales of this book to the Software Freedom Conservancy (*http://www.softwarefreedom.org/*), which provides clerical and legal support to Mercurial and a number of other prominent and worthy open source software projects.

Conventions Used in This Book

The following typographical conventions are used in this book:

Italic
> Indicates new terms, URLs, email addresses, filenames, and file extensions.

Constant width

> Used for program listings, as well as within paragraphs to refer to program elements such as variable or function names, databases, commands, data types, environment variables, statements, and keywords.

Constant width bold

> Shows commands or other text that should be typed literally by the user.

Constant width italic

> Shows text that should be replaced with user-supplied values or by values determined by context.

 This icon signifies a tip, suggestion, or general note.

 This icon indicates a warning or caution.

Using Code Examples

This book is here to help you get your job done. In general, you may use the code in this book in your programs and documentation. You do not need to contact us for permission unless you're reproducing a significant portion of the code. For example, writing a program that uses several chunks of code from this book does not require permission. Selling or distributing a CD-ROM of examples from O'Reilly books does require permission. Answering a question by citing this book and quoting example code does not require permission. Incorporating a significant amount of example code from this book into your product's documentation does require permission.

We appreciate, but do not require, attribution. An attribution usually includes the title, author, publisher, and ISBN. For example: "*Mercurial: The Definitive Guide* by Bryan O'Sullivan. Copyright 2009 Bryan O'Sullivan, 978-0-596-80067-3."

If you feel your use of code examples falls outside fair use or the permission given above, feel free to contact us at *permissions@oreilly.com*.

Safari® Books Online

Safari When you see a Safari® Books Online icon on the cover of your favorite technology book, that means the book is available online through the O'Reilly Network Safari Bookshelf.

Safari offers a solution that's better than e-books. It's a virtual library that lets you easily search thousands of top tech books, cut and paste code samples, download chapters, and find quick answers when you need the most accurate, current information. Try it for free at *http://my.safaribooksonline.com*.

How to Contact Us

Please address comments and questions concerning this book to the publisher:

O'Reilly Media, Inc.
1005 Gravenstein Highway North
Sebastopol, CA 95472
800-998-9938 (in the United States or Canada)
707-829-0515 (international or local)
707 829-0104 (fax)

We have a web page for this book, where we list errata, examples, and any additional information. You can access this page at:

http://oreilly.com/catalog/9780596800673

To comment or ask technical questions about this book, send email to:

bookquestions@oreilly.com

For more information about our books, conferences, Resource Centers, and the O'Reilly Network, see our website at:

http://oreilly.com

This Book Is Free

The complete source code for this book is published as a Mercurial repository, at *http://hg.serpentine.com/mercurial/book*.

Acknowledgments

This book would not exist were it not for the efforts of Matt Mackall, the author and project lead of Mercurial. He is ably assisted by hundreds of volunteer contributors across the world.

My children, Cian and Ruairi, always stood ready to help me unwind with wonderful, madcap little-boy games. I'd also like to thank my ex-wife, Shannon, for her support.

My colleagues and friends provided help and support in innumerable ways. This list of people is necessarily very incomplete: Stephen Hahn, Karyn Ritter, Bonnie Corwin, James Vasile, Matt Norwood, Eben Moglen, Bradley Kuhn, Robert Walsh, Jeremy Fitzhardinge, Rachel Chalmers.

I developed this book in the open, posting drafts of chapters to the book website as I completed them. Readers then submitted feedback using a web application that I developed. By the time I finished writing the book, more than 100 people had submitted comments, an amazing number considering that the comment system was live for only about two months toward the end of the writing process.

I would particularly like to recognize the following people, who between them contributed over a third of the total number of comments. I would like to thank them for their care and effort in providing so much detailed feedback: Martin Geisler, Damien Cassou, Alexey Bakhirkin, Till Plewe, Dan Himes, Paul Sargent, Gokberk Hamurcu, Matthijs van der Vleuten, Michael Chermside, John Mulligan, Jordi Fita, Jon Parise.

I also want to acknowledge the help of the many people who caught errors and provided helpful suggestions throughout the book: Jeremy W. Sherman, Brian Mearns, Vincent Furia, Iwan Luijks, Billy Edwards, Andreas Sliwka, Paweł Sołyga, Eric Hanchrow, Steve Nicolai, Michał Masłowski, Kevin Fitch, Johan Holmberg, Hal Wine, Volker Simonis, Thomas P Jakobsen, Ted Stresen-Reuter, Stephen Rasku, Raphael Das Gupta, Ned Batchelder, Lou Keeble, Li Linxiao, Kao Cardoso Félix, Joseph Wecker, Jon Prescot, Jon Maken, John Yeary, Jason Harris, Geoffrey Zheng, Fredrik Jonson, Ed Davies, David Zumbrunnen, David Mercer, David Cabana, Ben Karel, Alan Franzoni, Yousry Abdallah, Whitney Young, Vinay Sajip, Tom Towle, Tim Ottinger, Thomas Schraitle, Tero Saarni, Ted Mielczarek, Svetoslav Agafonkin, Shaun Rowland, Rocco Rutte, Polo-Francois Poli, Philip Jenvey, Petr Tesałék, Peter R. Annema, Paul Bonser, Olivier Scherler, Olivier Fournier, Nick Parker, Nick Fabry, Nicholas Guarracino, Mike Driscoll, Mike Coleman, Mietek Bák, Michael Maloney, László Nagy, Kent Johnson, Julio Nobrega, Jord Fita, Jonathan March, Jonas Nockert, Jim Tittsler, Jeduan Cornejo Legorreta, Jan Larres, James Murphy, Henri Wiechers, Hagen Möbius, Gábor Farkas, Fabien Engels, Evert Rol, Evan Willms, Eduardo Felipe Castegnaro, Dennis Decker Jensen, Deniz Dogan, David Smith, Daed Lee, Christine Slotty, Charles Merriam, Guillaume Catto, Brian Dorsey, Bob Nystrom, Benoit Boissinot, Avi Rosenschein, Andrew Watts, Andrew Donkin, Alexey Rodriguez, Ahmed Chaudhary.

## CHAPTER 1

A Brief History of Revision Control

Why Revision Control? Why Mercurial?

Revision control is the process of managing multiple versions of a piece of information. In its simplest form, this is something that many people do by hand: every time you modify a file, save it under a new name that contains a number, each one higher than the number of the preceding version.

Manually managing multiple versions of even a single file is an error-prone task, though, so software tools to help automate this process have long been available. The earliest automated revision control tools were intended to help a single user to manage revisions of a single file. Over the past few decades, the scope of revision control tools has expanded greatly; they now manage multiple files, and help multiple people to work together. The best modern revision control tools have no problem coping with thousands of people working together on projects that consist of hundreds of thousands of files.

The arrival of distributed revision control is relatively recent, and so far this new field has grown due to people's willingness to explore ill-charted territory.

I am writing a book about distributed revision control because I believe that it is an important subject that deserves a field guide. I chose to write about Mercurial because it is the easiest tool to learn the terrain with, and yet it scales to the demands of real, challenging environments where many other revision control tools buckle.

Why Use Revision Control?

There are a number of reasons why you or your team might want to use an automated revision control tool for a project:

- It will track the history and evolution of your project, so you don't have to. For every change, you'll have a log of *who* made it; *why* they made it; *when* they made it; and *what* the change was.

- When you're working with other people, revision control software makes it easier for you to collaborate. For example, when people more or less simultaneously make potentially incompatible changes, the software will help you to identify and resolve those conflicts.

- It can help you to recover from mistakes. If you make a change that later turns out to be in error, you can revert to an earlier version of one or more files. In fact, a *really* good revision control tool will even help you to efficiently figure out exactly when a problem was introduced (see "Finding the Source of a Bug" on page 137 for details).

- It will help you to work simultaneously on, and manage the drift between, multiple versions of your project.

Most of these reasons are equally valid—at least in theory—whether you're working on a project by yourself, or with a hundred other people.

A key question about the practicality of revision control at these two different scales ("lone hacker" and "huge team") is how its *benefits* compare to its *costs*. A revision control tool that's difficult to understand or use is going to impose a high cost.

A 500 person project is likely to collapse under its own weight almost immediately without a revision control tool and process. In this case, the cost of using revision control might hardly seem worth considering, since *without* it, failure is almost guaranteed.

On the other hand, a one-person "quick hack" might seem like a poor place to use a revision control tool, because surely the cost of using one must be close to the overall cost of the project. Right?

Mercurial uniquely supports *both* of these scales of development. You can learn the basics in just a few minutes, and due to its low overhead, you can apply revision control to the smallest of projects with ease. Its simplicity means you won't have a lot of abstruse concepts or command sequences competing for mental space with whatever you're *really* trying to do. At the same time, Mercurial's high performance and peer-to-peer nature let you scale painlessly to handle large projects.

No revision control tool can rescue a poorly run project, but a good choice of tools can make a huge difference to the fluidity with which you can work on a project.

The Many Names of Revision Control

Revision control is a diverse field, so much so that it is referred to by many names and acronyms. Here are a few of the more common variations you'll encounter:

- Revision control system (RCS)
- Software configuration management (SCM), or configuration management
- Source code management

- Source code control, or source control
- Version control system (VCS)

Some people claim that these terms actually have different meanings, but in practice they overlap so much that there's no agreed-upon or even useful way to tease them apart.

This Book Is a Work in Progress

I am releasing this book while I am still writing it (*http://hgbook.red-bean.com/*), in the hope that it will prove useful to others. I am writing under an open license in the hope that you, my readers, will contribute feedback and perhaps content of your own.

About the Examples in This Book

This book takes an unusual approach to code samples. Every example is "live"—each one is actually the result of a shell script that executes the Mercurial commands you see. Every time an image of the book is built from its sources, all the example scripts are automatically run, and their current results compared against their expected results.

The advantage of this approach is that the examples are always accurate; they describe *exactly* the behavior of the version of Mercurial that's mentioned at the front of the book. If I update the version of Mercurial that I'm documenting, and the output of some command changes, the build fails.

There is a small disadvantage to this approach, which is that the dates and times you'll see in examples tend to be "squashed" together in a way that they wouldn't be if the same commands were being typed by a human. Where a human can issue no more than one command every few seconds, with any resulting timestamps correspondingly spread out, my automated example scripts run many commands in one second.

As an instance of this, several consecutive commits in an example can show up as having occurred during the same second. You can see this occur in the `bisect` example in "Finding the Source of a Bug" on page 137, for instance.

So when you're reading examples, don't place too much weight on the dates or times you see in the output of commands. But *do* be confident that the behavior you're seeing is consistent and reproducible.

Trends in the Field

There has been an unmistakable trend in the development and use of revision control tools over the past four decades, as people have become familiar with the capabilities of their tools and constrained by their limitations.

The first generation began by managing single files on individual computers. Although these tools represented a huge advance over ad-hoc manual revision control, their locking model and reliance on a single computer limited them to small, tightly knit teams.

The second generation loosened these constraints by moving to network-centered architectures and managing entire projects at a time. As projects grew larger, they ran into new problems. With clients needing to talk to servers very frequently, server scaling became an issue for large projects. An unreliable network connection could prevent remote users from being able to talk to the server at all. As open source projects started making read-only access available anonymously to anyone, people without commit privileges found that they could not use the tools to interact with a project in a natural way, as they could not record their changes.

The current generation of revision control tools is peer-to-peer in nature. All of these systems have dropped the dependency on a single central server, and allow people to distribute their revision control data to where it's actually needed. Collaboration over the Internet has moved from being constrained by technology to a matter of choice and consensus. Modern tools can operate offline indefinitely and autonomously, with a network connection only needed when syncing changes with another repository.

A Few Advantages of Distributed Revision Control

Even though distributed revision control tools have for several years been as robust and usable as their previous-generation counterparts, people using older tools have not yet necessarily woken up to their advantages. There are a number of ways in which distributed tools shine relative to centralized ones.

For an individual developer, distributed tools are almost always much faster than centralized tools. This is for a simple reason: a centralized tool needs to talk over the network for many common operations, because most metadata is stored in a single copy on the central server. A distributed tool stores all of its metadata locally. All else being equal, talking over the network adds overhead to a centralized tool. Don't underestimate the value of a snappy, responsive tool: you're going to spend a lot of time interacting with your revision control software.

Distributed tools are indifferent to the vagaries of your server infrastructure, again because they replicate metadata to so many locations. If you use a centralized system and your server catches fire, you'd better hope that your backup media are reliable, and that your last backup was recent and actually worked. With a distributed tool, you have many backups available on every contributor's computer.

The reliability of your network will affect distributed tools far less than it will centralized tools. You can't even use a centralized tool without a network connection, except for a few highly constrained commands. With a distributed tool, if your network connection goes down while you're working, you may not even notice. The only thing you won't be able to do is talk to repositories on other computers, something that is relatively rare compared with local operations. If you have a far-flung team of collaborators, this may be significant.

Advantages for Open Source Projects

If you take a shine to an open source project and decide that you would like to start hacking on it, and that project uses a distributed revision control tool, you are at once a peer with the people who consider themselves the "core" of that project. If they publish their repositories, you can immediately copy their project history, start making changes, and record your work, using the same tools in the same ways as insiders. By contrast, with a centralized tool, you must use the software in a "read-only" mode unless someone grants you permission to commit changes to their central server. Until then, you won't be able to record changes, and your local modifications will be at risk of corruption any time you try to update your client's view of the repository.

The forking non-problem

It has been suggested that distributed revision control tools pose some sort of risk to open source projects because they make it easy to "fork" the development of a project. A fork happens when there are differences in opinion or attitude between groups of developers that cause them to decide that they can't work together any longer. Each side takes a more or less complete copy of the project's source code, and goes off in its own direction.

Sometimes the camps in a fork decide to reconcile their differences. With a centralized revision control system, the *technical* process of reconciliation is painful, and has to be performed largely by hand. You have to decide whose revision history is going to "win," and graft the other team's changes into the tree somehow. This usually loses some or all of one side's revision history.

What distributed tools do with respect to forking is they make forking the *only* way to develop a project. Every single change that you make is potentially a fork point. The great strength of this approach is that a distributed revision control tool has to be really good at *merging* forks, because forks are absolutely fundamental: they happen all the time.

If every piece of work that everybody does, all the time, is framed in terms of forking and merging, then what the open source world refers to as a "fork" becomes *purely* a social issue. If anything, distributed tools *lower* the likelihood of a fork:

- They eliminate the social distinction that centralized tools impose: that between insiders (people with commit access) and outsiders (people without).
- They make it easier to reconcile after a social fork, because all that's involved from the perspective of the revision control software is just another merge.

Some people resist distributed tools because they want to retain tight control over their projects, and they believe that centralized tools give them this control. However, if you're of this belief, and you publish your CVS or Subversion repositories publicly, there are plenty of tools available that can pull out your entire project's history (albeit slowly) and recreate it somewhere that you don't control. So while your control in this case is illusory, you are forgoing the ability to fluidly collaborate with whatever people feel compelled to mirror and fork your history.

Advantages for Commercial Projects

Many commercial projects are undertaken by teams that are scattered across the globe. Contributors who are far from a central server will see slower command execution and perhaps less reliability. Commercial revision control systems attempt to ameliorate these problems with remote-site replication add-ons that are typically expensive to buy and cantankerous to administer. A distributed system doesn't suffer from these problems in the first place. Better yet, you can easily set up multiple authoritative servers, say one per site, so that there's no redundant communication between repositories over expensive long-haul network links.

Centralized revision control systems tend to have relatively low scalability. It's not unusual for an expensive centralized system to fall over under the combined load of just a few dozen concurrent users. Once again, the typical response tends to be an expensive and clunky replication facility. Since the load on a central server—if you have one at all—is many times lower with a distributed tool (because all of the data is replicated everywhere), a single cheap server can handle the needs of a much larger team, and replication to balance load becomes a simple matter of scripting.

If you have an employee in the field, troubleshooting a problem at a customer's site, they'll benefit from distributed revision control. The tool will let them generate custom builds, try different fixes in isolation from each other, and search efficiently through history for the sources of bugs and regressions in the customer's environment, all without needing to connect to your company's network.

Why Choose Mercurial?

Mercurial has a unique set of properties that make it a particularly good choice as a revision control system:

- It is easy to learn and use.
- It is lightweight.
- It scales excellently.
- It is easy to customize.

If you are at all familiar with revision control systems, you should be able to get up and running with Mercurial in less than five minutes. Even if not, it will take no more than a few minutes longer. Mercurial's command and feature sets are generally uniform and consistent, so you can keep track of a few general rules instead of a host of exceptions.

On a small project, you can start working with Mercurial in moments. Creating new changes and branches, transferring changes around (whether locally or over a network), and history and status operations are all fast. Mercurial attempts to stay nimble and largely out of your way by combining low cognitive overhead with blazingly fast operations.

The usefulness of Mercurial is not limited to small projects: it is used by projects with hundreds to thousands of contributors, each containing tens of thousands of files and hundreds of megabytes of source code.

If the core functionality of Mercurial is not enough for you, it's easy to build on. Mercurial is well suited to scripting tasks, and its clean internals and implementation in Python make it easy to add features in the form of extensions. There are a number of popular and useful extensions already available, ranging from helping to identify bugs to improving performance.

Mercurial Compared with Other Tools

Before you read on, please understand that this section necessarily reflects my own experiences, interests, and (dare I say it) biases. I have used every one of the revision control tools listed below, in most cases for several years at a time.

Subversion

Subversion is a popular revision control tool, developed to replace CVS. It has a centralized client/server architecture.

Subversion and Mercurial have similarly named commands for performing the same operations, so if you're familiar with one, it is easy to learn to use the other. Both tools are portable to all popular operating systems.

Prior to version 1.5, Subversion had no useful support for merges. At the time of writing, its merge tracking capability is new, and known to be complicated and buggy (*http:// svnbook.red-bean.com/nightly/en/svn.branchmerge.advanced.html#svn.branchmerge .advanced.finalword*).

Mercurial has a substantial performance advantage over Subversion on every revision control operation I have benchmarked. I have measured its advantage as ranging from a factor of two to a factor of six when compared with Subversion 1.4.3's *ra_local* file store, which is the fastest access method available. In more realistic deployments involving a network-based store, Subversion will be at a substantially larger disadvantage. Because many Subversion commands must talk to the server and Subversion does not have useful replication facilities, server capacity and network bandwidth become bottlenecks for modestly large projects.

Additionally, Subversion incurs substantial storage overhead to avoid network transactions for a few common operations, such as finding modified files (`status`) and displaying modifications against the current revision (`diff`). As a result, a Subversion working copy is often the same size as, or larger than, a Mercurial repository and working directory, even though the Mercurial repository contains a complete history of the project.

Subversion is widely supported by third-party tools. Mercurial currently lags considerably in this area. This gap is closing, however, and indeed some of Mercurial's GUI tools now outshine their Subversion equivalents. Like Mercurial, Subversion has an excellent user manual.

Because Subversion doesn't store revision history on the client, it is well suited to managing projects that deal with lots of large, opaque binary files. If you check in fifty revisions to an incompressible 10MB file, Subversion's client-side space usage stays constant. The space used by any distributed SCM will grow rapidly in proportion to the number of revisions, because the differences between each revision are large.

In addition, it's often difficult (or more usually, impossible) to merge different versions of a binary file. Subversion's ability to let a user lock a file, so that they temporarily have the exclusive right to commit changes to it, can be a significant advantage to a project where binary files are widely used.

Mercurial can import revision history from a Subversion repository. It can also export revision history to a Subversion repository. This makes it easy to "test the waters" and use Mercurial and Subversion in parallel before deciding to switch. History conversion is incremental, so you can perform an initial conversion, then small additional conversions afterwards to bring in new changes.

Git

Git is a distributed revision control tool that was developed for managing the Linux kernel source tree. Like Mercurial, its early design was somewhat influenced by Monotone (described at the end of this chapter).

Git has a very large command set, with version 1.5.0 providing 139 individual commands. It has something of a reputation for being difficult to learn. Compared to Git, Mercurial has a strong focus on simplicity.

In terms of performance, Git is extremely fast. In several cases, it is faster than Mercurial, at least on Linux, while Mercurial performs better on other operations. However, on Windows, the performance and general level of support that Git provides is, at the time of writing, far behind that of Mercurial.

While a Mercurial repository needs no maintenance, a Git repository requires frequent manual "repacks" of its metadata. Without these, performance degrades, while space usage grows rapidly. A server that contains many Git repositories that are not rigorously and frequently repacked will become heavily disk-bound during backups, and there have been instances of daily backups taking far longer than 24 hours as a result. A freshly packed Git repository is slightly smaller than a Mercurial repository, but an unpacked repository is several orders of magnitude larger.

The core of Git is written in C. Many Git commands are implemented as shell or Perl scripts, and the quality of these scripts varies widely. I have encountered several instances where scripts charged along blindly in the presence of errors that should have been fatal.

Mercurial can import revision history from a Git repository.

CVS

CVS is probably the most widely used revision control tool in the world. Due to its age and internal untidiness, it has been only lightly maintained for many years.

It has a centralized client/server architecture. It does not group related file changes into atomic commits, making it easy for people to "break the build": one person can successfully commit part of a change and then be blocked by the need for a merge, causing other people to see only a portion of the work they intended to do. This also affects how you work with project history. If you want to see all of the modifications someone made as part of a task, you will need to manually inspect the descriptions and timestamps of the changes made to each file involved (if you even know what those files were).

CVS has a muddled notion of tags and branches that I will not attempt to even describe. It does not support renaming of files or directories well, making it easy to corrupt a repository. It has almost no internal consistency checking capabilities, so it is usually not even possible to tell whether or how a repository is corrupt. I would not recommend CVS for any project, existing or new.

Mercurial can import CVS revision history. However, there are a few caveats that apply; these are true of every other revision control tool's CVS importer, too. Due to CVS's lack of atomic changes and unversioned filesystem hierarchy, it is not possible to reconstruct CVS history completely accurately; some guesswork is involved, and renames will usually not show up. Because a lot of advanced CVS administration has to be done by hand and is hence error-prone, it's common for CVS importers to run into multiple problems with corrupted repositories (completely bogus revision timestamps and files that have remained locked for over a decade are just two of the less interesting problems I can recall from personal experience).

Mercurial can import revision history from a CVS repository.

Commercial Tools

Perforce has a centralized client/server architecture, with no client-side caching of any data. Unlike modern revision control tools, Perforce requires that a user run a command to inform the server about every file they intend to edit.

The performance of Perforce is quite good for small teams, but it falls off rapidly as the number of users grows beyond a few dozen. Modestly large Perforce installations require the deployment of proxies to cope with the load their users generate.

Choosing a Revision Control Tool

With the exception of CVS, all of the tools listed above have unique strengths that suit them to particular styles of work. There is no single revision control tool that is best in all situations.

As an example, Subversion is a good choice for working with frequently edited binary files, due to its centralized nature and support for file locking.

I personally find Mercurial's properties of simplicity, performance, and good merge support to be a compelling combination that has served me well for several years.

Switching from Another Tool to Mercurial

Mercurial is bundled with an extension named convert, which can incrementally import revision history from several other revision control tools. By "incremental," I mean that you can convert all of a project's history to date in one go, then rerun the conversion later to obtain new changes that happened after the initial conversion.

The revision control tools supported by convert are as follows:

- Subversion
- CVS
- Git
- Darcs

In addition, convert can export changes from Mercurial to Subversion. This makes it possible to try Subversion and Mercurial in parallel before committing to a switchover, without risking the loss of any work.

The convert command is easy to use. Simply point it at the path or URL of the source repository, optionally give it the name of the destination repository, and it will start working. After the initial conversion, just run the same command again to import new changes.

A Short History of Revision Control

The best known of the old-time revision control tools is SCCS (Source Code Control System), which Marc Rochkind wrote at Bell Labs in the early 1970s. SCCS operated on individual files, and required every person working on a project to have access to a shared workspace on a single system. Only one person could modify a file at any time; arbitration for access to files was via locks. It was common for people to lock files and later forget to unlock them, preventing anyone else from modifying those files without the help of an administrator.

Walter Tichy developed a free alternative to SCCS in the early 1980s; he called his program RCS (Revision Control System). Like SCCS, RCS required developers to work in a single shared workspace, and to lock files to prevent multiple people from modifying them simultaneously.

Later in the 1980s, Dick Grune used RCS as a building block for a set of shell scripts he initially called cmt, but then renamed to CVS (Concurrent Versions System). The big innovation of CVS was that it let developers work simultaneously and somewhat independently in their own personal workspaces. The personal workspaces prevented developers from stepping on each other's toes all the time, as was common with SCCS and RCS. Each developer had a copy of every project file, and could modify their copies independently. They had to merge their edits prior to committing changes to the central repository.

Brian Berliner took Grune's original scripts and rewrote them in C, releasing in 1989 the code that has since developed into the modern version of CVS. CVS subsequently acquired the ability to operate over a network connection, giving it a client/server architecture. CVS's architecture is centralized; only the server has a copy of the history of the project. Client workspaces just contain copies of recent versions of the project's files, and a little metadata to tell them where the server is. CVS has been enormously successful; it is probably the world's most widely used revision control system.

In the early 1990s, Sun Microsystems developed an early distributed revision control system called TeamWare. A TeamWare workspace contains a complete copy of the project's history. TeamWare has no notion of a central repository. (CVS relied upon RCS for its history storage; TeamWare used SCCS.)

As the 1990s progressed, awareness grew of a number of problems with CVS. It records simultaneous changes to multiple files individually, instead of grouping them together as a single logically atomic operation. It does not manage its file hierarchy well; it is easy to make a mess of a repository by renaming files and directories. Worse, its source code is difficult to read and maintain, which made the "pain level" of fixing these architectural problems prohibitive.

In 2001, Jim Blandy and Karl Fogel, two developers who had worked on CVS, started a project to replace it with a tool that would have a better architecture and cleaner code. The result, Subversion, does not stray from CVS's centralized client/server model, but it adds multi-file atomic commits, better namespace management, and a number of other features that make it a generally better tool than CVS. Since its initial release, it has rapidly grown in popularity.

More or less simultaneously, Graydon Hoare began working on an ambitious distributed revision control system that he named Monotone. While Monotone addresses many of CVS's design flaws and has a peer-to-peer architecture, it goes beyond earlier (and subsequent) revision control tools in a number of innovative ways. It uses cryptographic hashes as identifiers, and has an integral notion of "trust" for code from different sources.

Mercurial began life in 2005. While a few aspects of its design are influenced by Monotone, Mercurial focuses on ease of use, high performance, and scalability to very large projects.

## CHAPTER 2

A Tour of Mercurial: The Basics

Installing Mercurial on Your System

Prebuilt binary packages of Mercurial are available for every popular operating system. These make it easy to start using Mercurial on your computer immediately.

Windows

The best version of Mercurial for Windows is TortoiseHg, which can be found at *http://bitbucket.org/tortoisehg/stable/wiki/Home*. This package has no external dependencies; it "just works." It provides both command-line and graphical user interfaces.

Mac OS X

Lee Cantey publishes an installer of Mercurial for Mac OS X at *http://mercurial.berkwood.com*.

Linux

Because each Linux distribution has its own packaging tools, policies, and rate of development, it's difficult to give a comprehensive set of instructions on how to install Mercurial binaries. The version of Mercurial that you will end up with can vary depending on how active the person is who maintains the package for your distribution.

To keep things simple, I will focus on installing Mercurial from the command line under the most popular Linux distributions. Most of these distributions provide graphical package managers that will let you install Mercurial with a single click; the package name to look for is `mercurial`.

- Ubuntu and Debian:

        apt-get install mercurial

- Fedora:

```
    yum install mercurial
```
- OpenSUSE:
```
    zypper install mercurial
```
- Gentoo:
```
    emerge mercurial
```

Solaris

SunFreeWare, at *http://www.sunfreeware.com*, provides prebuilt packages of Mercurial.

Getting Started

To begin, we'll use the hg version command to find out whether Mercurial is installed properly. The actual version information that it prints isn't so important; we simply care whether the command runs and prints anything at all.

```
$ hg version
Mercurial Distributed SCM (version 5d25b2f59ade)

Copyright (C) 2005-2008 Matt Mackall <mpm@selenic.com> and others
This is free software; see the source for copying conditions. There is NO
warranty; not even for MERCHANTABILITY or FITNESS FOR A PARTICULAR PURPOSE.
```

Built-In Help

Mercurial provides a built-in help system. This is invaluable for those times when you find yourself stuck trying to remember how to run a command. If you are completely stuck, simply run hg help; it will print a brief list of commands, along with a description of what each does. If you ask for help on a specific command (as below), it prints more detailed information.

```
$ hg help init
hg init [-e CMD] [--remotecmd CMD] [DEST]

create a new repository in the given directory

    Initialize a new repository in the given directory. If the given
    directory does not exist, it is created.

    If no directory is given, the current directory is used.

    It is possible to specify an ssh:// URL as the destination.
    See 'hg help urls' for more information.

options:

 -e --ssh        specify ssh command to use
```

```
    --remotecmd  specify hg command to run on the remote side

  use "hg -v help init" to show global options
```

For a more impressive level of detail (which you won't usually need) run `hg help -v`. The `-v` option is short for `--verbose`, and tells Mercurial to print more information than it usually would.

Working with a Repository

In Mercurial, everything happens inside a *repository*. The repository for a project contains all of the files that "belong to" that project, along with a historical record of the project's files.

There's nothing particularly magical about a repository; it is simply a directory tree in your filesystem that Mercurial treats as special. You can rename or delete a repository any time you like, using either the command line or your file browser.

Making a Local Copy of a Repository

Copying a repository is just a little bit special. While you could use a normal file copying command to make a copy of a repository, it's best to use a built-in command that Mercurial provides. This command is called `hg clone`, because it makes an identical copy of an existing repository.

```
$ hg clone http://hg.serpentine.com/tutorial/hello
destination directory: hello
requesting all changes
adding changesets
adding manifests
adding file changes
added 5 changesets with 5 changes to 2 files
updating working directory
2 files updated, 0 files merged, 0 files removed, 0 files unresolved
```

One advantage of using `hg clone` is that, as we can see above, it lets us clone repositories over the network. Another is that it remembers where we cloned from, which we'll find useful soon when we want to fetch new changes from another repository.

If our clone succeeded, we should now have a local directory called *hello*. This directory will contain some files.

```
$ ls -l
total 4
drwxrwxr-x 3 bos bos 4096 May  5 06:44 hello
$ ls hello
Makefile  hello.c
```

These files have the same contents and history in our repository as they do in the repository we cloned.

Every Mercurial repository is complete, self-contained, and independent. It contains its own private copy of a project's files and history. As we just mentioned, a cloned repository remembers the location of the repository it was cloned from, but Mercurial will not communicate with that repository, or any other, unless you tell it to.

What this means for now is that we're free to experiment with our repository, safe in the knowledge that it's a private "sandbox" that won't affect anyone else.

What's in a Repository?

When we take a more detailed look inside a repository, we can see that it contains a directory named *.hg*. This is where Mercurial keeps all of its metadata for the repository.

```
$ cd hello
$ ls -a
.  ..  .hg  Makefile  hello.c
```

The contents of the *.hg* directory and its subdirectories are private to Mercurial. Every other file and directory in the repository is yours to do with as you please.

To introduce a little terminology, the *.hg* directory is the "real" repository, and all of the files and directories that coexist with it are said to live in the *working directory*. An easy way to remember the distinction is that the *repository* contains the *history* of your project, while the *working directory* contains a *snapshot* of your project at a particular point in history.

A Tour Through History

One of the first things we might want to do with a new, unfamiliar repository is understand its history. The hg log command gives us a view of the history of changes in the repository.

```
$ hg log
changeset:   4:2278160e78d4
tag:         tip
user:        Bryan O'Sullivan <bos@serpentine.com>
date:        Sat Aug 16 22:16:53 2008 +0200
summary:     Trim comments.

changeset:   3:0272e0d5a517
user:        Bryan O'Sullivan <bos@serpentine.com>
date:        Sat Aug 16 22:08:02 2008 +0200
summary:     Get make to generate the final binary from a .o file.

changeset:   2:fef857204a0c
user:        Bryan O'Sullivan <bos@serpentine.com>
date:        Sat Aug 16 22:05:04 2008 +0200
summary:     Introduce a typo into hello.c.

changeset:   1:82e55d328c8c
user:        mpm@selenic.com
```

```
date:           Fri Aug 26 01:21:28 2005 -0700
summary:        Create a makefile

changeset:      0:0a04b987be5a
user:           mpm@selenic.com
date:           Fri Aug 26 01:20:50 2005 -0700
summary:        Create a standard "hello, world" program
```

By default, this command prints a brief paragraph of output for each change to the project that was recorded. In Mercurial terminology, we call each of these recorded events a *changeset*, because it can contain a record of changes to several files.

The fields in a record of output from `hg log` are as follows:

- `changeset`: This field has the format of a number, followed by a colon, followed by a hexadecimal (or *hex*) string. These are *identifiers* for the changeset. The hex string is a unique identifier: the same hex string will always refer to the same changeset in every copy of this repository. The number is shorter and easier to type than the hex string, but it isn't unique: the same number in two different clones of a repository may identify different changesets.
- `user`: The identity of the person who created the changeset. This is a free-form field, but it most often contains a person's name and email address.
- `date`: The date and time on which the changeset was created, and the timezone in which it was created. (The date and time are local to that timezone; they display what time and date it was for the person who created the changeset.)
- `summary`: The first line of the text message that the creator of the changeset entered to describe the changeset.
- `tag`: Some changesets, such as the first in the list above, have a `tag` field. A tag is another way to identify a changeset, by giving it an easy-to-remember name. (The tag named `tip` is special: it always refers to the newest change in a repository.)

The default output printed by `hg log` is purely a summary; it is missing a lot of detail.

Figure 2-1 provides a graphical representation of the history of the *hello* repository, to make it a little easier to see which direction history is "flowing" in. We'll be returning to this figure several times in this chapter and the chapter that follows.

Changesets, Revisions, and Talking to Other People

As English is a notoriously sloppy language, and computer science has a hallowed history of terminological confusion (why use one term when four will do?), revision control has a variety of words and phrases that mean the same thing. If you are talking about Mercurial history with other people, you will find that the word "changeset" is often compressed to "change" or (when written) "cset", and sometimes a changeset is referred to as a "revision" or a "rev".

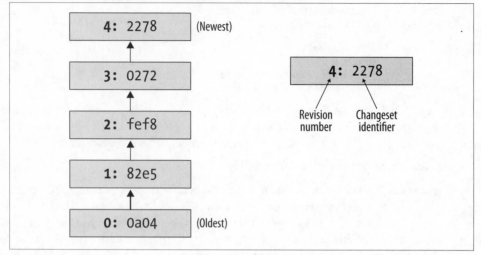

Figure 2-1. Graphical history of the hello repository

While it doesn't matter what *word* you use to refer to the concept of a changeset, the *identifier* that you use to refer to a *specific* changeset is of great importance. Recall that the changeset field in the output from hg log identifies a changeset using both a number and a hexadecimal string:

- The revision number is a handy notation that is *only valid in that repository*.
- The hexadecimal string is the *permanent, unchanging identifier* that will always identify that exact changeset in *every* copy of the repository.

This distinction is important. If you send someone an email talking about "revision 33," there's a high likelihood that their revision 33 will not be the same as yours. The reason for this is that a revision number depends on the order in which changes arrived in a repository, and there is no guarantee that the same changes will happen in the same order in different repositories. Three changes a,b,c can easily appear in one repository as 0,1,2, while in another as 0,2,1.

Mercurial uses revision numbers purely as a convenient shorthand. If you need to discuss a changeset with someone, or make a record of a changeset for some other reason (for example, in a bug report), use the hexadecimal identifier.

Viewing Specific Revisions

To narrow the output of hg log down to a single revision, use the -r (or --rev) option. You can use either a revision number or a hexadecimal identifier, and you can provide as many revisions as you want.

```
$ hg log -r 3
changeset:   3:0272e0d5a517
user:        Bryan O'Sullivan <bos@serpentine.com>
```

```
date:         Sat Aug 16 22:08:02 2008 +0200
summary:      Get make to generate the final binary from a .o file.

$ hg log -r 0272e0d5a517
changeset:    3:0272e0d5a517
user:         Bryan O'Sullivan <bos@serpentine.com>
date:         Sat Aug 16 22:08:02 2008 +0200
summary:      Get make to generate the final binary from a .o file.

$ hg log -r 1 -r 4
changeset:    1:82e55d328c8c
user:         mpm@selenic.com
date:         Fri Aug 26 01:21:28 2005 -0700
summary:      Create a makefile

changeset:    4:2278160e78d4
tag:          tip
user:         Bryan O'Sullivan <bos@serpentine.com>
date:         Sat Aug 16 22:16:53 2008 +0200
summary:      Trim comments.
```

If you want to see the history of several revisions without having to list each one, you can use *range notation*; this lets you express the idea "I want all revisions between abc and def, inclusive."

```
$ hg log -r 2:4
changeset:    2:fef857204a0c
user:         Bryan O'Sullivan <bos@serpentine.com>
date:         Sat Aug 16 22:05:04 2008 +0200
summary:      Introduce a typo into hello.c.

changeset:    3:0272e0d5a517
user:         Bryan O'Sullivan <bos@serpentine.com>
date:         Sat Aug 16 22:08:02 2008 +0200
summary:      Get make to generate the final binary from a .o file.

changeset:    4:2278160e78d4
tag:          tip
user:         Bryan O'Sullivan <bos@serpentine.com>
date:         Sat Aug 16 22:16:53 2008 +0200
summary:      Trim comments.
```

Mercurial also honors the order in which you specify revisions, so hg log -r 2:4 prints 2, 3, and 4 while hg log -r 4:2 prints 4, 3, and 2.

More Detailed Information

While the summary information printed by hg log is useful if you already know what you're looking for, you may need to see a complete description of the change, or a list of the files changed, if you're trying to decide whether a changeset is the one you're looking for. The hg log command's -v (or --verbose) option gives you this extra detail.

```
$ hg log -v -r 3
changeset:    3:0272e0d5a517
```

```
user:        Bryan O'Sullivan <bos@serpentine.com>
date:        Sat Aug 16 22:08:02 2008 +0200
files:       Makefile
description:
Get make to generate the final binary from a .o file.
```

If you want to see both the description and content of a change, add the -p (or --patch) option. This displays the content of a change as a *unified diff* (if you've never seen a unified diff before, see "Understanding Patches" on page 186 for an overview).

```
$ hg log -v -p -r 2
changeset:   2:fef857204a0c
user:        Bryan O'Sullivan <bos@serpentine.com>
date:        Sat Aug 16 22:05:04 2008 +0200
files:       hello.c
description:
Introduce a typo into hello.c.


diff -r 82e55d328c8c -r fef857204a0c hello.c
--- a/hello.c    Fri Aug 26 01:21:28 2005 -0700
+++ b/hello.c    Sat Aug 16 22:05:04 2008 +0200
@@ -11,6 +11,6 @@

 int main(int argc, char **argv)
 {
-    printf("hello, world!\n");
+    printf("hello, world!\");
     return 0;
 }
```

The -p option is tremendously useful, so it's well worth remembering.

All About Command Options

Let's take a brief break from exploring Mercurial commands to discuss a pattern in the way that they work; you may find this useful to keep in mind as we continue our tour.

Mercurial has a consistent and straightforward approach to dealing with the options that you can pass to commands. It follows the conventions for options that are common to modern Linux and Unix systems:

- Every option has a long name. For example, as we've already seen, the hg log command accepts a --rev option.

- Most options have short names, too. Instead of --rev, we can use -r. (The reason that some options don't have short names is that the options in question are rarely used.)

- Long options start with two dashes (e.g., --rev), while short options start with one (e.g., -r).

- Option naming and usage is consistent across commands. For example, every command that lets you specify a changeset ID or revision number accepts both `-r` and `--rev` arguments.

- If you are using short options, you can save typing by running them together. For example, the command `hg log -v -p -r 2` can be written as `hg log -vpr2`.

In the examples throughout this book, I usually use short options instead of long. This simply reflects my own preference, so don't read anything significant into it.

Most commands that print output of some kind will print more output when passed a `-v` (or `--verbose`) option, and less when passed `-q` (or `--quiet`).

Option naming consistency

Almost always, Mercurial commands use consistent option names to refer to the same concepts. For instance, if a command deals with changesets, you'll always identify them with `--rev` or `-r`. This consistent use of option names makes it easier to remember what options a particular command takes.

Making and Reviewing Changes

Now that we have a grasp of viewing history in Mercurial, let's take a look at making some changes and examining them.

The first thing we'll do is isolate our experiment in a repository of its own. We use the `hg clone` command, but we don't need to clone a copy of the remote repository. Since we already have a copy of it locally, we can just clone that instead. This is much faster than cloning over the network, and cloning a local repository uses less disk space in most cases, too.[*]

```
$ cd ..
$ hg clone hello my-hello
updating working directory
2 files updated, 0 files merged, 0 files removed, 0 files unresolved
$cd my-hello
```

As an aside, it's often good practice to keep a "pristine" copy of a remote repository around, which you can then make temporary clones of to create sandboxes for each task you want to work on. This lets you work on multiple tasks in parallel, each isolated from the others until it's complete and you're ready to integrate it back. Because local clones are so cheap, there's almost no overhead to cloning and destroying repositories whenever you want.

---

[*] The saving of space arises when source and destination repositories are on the same filesystem, in which case Mercurial will use hardlinks to do copy-on-write sharing of its internal metadata. If that explanation meant nothing to you, don't worry: everything happens transparently and automatically, and you don't need to understand it.

In our *my-hello* repository, we have a file *hello.c* that contains the classic "hello, world" program.

```
$ cat hello.c
/*
 * Placed in the public domain by Bryan O'Sullivan.  This program is
 * not covered by patents in the United States or other countries.
 */

#include <stdio.h>

int main(int argc, char **argv)
{
    printf("hello, world!\");
    return 0;
}
```

Let's edit this file so that it prints a second line of output:

```
# ... edit edit edit ...
$ cat hello.c
/*
 * Placed in the public domain by Bryan O'Sullivan.  This program is
 * not covered by patents in the United States or other countries.
 */

#include <stdio.h>

int main(int argc, char **argv)
{
    printf("hello, world!\");
    printf("hello again!\n");
    return 0;
}
```

Mercurial's hg status command will tell us what Mercurial knows about the files in the repository:

```
$ ls
Makefile  hello.c
$ hg status
M hello.c
```

The hg status command prints no output for some files, but a line starting with M for *hello.c*. Unless you tell it to, hg status will not print any output for files that have not been modified.

The M indicates that Mercurial has noticed that we modified *hello.c*. We didn't need to *inform* Mercurial that we were going to modify the file before we started, or that we had modified the file after we were done; it was able to figure this out itself.

It's somewhat helpful to know that we've modified *hello.c*, but we might prefer to know exactly what changes we've made to it. To do this, we use the hg diff command:

```
$ hg diff
diff -r 2278160e78d4 hello.c
```

```
--- a/hello.c      Sat Aug 16 22:16:53 2008 +0200
+++ b/hello.c      Tue May 05 06:44:49 2009 +0000
@@ -8,5 +8,6 @@
 int main(int argc, char **argv)
 {
     printf("hello, world!\");
+    printf("hello again!\n");
     return 0;
 }
```

 Understanding patches

Remember to take a look at "Understanding Patches" on page 186 if you don't know how to read the output above.

Recording Changes in a New Changeset

We can modify files, build and test our changes and use hg `status` and hg `diff` to review our changes, until we're satisfied with what we've done and arrive at a natural stopping point where we want to record our work in a new changeset.

The hg `commit` command lets us create a new changeset; we'll usually refer to this as "making a commit" or "committing."

Setting Up a Username

When you try to run hg `commit` for the first time, it is not guaranteed to succeed. Mercurial records your name and address with each change that you commit, so that you and others will later be able to tell who made each change. Mercurial tries to automatically figure out a sensible username to commit the change with. It will attempt each of the following methods, in order:

1. If you specify a -u option to the hg `commit` command on the command line, followed by a username, this is always given the highest precedence.

2. If you have set the HGUSER environment variable, this is checked next.

3. If you create a file in your home directory called *.hgrc* with a username entry, that will be used next. To see what the contents of this file should look like, refer to "Creating a Mercurial configuration file" on page 24.

4. If you have set the EMAIL environment variable, this will be used next.

5. Mercurial will query your system to find out your local user-name and host-name, and construct a username from these components. Since this often results in a username that is not very useful, it will print a warning if it has to do this.

If all of these mechanisms fail, Mercurial will fail, printing an error message. In this case, it will not let you commit until you set up a username.

You should think of the HGUSER environment variable and the -u option to the hg commit command as ways to *override* Mercurial's default selection of username. For normal use, the simplest and most robust way to set a username for yourself is by creating a *.hgrc* file; see below for details.

Creating a Mercurial configuration file

To set a username, use your favorite editor to create a file called *.hgrc* in your home directory. Mercurial will use this file to look up your personalized configuration settings. The initial contents of your *.hgrc* should look like this:

```
# This is a Mercurial configuration file.
[ui]
username = Firstname Lastname <email.address@example.net>
```

"Home directory" on Windows

When we refer to your home directory, on an English language installation of Windows this will usually be a folder named after your username in *C:\Documents and Settings*. You can find out the exact name of your home directory by opening a command prompt window and running the following command:

```
C:\> echo %UserProfile%
```

The [ui] line begins a *section* of the config file, so you can read the "username = ..." line as meaning "set the value of the username item in the ui section." A section continues until a new section begins, or the end of the file. Mercurial ignores empty lines and treats any text from # to the end of a line as a comment.

Choosing a username

You can use any text you like as the value of the username config item, since this information is for reading by other people, but will not be interpreted by Mercurial. The convention that most people follow is to use their name and email address, as in the example above.

Mercurial's built-in web server obfuscates email addresses, to make it more difficult for the email harvesting tools that spammers use. This reduces the likelihood that you'll start receiving more junk email if you publish a Mercurial repository on the Web.

Writing a Commit Message

When we commit a change, Mercurial drops us into a text editor to enter a message that will describe the modifications we've made in this changeset. This is called the *commit message*. It will be a record for readers of what we did and why, and it will be printed by hg log after we've finished committing:

```
$ hg commit
```

The editor that the hg commit command drops us into will contain an empty line or two, followed by a number of lines starting with HG:.

```
This is where I type my commit comment.

HG: Enter commit message.  Lines beginning with 'HG:' are removed.
HG: --
HG: user: Bryan O'Sullivan <bos@serpentine.com>
HG: branch 'default'
HG: changed hello.c
```

Mercurial ignores the lines that start with HG:; it uses them only to tell us which files it's recording changes to. Modifying or deleting these lines has no effect.

Writing a Good Commit Message

Since hg log only prints the first line of a commit message by default, it's best to write a commit message whose first line stands alone. Here's a real example of a commit message that *doesn't* follow this guideline, and hence has a summary that is not readable:

```
changeset:   73:584af0e231be
user:        Censored Person <censored.person@example.org>
date:        Tue Sep 26 21:37:07 2006 -0700
summary:     include buildmeister/commondefs. Add exports.
```

As far as the remainder of the contents of the commit message are concerned, there are no hard-and-fast rules. Mercurial itself doesn't interpret or care about the contents of the commit message, though your project may have policies that dictate a certain kind of formatting.

My personal preference is for short but informative commit messages that tell me something that I can't figure out with a quick glance at the output of hg log --patch.

If we run the hg commit command without any arguments, it records all of the changes we've made, as reported by hg status and hg diff.

A surprise for Subversion users

Like other Mercurial commands, if we don't supply explicit names to commit to the hg commit, it will operate across a repository's entire working directory. Be wary of this if you're coming from the Subversion or CVS world, since you might expect it to operate only on the current directory that you happen to be visiting and its subdirectories.

Aborting a Commit

If you decide that you don't want to commit while in the middle of editing a commit message, simply exit from your editor without saving the file that it's editing. This will cause nothing to happen to either the repository or the working directory.

Admiring Our New Handiwork

Once we've finished the commit, we can use the hg tip command to display the changeset we just created. This command produces output that is identical to hg log, but it only displays the newest revision in the repository:

```
$ hg tip -vp
changeset:    5:12efb75cbece
tag:          tip
user:         Bryan O'Sullivan <bos@serpentine.com>
date:         Tue May 05 06:44:49 2009 +0000
files:        hello.c
description:
Added an extra line of output


diff -r 2278160e78d4 -r 12efb75cbece hello.c
--- a/hello.c    Sat Aug 16 22:16:53 2008 +0200
+++ b/hello.c    Tue May 05 06:44:49 2009 +0000
@@ -8,5 +8,6 @@
 int main(int argc, char **argv)
 {
     printf("hello, world!\");
+    printf("hello again!\n");
     return 0;
 }
```

We refer to the newest revision in the repository as the *tip revision*, or simply the *tip*.

By the way, the hg tip command accepts many of the same options as hg log, so -v above indicates "be verbose" and -p specifies "print a patch." The use of -p to print patches is another example of the consistent naming we covered earlier.

Sharing Changes

I mentioned earlier that repositories in Mercurial are self-contained. This means that the changeset we just created exists only in our *my-hello* repository. Let's look at a few ways that we can propagate this change into other repositories.

Pulling Changes from Another Repository

To get started, let's clone our original *hello* repository, which does not contain the change we just committed. We'll call our temporary repository *hello-pull*:

```
$ cd ..
$ hg clone hello hello-pull
updating working directory
2 files updated, 0 files merged, 0 files removed, 0 files unresolved
```

We'll use the `hg pull` command to bring changes from *my-hello* into *hello-pull*. However, blindly pulling unknown changes into a repository is a somewhat scary prospect. Mercurial provides the `hg incoming` command to tell us what changes the `hg pull` command *would* pull into the repository, without actually pulling the changes in:

```
$ cd hello-pull
$ hg incoming ../my-hello
comparing with ../my-hello
searching for changes
changeset:   5:12efb75cbece
tag:         tip
user:        Bryan O'Sullivan <bos@serpentine.com>
date:        Tue May 05 06:44:49 2009 +0000
summary:     Added an extra line of output
```

Bringing changes into a repository is a simple matter of running the `hg pull` command, and optionally telling it which repository to pull from:

```
$ hg tip
changeset:   4:2278160e78d4
tag:         tip
user:        Bryan O'Sullivan <bos@serpentine.com>
date:        Sat Aug 16 22:16:53 2008 +0200
summary:     Trim comments.

$ hg pull ../my-hello
pulling from ../my-hello
searching for changes
adding changesets
adding manifests
adding file changes
added 1 changesets with 1 changes to 1 files
(run 'hg update' to get a working copy)
$ hg tip
changeset:   5:12efb75cbece
tag:         tip
user:        Bryan O'Sullivan <bos@serpentine.com>
date:        Tue May 05 06:44:49 2009 +0000
summary:     Added an extra line of output
```

As you can see from the before-and-after output of `hg tip`, we have successfully pulled changes into our repository. However, Mercurial separates pulling changes in from updating the working directory. There remains one step before we will see the changes that we just pulled appear in the working directory.

Pulling specific changes

It is possible that due to the delay between running `hg incoming` and `hg pull`, you may not see all changesets that will be brought from the other repository. Suppose you're pulling changes from a repository on the network somewhere. While you are looking at the `hg incoming` output, and before you pull those changes, someone might have committed something in the remote repository. This means that it's possible to pull more changes than you saw when using `hg incoming`.

If you only want to pull precisely the changes that were listed by `hg incoming`, or you have some other reason to pull a subset of changes, simply identify the change that you want to pull by its changeset ID, e.g., `hg pull -r7e95bb`.

Updating the Working Directory

We have so far glossed over the relationship between a repository and its working directory. The `hg pull` command that we ran in "Pulling Changes from Another Repository" on page 26 brought changes into the repository, but if we check, there's no sign of those changes in the working directory. This is because `hg pull` does not (by default) touch the working directory. Instead, we use the `hg update` command to do this:

```
$ grep printf hello.c
    printf("hello, world!\");
$ hg update tip
1 files updated, 0 files merged, 0 files removed, 0 files unresolved
$ grep printf hello.c
    printf("hello, world!\");
    printf("hello again!\n");
```

It might seem a bit strange that `hg pull` doesn't update the working directory automatically. There's actually a good reason for this: you can use `hg update` to update the working directory to the state it was in at *any revision* in the history of the repository. If you had the working directory updated to an old revision—to hunt down the origin of a bug, say—and ran an `hg pull` that automatically updated the working directory to a new revision, you might not be terribly happy.

Since pull-then-update is such a common sequence of operations, Mercurial lets you combine the two by passing the `-u` option to `hg pull`.

If you look back at the output of `hg pull` in "Pulling Changes from Another Repository" on page 26 when we ran it without `-u`, you can see that it printed a helpful reminder that we'd have to take an explicit step to update the working directory.

To find out what revision the working directory is at, use the `hg parents` command:

```
$ hg parents
changeset:   5:12efb75cbece
tag:         tip
user:        Bryan O'Sullivan <bos@serpentine.com>
```

```
date:          Tue May 05 06:44:49 2009 +0000
summary:       Added an extra line of output
```

If you look back at Figure 2-1, you'll see arrows connecting each changeset. The node that the arrow leads *from* in each case is a parent, and the node that the arrow leads *to* is its child. The working directory has a parent in just the same way; this is the changeset that the working directory currently contains.

To update the working directory to a particular revision, give a revision number or changeset ID to the hg update command:

```
$ hg update 2
2 files updated, 0 files merged, 0 files removed, 0 files unresolved
$ hg parents
changeset:     2:fef857204a0c
user:          Bryan O'Sullivan <bos@serpentine.com>
date:          Sat Aug 16 22:05:04 2008 +0200
summary:       Introduce a typo into hello.c.

$ hg update
2 files updated, 0 files merged, 0 files removed, 0 files unresolved
$ hg parents
changeset:     5:12efb75cbece
tag:           tip
user:          Bryan O'Sullivan <bos@serpentine.com>
date:          Tue May 05 06:44:49 2009 +0000
summary:       Added an extra line of output
```

If you omit an explicit revision, hg update will update to the tip revision, as shown by the second call to hg update in the example above.

Pushing Changes to Another Repository

Mercurial lets us push changes to another repository from the repository we're currently visiting. As with the example of hg pull above, we'll create a temporary repository to push our changes into:

```
$ cd ..
$ hg clone hello hello-push
updating working directory
2 files updated, 0 files merged, 0 files removed, 0 files unresolved
```

The hg outgoing command tells us what changes would be pushed into another repository:

```
$ cd my-hello
$ hg outgoing ../hello-push
comparing with ../hello-push
searching for changes
changeset:     5:12efb75cbece
tag:           tip
user:          Bryan O'Sullivan <bos@serpentine.com>
date:          Tue May 05 06:44:49 2009 +0000
summary:       Added an extra line of output
```

And the hg push command does the actual push:

```
$ hg push ../hello-push
pushing to ../hello-push
searching for changes
adding changesets
adding manifests
adding file changes
added 1 changesets with 1 changes to 1 files
```

As with hg pull, the hg push command does not update the working directory in the repository that it's pushing changes into. Unlike hg pull, hg push does not provide a -u option that updates the other repository's working directory. This asymmetry is deliberate: the repository we're pushing to might be on a remote server and shared between several people. If we were to update its working directory while someone was working in it, their work would be disrupted.

What happens if we try to pull or push changes and the receiving repository already has those changes? Nothing too exciting:

```
$ hg push ../hello-push
pushing to ../hello-push
searching for changes
no changes found
```

Default Locations

When we clone a repository, Mercurial records the location of the repository we cloned in the *.hg/hgrc* file of the new repository. If we don't supply a location to hg pull from or hg push to, those commands will use this location as a default. The hg incoming and hg outgoing commands do so too.

If you open a repository's *.hg/hgrc* file in a text editor, you will see contents like the following:

```
[paths]
default = http://www.selenic.com/repo/hg
```

It is possible—and often useful—to have the default location for hg push and hg outgoing be different from those for hg pull and hg incoming. We can do this by adding a default-push entry to the [paths] section of the *.hg/hgrc* file, as follows:

```
[paths]
default = http://www.selenic.com/repo/hg
default-push = http://hg.example.com/hg
```

Sharing Changes over a Network

The commands we have covered in the previous few sections are not limited to working with local repositories. Each works in exactly the same fashion over a network connection; simply pass in a URL instead of a local path:

```
$ hg outgoing http://hg.serpentine.com/tutorial/hello
comparing with http://hg.serpentine.com/tutorial/hello
searching for changes
changeset:   5:12efb75cbece
tag:         tip
user:        Bryan O'Sullivan <bos@serpentine.com>
date:        Tue May 05 06:44:49 2009 +0000
summary:     Added an extra line of output
```

In this example, we can see what changes we could push to the remote repository, but the repository is understandably not set up to let anonymous users push to it:

```
$ hg push http://hg.serpentine.com/tutorial/hello
pushing to http://hg.serpentine.com/tutorial/hello
searching for changes
ssl required
```

Starting a New Project

It is just as easy to begin a new project as to work on one that already exists. The hg init command creates a new, empty Mercurial repository:

```
$ hg init myproject
```

This simply creates a repository named *myproject* in the current directory:

```
$ ls -l
total 12
-rw-rw-r-- 1 bos bos   47 May  5 06:44 goodbye.c
-rw-rw-r-- 1 bos bos   45 May  5 06:44 hello.c
drwxrwxr-x 3 bos bos 4096 May  5 06:44 myproject
```

We can tell that *myproject* is a Mercurial repository, because it contains a *.hg* directory:

```
$ ls -al myproject
total 12
drwxrwxr-x 3 bos bos 4096 May  5 06:44 .
drwx------ 3 bos bos 4096 May  5 06:44 ..
drwxrwxr-x 3 bos bos 4096 May  5 06:44 .hg
```

If we want to add some pre-existing files to the repository, we copy them into place and tell Mercurial to start tracking them using the hg add command:

```
$ cd myproject
$ cp ../hello.c .
$ cp ../goodbye.c .
$ hg add
adding goodbye.c
adding hello.c
$ hg status
A goodbye.c
A hello.c
```

Once we are satisfied that our project looks right, we commit our changes:

```
$ hg commit -m 'Initial commit'
```

It takes just a few moments to start using Mercurial on a new project, which is part of its appeal. Revision control is now so easy to work with, we can use it on the smallest of projects that we might not have considered with a more complicated tool.

## CHAPTER 3

A Tour of Mercurial: Merging Work

We've now covered cloning a repository, making changes in a repository, and pulling or pushing changes from one repository into another. Our next step is *merging* changes from separate repositories.

Merging Streams of Work

Merging is a fundamental part of working with a distributed revision control tool. Here are a few cases in which the need to merge work arises:

- Alice and Bob each have a personal copy of a repository for a project they're collaborating on. Alice fixes a bug in her repository; Bob adds a new feature in his. They want the shared repository to contain both the bug fix and the new feature.

- Cynthia frequently works on several different tasks for a single project at once, each safely isolated in its own repository. Working this way means that she often needs to merge one piece of her own work with another.

Because we need to merge often, Mercurial makes the process easy. Let's walk through a merge. We'll begin by cloning yet another repository (see how often they spring up?) and making a change in it:

```
$ cd ..
$ hg clone hello my-new-hello
updating working directory
2 files updated, 0 files merged, 0 files removed, 0 files unresolved
$ cd my-new-hello
# Make some simple edits to hello.c.
$ my-text-editor hello.c
$ hg commit -m 'A new hello for a new day.'
```

We should now have two copies of *hello.c* with different contents. The histories of the two repositories have also diverged, as illustrated in Figure 3-1. Here is a copy of our file from one repository:

```
$ cat hello.c
/*
```

```
 * Placed in the public domain by Bryan O'Sullivan.  This program is
 * not covered by patents in the United States or other countries.
 */

#include <stdio.h>

int main(int argc, char **argv)
{
    printf("once more, hello.\n");
    printf("hello, world!\");
    printf("hello again!\n");
    return 0;
}
```

And here is our slightly different version from the other repository:

```
$ cat ../my-hello/hello.c
/*
 * Placed in the public domain by Bryan O'Sullivan.  This program is
 * not covered by patents in the United States or other countries.
 */

#include <stdio.h>

int main(int argc, char **argv)
{
    printf("hello, world!\");
    printf("hello again!\n");
    return 0;
}
```

We already know that pulling changes from our *my-hello* repository will have no effect on the working directory:

```
$ hg pull ../my-hello
pulling from ../my-hello
searching for changes
adding changesets
adding manifests
adding file changes
added 1 changesets with 1 changes to 1 files (+1 heads)
(run 'hg heads' to see heads, 'hg merge' to merge)
```

However, the hg pull command says something about "heads."

Head Changesets

Remember that Mercurial records what the parent of each change is. If a change has a parent, we call it a child or descendant of the parent. A head is a change that has no children. The tip revision is thus a head, because the newest revision in a repository doesn't have any children. There are times when a repository can contain more than one head.

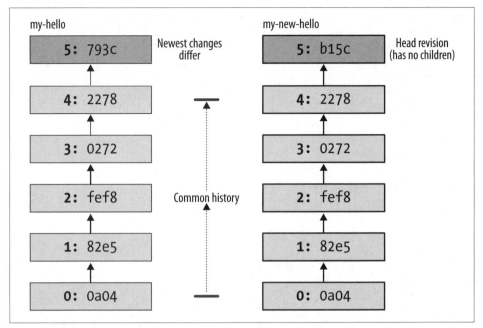

Figure 3-1. Divergent recent histories of the my-hello and my-new-hello repositories

In Figure 3-2, you can see the effect of the pull from *my-hello* into *my-new-hello*. The history that was already present in *my-new-hello* is untouched, but a new revision has been added. By referring to Figure 3-1, we can see that the changeset ID remains the same in the new repository, but the revision number has changed. (This, incidentally, is a fine example of why it's not safe to use revision numbers when discussing change-sets.) We can view the heads in a repository using the hg heads command:

```
$ hg heads
changeset:   6:12efb75cbece
tag:         tip
parent:      4:2278160e78d4
user:        Bryan O'Sullivan <bos@serpentine.com>
date:        Tue May 05 06:44:49 2009 +0000
summary:     Added an extra line of output

changeset:   5:cbfc9ee6ea99
user:        Bryan O'Sullivan <bos@serpentine.com>
date:        Tue May 05 06:44:52 2009 +0000
summary:     A new hello for a new day.
```

Performing the Merge

What happens if we try to use the normal hg update command to update to the new tip?

```
$ hg update
abort: crosses branches (use 'hg merge' or 'hg update -C')
```

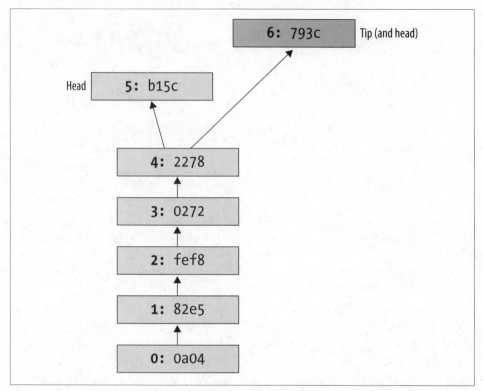

Figure 3-2. Repository contents after pulling from my-hello into my-new-hello

Mercurial is telling us that the `hg update` command won't do a merge; it won't update the working directory when it thinks we might want to do a merge, unless we force it to do so. (Incidentally, forcing the update with `hg update -C` would revert any uncommitted changes in the working directory.)

To start a merge between the two heads, we use the `hg merge` command:

```
$ hg merge
merging hello.c
0 files updated, 1 files merged, 0 files removed, 0 files unresolved
(branch merge, don't forget to commit)
```

We resolve the contents of *hello.c*. This updates the working directory so that it contains changes from *both* heads, which is reflected in both the output of `hg parents` and the contents of *hello.c*:

```
$ hg parents
changeset:   5:cbfc9ee6ea99
user:        Bryan O'Sullivan <bos@serpentine.com>
date:        Tue May 05 06:44:52 2009 +0000
summary:     A new hello for a new day.
```

```
changeset:   6:12efb75cbece
tag:         tip
parent:      4:2278160e78d4
user:        Bryan O'Sullivan <bos@serpentine.com>
date:        Tue May 05 06:44:49 2009 +0000
summary:     Added an extra line of output

$ cat hello.c
/*
 * Placed in the public domain by Bryan O'Sullivan.  This program is
 * not covered by patents in the United States or other countries.
 */

#include <stdio.h>

int main(int argc, char **argv)
{
    printf("once more, hello.\n");
    printf("hello, world!\");
    printf("hello again!\n");
    return 0;
}
```

Committing the Results of the Merge

Whenever we've done a merge, `hg parents` will display two parents until we `hg commit` the results of the merge:

```
$ hg commit -m 'Merged changes'
```

We now have a new tip revision; notice that it has *both* of our former heads as its parents. These are the same revisions that were previously displayed by `hg parents`:

```
$ hg tip
changeset:   7:41ec93b29030
tag:         tip
parent:      5:cbfc9ee6ea99
parent:      6:12efb75cbece
user:        Bryan O'Sullivan <bos@serpentine.com>
date:        Tue May 05 06:44:52 2009 +0000
summary:     Merged changes
```

In Figure 3-3, you can see a representation of what happens to the working directory during the merge, and how this affects the repository when the commit happens. During the merge, the working directory has two parent changesets, and these become the parents of the new changeset.

We sometimes talk about a merge having *sides*: the left side is the first parent in the output of `hg parents`, and the right side is the second. If the working directory was at revision 5 before we began a merge, that revision will become the left side of the merge.

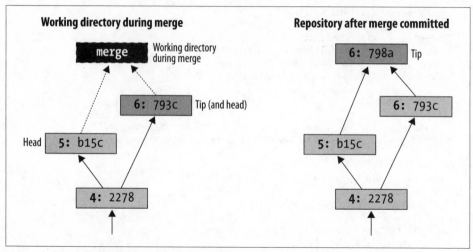

Figure 3-3. Working directory and repository during merge, and following commit

Merging Conflicting Changes

Most merges are simple affairs, but sometimes you'll find yourself merging changes where each side modifies the same portions of the same files. Unless both modifications are identical, this results in a *conflict*, where you have to decide how to reconcile the different changes into something coherent.

Figure 3-4 illustrates an instance of two conflicting changes to a document. We started with a single version of the file; then we made some changes, while someone else made different changes to the same text. Our task in resolving the conflicting changes is to decide what the file should look like.

Mercurial doesn't have a built-in facility for handling conflicts. Instead, it runs an external program, usually one that displays some kind of graphical conflict resolution interface. By default, Mercurial tries to find one of several different merging tools that are likely to be installed on your system. It first tries a few fully automatic merging tools; if these don't succeed (because the resolution process requires human guidance) or aren't present, it tries a few different graphical merging tools.

It's also possible to get Mercurial to run a specific program or script by setting the HGMERGE environment variable to the name of your preferred program.

Using a Graphical Merge Tool

My preferred graphical merge tool is kdiff3, which I'll use to describe the features that are common to graphical file merging tools. You can see a screenshot of kdiff3 in action in Figure 3-5. The kind of merge it is performing is called a *three-way merge*, because there are three different versions of the file of interest to us. The tool thus splits the upper portion of the window into three panes:

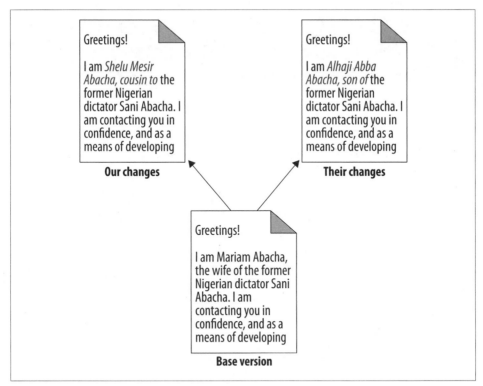

Our changes

Greetings!

I am *Shelu Mesir Abacha, cousin to* the former Nigerian dictator Sani Abacha. I am contacting you in confidence, and as a means of developing

Their changes

Greetings!

I am *Alhaji Abba Abacha, son of* the former Nigerian dictator Sani Abacha. I am contacting you in confidence, and as a means of developing

Base version

Greetings!

I am Mariam Abacha, the wife of the former Nigerian dictator Sani Abacha. I am contacting you in confidence, and as a means of developing

Figure 3-4. Conflicting changes to a document

- At the left is the *base* version of the file, i.e., the most recent version from which the two versions we're trying to merge are descended.
- In the middle is "our" version of the file, with the contents that we modified.
- On the right is "their" version of the file, the one from the changeset that we're trying to merge with.

In the pane below these is the current *result* of the merge. Our task is to replace all of the red text, which indicates unresolved conflicts, with some sensible merger of the "ours" and "theirs" versions of the file.

All four of these panes are *locked together*; if we scroll vertically or horizontally in any of them, the others are updated to display the corresponding sections of their respective files.

For each conflicting portion of the file, we can choose to resolve the conflict using some combination of text from the base version, ours, or theirs. We can also manually edit the merged file at any time, in case we need to make further modifications.

There are *many* file merging tools available, too many to cover here. They vary in which platforms they are available for, and in their particular strengths and weaknesses. Most

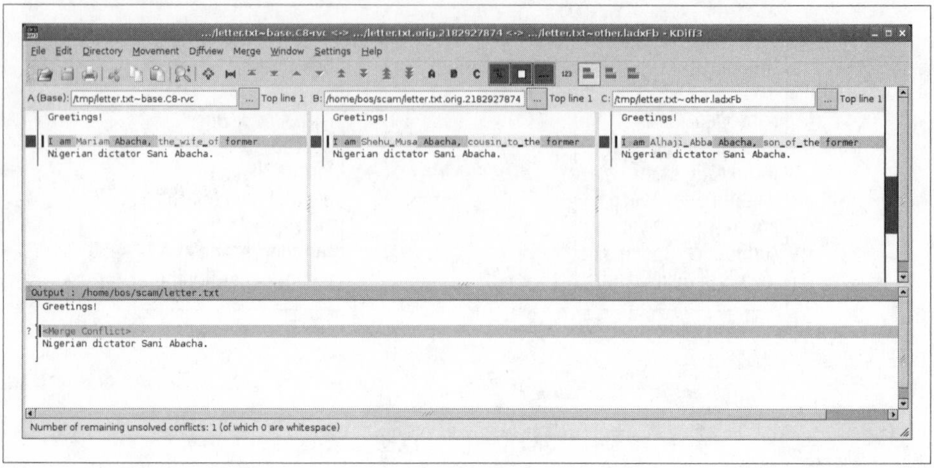

Figure 3-5. Using kdiff3 to merge versions of a file

are tuned for merging files containing plain text, while a few are aimed at specialized file formats (generally XML).

A Worked Example

In this example, we will reproduce the file modification history of Figure 3-4. Let's begin by creating a repository with a base version of our document:

```
$ cat > letter.txt <<EOF
> Greetings!
> I am Mariam Abacha, the wife of former
> Nigerian dictator Sani Abacha.
> EOF
$ hg add letter.txt
$ hg commit -m '419 scam, first draft'
```

We'll clone the repository and make a change to the file:

```
$ cd ..
$ hg clone scam scam-cousin
updating working directory
1 files updated, 0 files merged, 0 files removed, 0 files unresolved
$ cd scam-cousin
$ cat > letter.txt <<EOF
> Greetings!
> I am Shehu Musa Abacha, cousin to the former
> Nigerian dictator Sani Abacha.
> EOF
$ hg commit -m '419 scam, with cousin'
```

And another clone, to simulate someone else making a change to the file. (This hints at the idea that it's not all that unusual to merge with yourself when you isolate tasks in separate repositories, and indeed to find and resolve conflicts while doing so.)

```
$ cd ..
$ hg clone scam scam-son
updating working directory
1 files updated, 0 files merged, 0 files removed, 0 files unresolved
$ cd scam-son
$ cat > letter.txt <<EOF
> Greetings!
> I am Alhaji Abba Abacha, son of the former
> Nigerian dictator Sani Abacha.
> EOF
$ hg commit -m '419 scam, with son'
```

Having created two different versions of the file, we'll set up an environment suitable for running our merge:

```
$ cd ..
$ hg clone scam-cousin scam-merge
updating working directory
1 files updated, 0 files merged, 0 files removed, 0 files unresolved
$ cd scam-merge
$ hg pull -u ../scam-son
pulling from ../scam-son
searching for changes
adding changesets
adding manifests
adding file changes
added 1 changesets with 1 changes to 1 files (+1 heads)
not updating, since new heads added
(run 'hg heads' to see heads, 'hg merge' to merge)
```

In this example, I'll set HGMERGE to tell Mercurial to use the non-interactive merge command. This is bundled with many Unix-like systems. (If you're following this example on your computer, don't bother setting HGMERGE. You'll get dropped into a GUI file merge tool instead, which is much preferable.)

```
$ export HGMERGE=merge
$ hg merge
merging letter.txt
merge: warning: conflicts during merge
merging letter.txt failed!
0 files updated, 0 files merged, 0 files removed, 1 files unresolved
use 'hg resolve' to retry unresolved file merges
$ cat letter.txt
Greetings!
<<<<<<< /tmp/tour-merge-conflict_ULNXe/scam-merge/letter.txt
I am Shehu Musa Abacha, cousin to the former
=======
I am Alhaji Abba Abacha, son of the former
>>>>>>> /tmp/letter.txt~other.9ZxyYj
Nigerian dictator Sani Abacha.
```

Because merge can't resolve the conflicting changes, it leaves *merge markers* inside the file that has conflicts, indicating which lines have conflicts, and whether they came from our version of the file or theirs.

Mercurial can tell from the way merge exits that it wasn't able to merge successfully, so it tells us what commands we'll need to run if we want to redo the merging operation. This could be useful if, for example, we were running a graphical merge tool and quit because we were confused or realized we had made a mistake.

If automatic or manual merges fail, there's nothing to prevent us from "fixing up" the affected files ourselves, and committing the results of our merge:

```
$ cat > letter.txt <<EOF
> Greetings!
> I am Bryan O'Sullivan, no relation of the former
> Nigerian dictator Sani Abacha.
> EOF
$ hg resolve -m letter.txt
$ hg commit -m 'Send me your money'
$ hg tip
changeset:    3:cef275730d6e
tag:          tip
parent:       1:4a31891298cb
parent:       2:44d8436f9b83
user:         Bryan O'Sullivan <bos@serpentine.com>
date:         Tue May 05 06:44:53 2009 +0000
summary:      Send me your money
```

 Where is the hg resolve command?

The hg resolve command was introduced in Mercurial 1.1, which was released in December 2008. If you are using an older version of Mercurial (run hg version to see), this command will not be present. If your version of Mercurial is older than 1.1, you should strongly consider upgrading to a newer version before trying to tackle complicated merges.

Simplifying the Pull-Merge-Commit Sequence

The process of merging changes as outlined above is straightforward, but requires running three commands in sequence:

```
hg pull -u
hg merge
hg commit -m 'Merged remote changes'
```

In the case of the final commit, you also need to enter a commit message, which is almost always going to be a piece of uninteresting "boilerplate" text.

It would be nice to reduce the number of steps needed, if this were possible. Indeed, Mercurial is distributed with an extension called fetch that does just this.

Mercurial provides a flexible extension mechanism that lets people extend its functionality, while keeping the core of Mercurial small and easy to deal with. Some extensions add new commands that you can use from the command line, while others work "behind the scenes," for example adding capabilities to Mercurial's built-in server mode.

The `fetch` extension adds a new command called, not surprisingly, `hg fetch`. This extension acts as a combination of `hg pull -u`, `hg merge`, and `hg commit`. It begins by pulling changes from another repository into the current repository. If it finds that the changes added a new head to the repository, it updates to the new head, begins a merge, then (if the merge succeeded) commits the result of the merge with an automatically generated commit message. If no new heads were added, it updates the working directory to the new tip changeset.

Enabling the `fetch` extension is easy. Edit the *.hgrc* file in your home directory, and either go to or create the `extensions` section. Then add a line that simply reads fetch=:

```
[extensions]
fetch =
```

(Normally, the right-hand side of the = would indicate where to find the extension, but since the `fetch` extension is in the standard distribution, Mercurial knows where to search for it.)

Renaming, Copying, and Merging

During the life of a project, we will often want to change the layout of its files and directories. This can be as simple as renaming a single file, or as complex as restructuring the entire hierarchy of files within the project.

Mercurial supports these kinds of complex changes fluently, provided we tell it what we're doing. If we want to rename a file, we should use the `hg rename`* command to do so, so that Mercurial can do the right thing later when we merge.

We will cover the use of these commands in more detail in "Copying Files" on page 65.

---

* If you're a Unix user, you'll be glad to know that the `hg rename` command can be abbreviated as `hg mv`.

## CHAPTER 4

Behind the Scenes

Unlike many revision control systems, the concepts upon which Mercurial is built are simple enough that it's easy to understand how the software really works. Knowing these details certainly isn't necessary, so it is safe to skip this chapter. However, I think you will get more out of the software with a "mental model" of what's going on.

Being able to understand what's going on behind the scenes gives me confidence that Mercurial has been carefully designed to be both *safe* and *efficient*. And just as importantly, if it's easy for me to retain a good idea of what the software is doing when I perform a revision control task, I'm less likely to be surprised by its behavior.

In this chapter, we'll initially cover the core concepts behind Mercurial's design, then continue to discuss some of the interesting details of its implementation.

Mercurial's Historical Record

Tracking the History of a Single File

When Mercurial tracks modifications to a file, it stores the history of that file in a metadata object called a *filelog*. Each entry in the filelog contains enough information to reconstruct one revision of the file that is being tracked. Filelogs are stored as files in the *.hg/store/data* directory. A filelog contains two kinds of information: revision data, and an index to help Mercurial find a revision efficiently.

A file that is large, or has a lot of history, has its filelog stored in separate data (*.d* suffix) and index (*.i* suffix) files. For small files without much history, the revision data and index are combined in a single *.i* file. The correspondence between a file in the working directory and the filelog that tracks its history in the repository is illustrated in Figure 4-1.

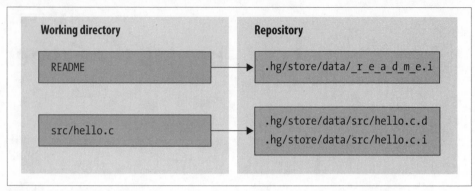

Figure 4-1. Relationships between files in working directory and filelogs in repository

Managing Tracked Files

Mercurial uses a structure called a *manifest* to collect together information about the files that it tracks. Each entry in the manifest contains information about the files present in a single changeset. An entry records which files are present in the changeset, the revision of each file, and a few other pieces of file metadata.

Recording Changeset Information

The *changelog* contains information about each changeset. Each revision records who committed a change, the changeset comment, other pieces of changeset-related information, and the revision of the manifest to use.

Relationships Between Revisions

Within a changelog, a manifest, or a filelog, each revision stores a pointer to its immediate parent (or to its two parents, if it's a merge revision). As I mentioned above, there are also relationships between revisions *across* these structures, and they are hierarchical in nature.

For every changeset in a repository, there is exactly one revision stored in the changelog. Each revision of the changelog contains a pointer to a single revision of the manifest. A revision of the manifest stores a pointer to a single revision of each filelog tracked when that changeset was created. These relationships are illustrated in Figure 4-2.

As the illustration shows, there is *not* a "one to one" relationship between revisions in the changelog, manifest, or filelog. If a file that Mercurial tracks hasn't changed between two changesets, the entry for that file in the two revisions of the manifest will point to the same revision of its filelog.[*]

---

[*] It is possible (though unusual) for the manifest to remain the same between two changesets, in which case the changelog entries for those changesets will point to the same revision of the manifest.

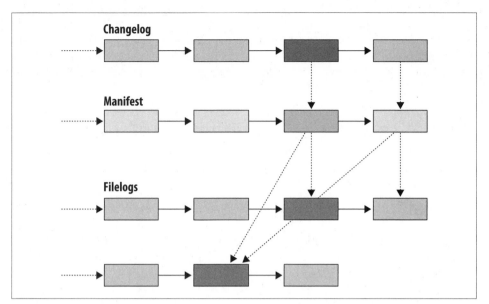

Figure 4-2. Metadata relationships

Safe, Efficient Storage

The underpinnings of changelogs, manifests, and filelogs are provided by a single structure called the *revlog*.

Efficient Storage

The revlog provides efficient storage of revisions using a *delta* mechanism. Instead of storing a complete copy of a file for each revision, it stores the changes needed to transform an older revision into the new revision. For many kinds of file data, these deltas are typically a fraction of a percent of the size of a full copy of a file.

Some obsolete revision control systems can only work with deltas of text files. They must either store binary files as complete snapshots or encoded into a text representation, both of which are wasteful approaches. Mercurial can efficiently handle deltas of files with arbitrary binary contents; it doesn't need to treat text as special.

Safe Operation

Mercurial only ever *appends* data to the end of a revlog file. It never modifies a section of a file after it has written it. This is both more robust and more efficient than schemes that need to modify or rewrite data.

In addition, Mercurial treats every write as part of a *transaction* that can span a number of files. A transaction is *atomic*: either the entire transaction succeeds and all its effects are visible to readers in one go, or the whole thing is undone. This guarantee of atomicity means that if you're running two copies of Mercurial, where one is reading data and one is writing it, the reader will never see a partially written result that might cause confusion.

The fact that Mercurial only appends to files makes it easier to provide this transactional guarantee. The easier it is to do stuff like this, the more confident you should be that it's done correctly.

Fast Retrieval

Mercurial cleverly avoids a pitfall common to all earlier revision control systems: the problem of *inefficient retrieval*. Most revision control systems store the contents of a revision as an incremental series of modifications against a "snapshot." (Some base the snapshot on the oldest revision, others on the newest.) To reconstruct a specific revision, you must first read the snapshot, and then every one of the revisions between the snapshot and your target revision. The more history that a file accumulates, the more revisions you must read, and hence the longer it takes to reconstruct a particular revision.

The innovation that Mercurial applies to this problem is simple but effective. Once the cumulative amount of delta information stored since the last snapshot exceeds a fixed threshold, it stores a new snapshot (compressed, of course) instead of another delta. This makes it possible to reconstruct *any* revision of a file quickly. This approach works so well that it has since been copied by several other revision control systems.

Figure 4-3 illustrates the idea. In an entry in a revlog's index file, Mercurial stores the range of entries from the data file that it must read to reconstruct a particular revision.

Aside: the influence of video compression

If you're familiar with video compression or have ever watched a TV feed through a digital cable or satellite service, you may know that most video compression schemes store each frame of video as a delta against its predecessor frame.

Mercurial borrows this idea to make it possible to reconstruct a revision from a snapshot and a small number of deltas.

Identification and Strong Integrity

Along with delta or snapshot information, a revlog entry contains a cryptographic hash of the data that it represents. This makes it difficult to forge the contents of a revision, and easy to detect accidental corruption.

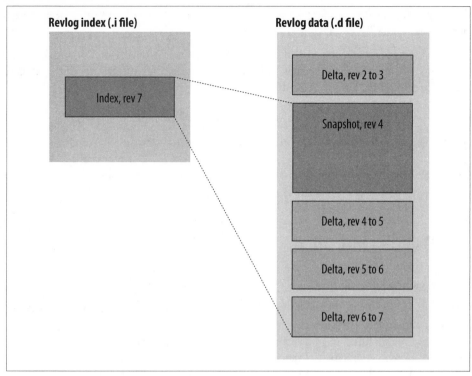

Figure 4-3. Snapshot of a revlog, with incremental deltas

Hashes provide more than a mere check against corruption; they are used as the identifiers for revisions. The changeset identification hashes that you see as an end user are from revisions of the changelog. Although filelogs and the manifest also use hashes, Mercurial only uses these behind the scenes.

Mercurial verifies that hashes are correct when it retrieves file revisions and when it pulls changes from another repository. If it encounters an integrity problem, it will complain and stop whatever it's doing.

In addition to the effect it has on retrieval efficiency, Mercurial's use of periodic snapshots makes it more robust against partial data corruption. If a revlog becomes partly corrupted due to a hardware error or system bug, it's often possible to reconstruct some or most revisions from the uncorrupted sections of the revlog, both before and after the corrupted section. This would not be possible with a delta-only storage model.

Revision History, Branching, and Merging

Every entry in a Mercurial revlog knows the identity of its immediate ancestor revision, usually referred to as its *parent*. In fact, a revision contains room for not one parent, but two. Mercurial uses a special hash, called the *null ID*, to represent the idea "there is no parent here." This hash is simply a string of zeros.

In Figure 4-4, you can see an example of the conceptual structure of a revlog. Filelogs, manifests, and changelogs all have this same structure; they differ only in the kind of data stored in each delta or snapshot.

The first revision in a revlog (at the bottom of the image) has the null ID in both of its parent slots. For a "normal" revision, its first parent slot contains the ID of its parent revision, and its second contains the null ID, indicating that the revision has only one real parent. Any two revisions that have the same parent ID are branches. A revision that represents a merge between branches has two normal revision IDs in its parent slots.

The Working Directory

In the working directory, Mercurial stores a snapshot of the files from the repository as of a particular changeset.

The working directory "knows" which changeset it contains. When you update the working directory to contain a particular changeset, Mercurial looks up the appropriate revision of the manifest to find out which files it was tracking at the time that changeset was committed, and which revision of each file was then current. It then recreates a copy of each of those files, with the same contents it had when the changeset was committed.

The *dirstate* is a special structure that contains Mercurial's knowledge of the working directory. It is maintained as a file named *.hg/dirstate* inside a repository. The dirstate details which changeset the working directory is updated to, and all of the files that Mercurial is tracking in the working directory. It also lets Mercurial quickly notice changed files, by recording their checkout times and sizes.

Just as a revision of a revlog has room for two parents, so that it can represent either a normal revision (with one parent) or a merge of two earlier revisions, the dirstate also has slots for two parents. When you use the `hg update` command, the changeset that you update to is stored in the "first parent" slot, and the null ID in the second. When you `hg merge` with another changeset, the first parent remains unchanged, and the second parent is filled in with the changeset you're merging with. The `hg parents` command tells you what the parents of the dirstate are.

What Happens When You Commit

The dirstate stores parent information for more than just book-keeping purposes. Mercurial uses the parents of the dirstate as *the parents of a new changeset* when you perform a commit.

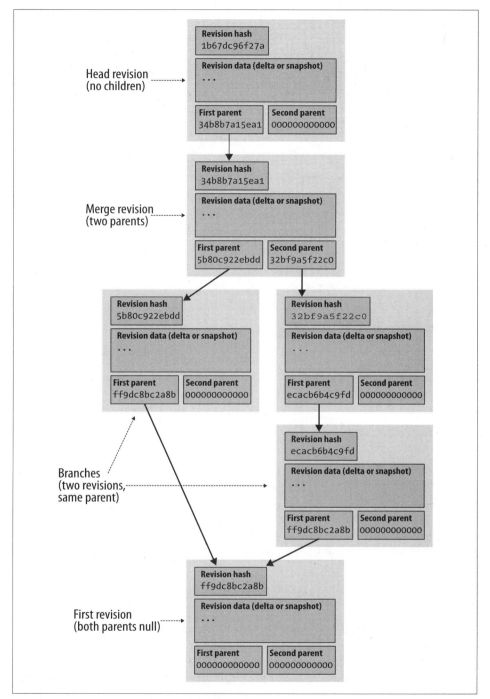

Figure 4-4. The conceptual structure of a revlog

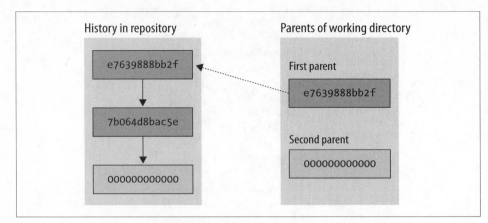

Figure 4-5. The working directory can have two parents

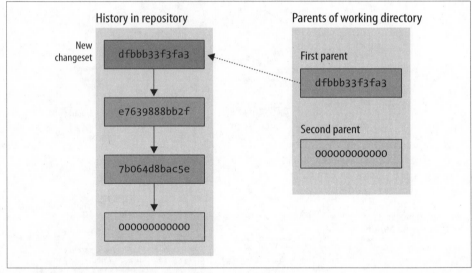

Figure 4-6. The working directory gains new parents after a commit

Figure 4-5 shows the normal state of the working directory, where it has a single changeset as parent. That changeset is the *tip*, the newest changeset in the repository that has no children.

It's useful to think of the working directory as "the changeset I'm about to commit." Any files that you tell Mercurial that you've added, removed, renamed, or copied will be reflected in that changeset, as will modifications to any files that Mercurial is already tracking; the new changeset will have the parents of the working directory as its parents.

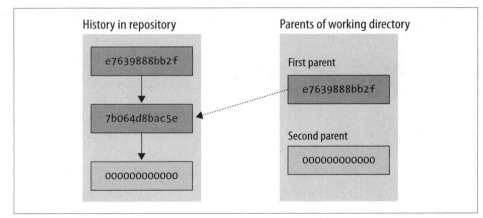

Figure 4-7. The working directory, updated to an older changeset

After a commit, Mercurial will update the parents of the working directory, so that the first parent is the ID of the new changeset, and the second is the null ID. This is shown in Figure 4-6. Mercurial doesn't touch any of the files in the working directory when you commit; it just modifies the dirstate to note its new parents.

Creating a New Head

It's perfectly normal to update the working directory to a changeset other than the current tip. For example, you might want to know what your project looked like last Tuesday, or you could be looking through changesets to see which one introduced a bug. In cases like this, the natural thing to do is update the working directory to the changeset you're interested in, and then examine the files in the working directory directly to see their contents as they were when you committed that changeset. The effect of this is shown in Figure 4-7.

Having updated the working directory to an older changeset, what happens if you make some changes, and then commit? Mercurial behaves in the same way as I outlined above. The parents of the working directory become the parents of the new changeset. This new changeset has no children, so it becomes the new tip. And the repository now contains two changesets that have no children; we call these *heads*. You can see the structure that this creates in Figure 4-8.

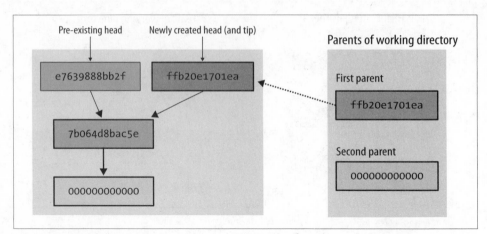

Figure 4-8. After a commit made while synced to an older changeset

 If you're new to Mercurial, you should keep in mind a common "error," which is to use the `hg pull` command without any options. By default, the `hg pull` command does *not* update the working directory, so you'll bring new changesets into your repository, but the working directory will stay synced at the same changeset as before the pull. If you make some changes and commit afterwards, you'll thus create a new head, because your working directory isn't synced to whatever the current tip is. To combine the operation of a pull, followed by an update, run `hg pull -u`.

I put the word "error" in quotes because all that you need to do to rectify the situation where you created a new head by accident is `hg merge`, then `hg commit`. In other words, this almost never has negative consequences; it's just something of a surprise for newcomers. I'll discuss other ways to avoid this behavior, and why Mercurial behaves in this initially surprising way, later on.

Merging Changes

When you run the `hg merge` command, Mercurial leaves the first parent of the working directory unchanged, and sets the second parent to the changeset you're merging with, as shown in Figure 4-9.

Mercurial also has to modify the working directory, to merge the files managed in the two changesets. Simplified a little, the merging process goes like this, for every file in the manifests of both changesets:

- If neither changeset has modified a file, do nothing with that file.
- If one changeset has modified a file and the other hasn't, create the modified copy of the file in the working directory.

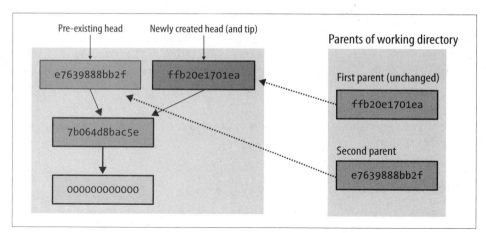

Figure 4-9. Merging two heads

- If one changeset has removed a file and the other hasn't (or has also deleted it), delete the file from the working directory.

- If one changeset has removed a file but the other has modified the file, ask the user what to do: keep the modified file, or remove it?

- If both changesets have modified a file, invoke an external merge program to choose the new contents for the merged file. This may require input from the user.

- If one changeset has modified a file and the other has renamed or copied the file, make sure that the changes follow the new name of the file.

There are more details—merging has plenty of corner cases—but these are the most common choices that are involved in a merge. As you can see, most cases are completely automatic, and indeed most merges finish automatically, without requiring your input to resolve any conflicts.

When you're thinking about what happens when you commit after a merge, once again the working directory is "the changeset I'm about to commit." After the `hg merge` command completes, the working directory has two parents; these will become the parents of the new changeset.

Mercurial lets you perform multiple merges, but you must commit the results of each individual merge as you go. This is necessary because Mercurial only tracks two parents for both revisions and the working directory. While it would be technically feasible to merge multiple changesets at once, Mercurial avoids this for simplicity. With multi-way merges, the risks of user confusion, nasty conflict resolution, and making a terrible mess of a merge would grow intolerable.

Merging and Renames

A surprising number of revision control systems pay little or no attention to a file's *name* over time. For instance, it used to be common that if a file got renamed on one side of a merge, the changes from the other side would be silently dropped.

Mercurial records metadata when you tell it to perform a rename or copy. It uses this metadata to do the right thing during a merge. For instance, if I rename a file, and you edit it without renaming it, when we merge our work the file will be renamed and have your edits applied.

Other Interesting Design Features

In the sections above, I've tried to highlight some of the most important aspects of Mercurial's design, to illustrate that it pays careful attention to reliability and performance. However, the attention to detail doesn't stop there. There are a number of other aspects of Mercurial's construction that I personally find interesting. I'll detail a few of them here, separate from the "big ticket" items above, so that if you're interested, you can gain a better idea of the amount of thinking that goes into a well-designed system.

Clever Compression

When appropriate, Mercurial will store both snapshots and deltas in compressed form. It does this by always *trying* to compress a snapshot or delta, but only storing the compressed version if it's smaller than the uncompressed version.

This means that Mercurial does "the right thing" when storing a file whose native form is compressed, such as a zip archive or a JPEG image. When these types of files are compressed a second time, the resulting file is usually bigger than the once-compressed form, and so Mercurial will store the plain zip or JPEG.

Deltas between revisions of a compressed file are usually larger than snapshots of the file, and Mercurial again does "the right thing" in these cases. It finds that such a delta exceeds the threshold at which it should store a complete snapshot of the file, so it stores the snapshot, again saving space compared to a naive delta-only approach.

Network recompression

When storing revisions on disk, Mercurial uses the "deflate" compression algorithm (the same one used by the popular `zip` archive format), which balances good speed with a respectable compression ratio. However, when transmitting revision data over a network connection, Mercurial uncompresses the compressed revision data.

If the connection is over HTTP, Mercurial recompresses the entire stream of data using a compression algorithm that gives a better compression ratio (the Burrows-Wheeler algorithm from the widely used `bzip2` compression package). This combination of algorithm and compression of the entire stream (instead of a revision at a time) substantially reduces the number of bytes to be transferred, yielding better network performance over most kinds of network.

If the connection is over ssh, Mercurial *doesn't* recompress the stream, because ssh can already do this itself. You can tell Mercurial to always use ssh's compression feature by editing the *.hgrc* file in your home directory as follows:

```
[ui]
ssh = ssh -C
```

Read/Write Ordering and Atomicity

Appending to files isn't the whole story when it comes to guaranteeing that a reader won't see a partial write. If you recall Figure 4-2, revisions in the changelog point to revisions in the manifest, and revisions in the manifest point to revisions in filelogs. This hierarchy is deliberate.

A writer starts a transaction by writing filelog and manifest data, and doesn't write any changelog data until those are finished. A reader starts by reading changelog data, then manifest data, followed by filelog data.

Since the writer has always finished writing filelog and manifest data before it writes to the changelog, a reader will never read a pointer to a partially written manifest revision from the changelog, and it will never read a pointer to a partially written filelog revision from the manifest.

Concurrent Access

The read/write ordering and atomicity guarantees mean that Mercurial never needs to *lock* a repository when it's reading data, even if the repository is being written to while the read is occurring. This has a big effect on scalability; you can have an arbitrary number of Mercurial processes safely reading data from a repository all at once, no matter whether it's being written to or not.

The lockless nature of reading means that if you're sharing a repository on a multi-user system, you don't need to grant other local users permission to *write* to your repository in order for them to be able to clone it or pull changes from it; they only need *read* permission. (This is *not* a common feature among revision control systems, so don't take it for granted! Most require readers to be able to lock a repository to access it safely, and this requires write permission on at least one directory, which of course makes for all kinds of nasty and annoying security and administrative problems.)

Mercurial uses locks to ensure that only one process can write to a repository at a time (the locking mechanism is safe even over filesystems that are notoriously hostile to locking, such as NFS). If a repository is locked, a writer will wait for a while to retry if the repository becomes unlocked, but if the repository remains locked for too long, the process attempting to write will time out after a while. This means that your daily automated scripts won't get stuck forever and pile up if a system crashes unnoticed, for example. (Yes, the timeout is configurable, from zero to infinity.)

Safe dirstate access

As with revision data, Mercurial doesn't take a lock to read the dirstate file; it does acquire a lock to write it. To avoid the possibility of reading a partially written copy of the dirstate file, Mercurial writes to a file with a unique name in the same directory as the dirstate file, then renames the temporary file atomically to *dirstate*. The file named *dirstate* is thus guaranteed to be complete, not partially written.

Avoiding Seeks

Critical to Mercurial's performance is the avoidance of seeks of the disk head, since any seek is far more expensive than even a comparatively large read operation.

This is why, for example, the dirstate is stored in a single file. If there were a dirstate file per directory that Mercurial tracked, the disk would seek once per directory. Instead, Mercurial reads the entire single dirstate file in one step.

Mercurial also uses a "copy on write" scheme when cloning a repository on local storage. Instead of copying every revlog file from the old repository into the new repository, it makes a "hard link," which is a shorthand way to say "these two names point to the same file." When Mercurial is about to write to one of a revlog's files, it checks to see if the number of names pointing at the file is greater than one. If it is, more than one repository is using the file, so Mercurial makes a new copy of the file that is private to this repository.

A few revision control developers have pointed out that this idea of making a complete private copy of a file is not very efficient in its use of storage. While this is true, storage is cheap, and this method gives the highest performance while deferring most bookkeeping to the operating system. An alternative scheme would most likely reduce performance and increase the complexity of the software, but speed and simplicity are key to the "feel" of day-to-day use.

Other Contents of the Dirstate

Because Mercurial doesn't force you to tell it when you're modifying a file, it uses the dirstate to store some extra information so it can determine efficiently whether you have modified a file. For each file in the working directory, it stores the time that it last modified the file itself, and the size of the file at that time.

When you explicitly hg add, hg remove, hg rename, or hg copy files, Mercurial updates the dirstate so that it knows what to do with those files when you commit.

The dirstate helps Mercurial to efficiently check the status of files in a repository:

- When Mercurial checks the state of a file in the working directory, it first checks a file's modification time against the time in the dirstate that records when Mercurial last wrote the file. If the last modified time is the same as the time when Mercurial wrote the file, the file must not have been modified, so Mercurial does not need to check any further.

- If the file's size has changed, the file must have been modified. If the modification time has changed but the size has not, only then does Mercurial need to actually read the contents of the file to see if it has changed.

Storing the modification time and size dramatically reduces the number of read operations that Mercurial needs to perform when we run commands like hg status. This results in large performance improvements.

## CHAPTER 5

Mercurial in Daily Use

Telling Mercurial Which Files to Track

Mercurial does not work with files in your repository unless you tell it to manage them. The hg status command will tell you which files Mercurial doesn't know about; it uses a ? to display such files.

To tell Mercurial to track a file, use the hg add command. Once you have added a file, the entry in the output of hg status for that file changes from ? to A.

```
$ hg init add-example
$ cd add-example
$ echo a > myfile.txt
$ hg status
? myfile.txt
$ hg add myfile.txt
$ hg status
A myfile.txt
$ hg commit -m 'Added one file'
$ hg status
```

After you run a hg commit, the files that you added before the commit will no longer be listed in the output of hg status. The reason for this is that by default, hg status only tells you about "interesting" files—those that you have (for example) modified, removed, or renamed. If you have a repository that contains thousands of files, you will rarely want to know about files that Mercurial is tracking, but that have not changed. (You can still get this information; we'll return to this later.)

Once you add a file, Mercurial doesn't do anything with it immediately. Instead, it will take a snapshot of the file's state the next time you perform a commit. It will then continue to track the changes you make to the file every time you commit, until you remove the file.

Explicit Versus Implicit File Naming

A useful behavior that Mercurial has is that if you pass the name of a directory to a command, every Mercurial command will treat this as "I want to operate on every file in this directory and its subdirectories."

```
$ mkdir b
$ echo b > b/somefile.txt
$ echo c > b/source.cpp
$ mkdir b/d
$ echo d > b/d/test.h
$ hg add b
adding b/d/test.h
adding b/somefile.txt
adding b/source.cpp
$ hg commit -m 'Added all files in subdirectory'
```

Notice in this example that Mercurial printed the names of the files it added, whereas it didn't do so when we added the file named *myfile.txt* in the earlier example.

What's going on is that in the former case, we explicitly named the file to add on the command line. The assumption that Mercurial makes in such cases is that we know what we are doing, and it doesn't print any output.

However, when we *imply* the names of files by giving the name of a directory, Mercurial takes the extra step of printing the name of each file that it does something with. This makes it more clear what is happening, and reduces the likelihood of a silent and nasty surprise. This behavior is common to most Mercurial commands.

Mercurial Tracks Files, Not Directories

Mercurial does not track directory information. Instead, it tracks the path to a file. Before creating a file, it first creates any missing directory components of the path. After it deletes a file, it then deletes any empty directories that were in the deleted file's path. This sounds like a trivial distinction, but it has one minor practical consequence: it is not possible to represent a completely empty directory in Mercurial.

Empty directories are rarely useful, and there are unintrusive workarounds that you can use to achieve an appropriate effect. The developers of Mercurial thus felt that the complexity that would be required to manage empty directories was not worth the limited benefit this feature would bring.

If you need an empty directory in your repository, there are a few ways to achieve this. One is to create a directory, then `hg add` a "hidden" file to that directory. On Unix-like systems, any filename that begins with a period (.) is treated as hidden by most commands and GUI tools. This approach is illustrated below.

```
$ hg init hidden-example
$ cd hidden-example
$ mkdir empty
$ touch empty/.hidden
```

```
$ hg add empty/.hidden
$ hg commit -m 'Manage an empty-looking directory'
$ ls empty
$ cd ..
$ hg clone hidden-example tmp
updating working directory
1 files updated, 0 files merged, 0 files removed, 0 files unresolved
$ ls tmp
empty
$ ls tmp/empty
```

Another way to tackle a need for an empty directory is to simply create one in your automated build scripts before they will need it.

How to Stop Tracking a File

Once you decide that a file no longer belongs in your repository, use the `hg remove` command. This deletes the file, and tells Mercurial to stop tracking it (which will occur at the next commit). A removed file is represented in the output of `hg status` with an R.

```
$ hg init remove-example
$ cd remove-example
$ echo a > a
$ mkdir b
$ echo b > b/b
$ hg add a b
adding b/b
$ hg commit -m 'Small example for file removal'
$ hg remove a
$ hg status
R a
$ hg remove b
removing b/b
```

After you `hg remove` a file, Mercurial will no longer track changes to that file, even if you recreate a file with the same name in your working directory. If you do recreate a file with the same name and want Mercurial to track the new file, simply `hg add` it. Mercurial will know that the newly added file is not related to the old file of the same name.

Removing a File Does Not Affect Its History

It is important to understand that removing a file has only two effects:

- It removes the current version of the file from the working directory.
- It stops Mercurial from tracking changes to the file, from the time of the next commit.

Removing a file does not in any way alter the history of the file.

If you update the working directory to a changeset that was committed when it was still tracking a file that you later removed, the file will reappear in the working directory, with the contents it had when you committed that changeset. If you then update the working directory to a later changeset, in which the file had been removed, Mercurial will once again remove the file from the working directory.

Missing Files

Mercurial considers a file that you have deleted, but not used `hg remove` to delete, to be *missing*. A missing file is represented with ! in the output of `hg status`. Mercurial commands will not generally do anything with missing files.

```
$ hg init missing-example
$ cd missing-example
$ echo a > a
$ hg add a
$ hg commit -m 'File about to be missing'
$ rm a
$ hg status
! a
```

If your repository contains a file that `hg status` reports as missing, and you want the file to stay gone, you can run `hg remove --after` at any time later on, to tell Mercurial that you really did mean to remove the file.

```
$ hg remove --after a
$ hg status
R a
```

On the other hand, if you deleted the missing file by accident, give `hg revert` the name of the file to recover. It will reappear in unmodified form.

```
$ hg revert a
$ cat a
a
$ hg status
```

Aside: Why tell Mercurial explicitly to remove a file?

You might wonder why Mercurial requires you to explicitly tell it that you are deleting a file. Early in its development, Mercurial let you delete a file however you pleased; it would notice the absence of the file automatically when you next ran a `hg commit`, and stop tracking the file. In practice, this made it too easy to accidentally remove a file without noticing.

Useful Shorthand: Adding and Removing Files in One Step

Mercurial offers a combination command, `hg addremove`, that adds untracked files and marks missing files as removed.

```
$ hg init addremove-example
$ cd addremove-example
$ echo a > a
$ echo b > b
$ hg addremove
adding a
adding b
```

The hg commit command also provides a -A option that performs this same add-and-remove, immediately followed by a commit.

```
$ echo c > c
$ hg commit -A -m 'Commit with addremove'
adding c
```

Copying Files

Mercurial provides a hg copy command that lets you make a new copy of a file. When you copy a file using this command, Mercurial makes a record of the fact that the new file is a copy of the original file. It treats these copied files specially when you merge your work with someone else's.

The Results of Copying During a Merge

What happens during a merge is that changes "follow" a copy. To best illustrate what this means, let's create an example. We'll start with the usual tiny repository that contains a single file.

```
$ hg init my-copy
$ cd my-copy
$ echo line > file
$ hg add file
$ hg commit -m 'Added a file'
```

We need to do some work in parallel, so that we'll have something to merge. So let's clone our repository.

```
$ cd ..
$ hg clone my-copy your-copy
updating working directory
1 files updated, 0 files merged, 0 files removed, 0 files unresolved
```

Back in our initial repository, let's use the hg copy command to make a copy of the first file we created.

```
$ cd my-copy
$ hg copy file new-file
```

If we look at the output of the hg status command afterwards, the copied file looks just like a normal added file.

```
$ hg status
A new-file
```

But if we pass the -C option to `hg status`, it prints another line of output: this is the file that our newly added file was copied *from*.

```
$ hg status -C
A new-file
  file
$ hg commit -m 'Copied file'
```

Now, back in the repository we cloned, let's make a change in parallel. We'll add a line of content to the original file that we created.

```
$ cd ../your-copy
$ echo 'new contents' >> file
$ hg commit -m 'Changed file'
```

Now we have a modified *file* in this repository. When we pull the changes from the first repository, and merge the two heads, Mercurial will propagate the changes that we made locally to *file* into its copy, *new-file*.

```
$ hg pull ../my-copy
pulling from ../my-copy
searching for changes
adding changesets
adding manifests
adding file changes
added 1 changesets with 1 changes to 1 files (+1 heads)
(run 'hg heads' to see heads, 'hg merge' to merge)
$ hg merge
merging file and new-file to new-file
0 files updated, 1 files merged, 0 files removed, 0 files unresolved
(branch merge, don't forget to commit)
$ cat new-file
line
new contents
```

Why Should Changes Follow Copies?

This behavior—of changes to a file propagating out to copies of the file—might seem esoteric, but in most cases it's highly desirable.

First of all, remember that this propagation *only* happens when you merge. So if you `hg copy` a file, and subsequently modify the original file during the normal course of your work, nothing will happen.

The second thing to know is that modifications will only propagate across a copy as long as the changeset that you're merging changes from *hasn't yet seen* the copy.

The reason that Mercurial does this is as follows. Let's say I make an important bug fix in a source file, and commit my changes. Meanwhile, you've decided to `hg copy` the file in your repository, without knowing about the bug or having seen the fix, and you have started hacking on your copy of the file.

If you pulled and merged my changes, and Mercurial *didn't* propagate changes across copies, your new source file would now contain the bug, and unless you knew to propagate the bug fix by hand, the bug would remain in your copy of the file.

By automatically propagating the change that fixed the bug from the original file to the copy, Mercurial prevents this class of problem. To my knowledge, Mercurial is the only revision control system that propagates changes across copies like this.

Once your change history has a record that the copy and subsequent merge occurred, there's usually no further need to propagate changes from the original file to the copied file, and that's why Mercurial only propagates changes across copies at the first merge, and not afterwards.

How to Make Changes Not Follow a Copy

If, for some reason, you decide that this business of automatically propagating changes across copies is not for you, simply use your system's normal file copy command (on Unix-like systems, that's cp) to make a copy of a file, then hg add the new copy by hand. Before you do so, though, please do reread the previous section, and make an informed decision that this behavior is not appropriate to your specific case.

Behavior of the hg copy Command

When you use the hg copy command, Mercurial makes a copy of each source file as it currently stands in the working directory. This means that if you make some modifications to a file, then hg copy it without first having committed those changes, the new copy will also contain the modifications you have made up until that point. (I find this behavior a little counterintuitive, which is why I mention it here.)

The hg copy command acts similarly to the Unix cp command (you can use the hg cp alias if you prefer). We must supply two or more arguments, of which the last is treated as the *destination*, and all others are *sources*.

If you pass hg copy a single file as the source, and the destination does not exist, it creates a new file with that name.

```
$ mkdir k
$ hg copy a k
$ ls k
a
```

If the destination is a directory, Mercurial copies its sources into that directory.

```
$ mkdir d
$ hg copy a b d
$ ls d
a  b
```

Copying a directory is recursive, and preserves the directory structure of the source.

```
$ hg copy z e
copying z/a/c to e/a/c
```

If the source and destination are both directories, the source tree is recreated in the destination directory.

```
$ hg copy z d
copying z/a/c to d/z/a/c
```

As with the hg remove command, if you copy a file manually and then want Mercurial to know that you've copied the file, simply use the --after option to hg copy.

```
$ cp a n
$ hg copy --after a n
```

Renaming Files

It's rather more common to need to rename a file than to make a copy of it. The reason I discussed the hg copy command before talking about renaming files is that Mercurial treats a rename in essentially the same way as a copy. Therefore, knowing what Mercurial does when you copy a file tells you what to expect when you rename a file.

When you use the hg rename command, Mercurial makes a copy of each source file, then deletes it and marks the file as removed.

```
$ hg rename a b
```

The hg status command shows the newly copied file as added, and the copied-from file as removed.

```
$ hg status
A b
R a
```

As with the results of a hg copy, we must use the -C option to hg status to see that the added file is really being tracked by Mercurial as a copy of the original, now removed, file.

```
$ hg status -C
A b
  a
R a
```

As with hg remove and hg copy, you can tell Mercurial about a rename after the fact using the --after option. In most other respects, the behavior of the hg rename command, and the options it accepts, are similar to the hg copy command.

If you're familiar with the Unix command line, you'll be glad to know that the hg rename command can be invoked as hg mv.

Renaming Files and Merging Changes

Since Mercurial's rename is implemented as copy-and-remove, the same propagation of changes happens when you merge after a rename as after a copy.

If I modify a file, and you rename it to a new name, and then we merge our respective changes, my modifications to the file under its original name will be propagated into the file under its new name. (This is something you might expect to "simply work," but not all revision control systems actually do this.)

Whereas having changes follow a copy is a feature where you can perhaps nod and say "yes, that might be useful," it should be clear that having them follow a rename is definitely important. Without this facility, it would simply be too easy for changes to become orphaned when files are renamed.

Divergent Renames and Merging

The case of diverging names occurs when two developers start with a file—let's call it *foo*—in their respective repositories.

```
$ hg clone orig anne
updating working directory
1 files updated, 0 files merged, 0 files removed, 0 files unresolved
$ hg clone orig bob
updating working directory
1 files updated, 0 files merged, 0 files removed, 0 files unresolved
```

Anne renames the file to *bar*.

```
$ cd anne
$ hg rename foo bar
$ hg ci -m 'Rename foo to bar'
```

Meanwhile, Bob renames it to *quux*. (Remember that hg mv is an alias for hg rename.)

```
$ cd ../bob
$ hg mv foo quux
$ hg ci -m 'Rename foo to quux'
```

I like to think of this as a conflict because each developer has expressed different intentions about what the file ought to be named.

What do you think should happen when they merge their work? Mercurial's actual behavior is that it always preserves *both* names when it merges changesets that contain divergent renames.

```
# See http://www.selenic.com/mercurial/bts/issue455
$ cd ../orig
$ hg pull -u ../anne
pulling from ../anne
searching for changes
adding changesets
adding manifests
adding file changes
```

```
added 1 changesets with 1 changes to 1 files
1 files updated, 0 files merged, 1 files removed, 0 files unresolved
$ hg pull ../bob
pulling from ../bob
searching for changes
adding changesets
adding manifests
adding file changes
added 1 changesets with 1 changes to 1 files (+1 heads)
(run 'hg heads' to see heads, 'hg merge' to merge)
$ hg merge
warning: detected divergent renames of foo to:
 bar
 quux
1 files updated, 0 files merged, 0 files removed, 0 files unresolved
(branch merge, don't forget to commit)
$ ls
bar  quux
```

Notice that while Mercurial warns about the divergent renames, it leaves it up to you
to do something about the divergence after the merge.

Convergent Renames and Merging

Another kind of rename conflict occurs when two people choose to rename different
source files to the same *destination*. In this case, Mercurial runs its normal merge machinery, and lets you guide it to a suitable resolution.

Other Name-Related Corner Cases

Mercurial has a longstanding bug in which it fails to handle a merge where one side
has a file with a given name, while another has a directory with the same name. This
is documented as issue 29 (*http://www.selenic.com/mercurial/bts/issue29*).

```
$ hg init issue29
$ cd issue29
$ echo a > a
$ hg ci -Ama
adding a
$ echo b > b
$ hg ci -Amb
adding b
$ hg up 0
0 files updated, 0 files merged, 1 files removed, 0 files unresolved
$ mkdir b
$ echo b > b/b
$ hg ci -Amc
adding b/b
created new head
$ hg merge
abort: Is a directory: /tmp/issue29Awb9eV/issue29/b
```

Recovering from Mistakes

Mercurial has some useful commands that will help you to recover from some common mistakes.

The `hg revert` command lets you undo changes that you have made to your working directory. For example, if you `hg add` a file by accident, just run `hg revert` with the name of the file you added, and while the file won't be touched in any way, it won't be tracked by Mercurial any longer, either. You can also use `hg revert` to get rid of erroneous changes to a file.

It is helpful to remember that the `hg revert` command is useful for changes that you have not yet committed. Once you've committed a change and then decide it was a mistake, you can still do something about it, though your options may be more limited.

For more information about the `hg revert` command, and details about how to deal with changes you have already committed, see Chapter 9.

Dealing with Tricky Merges

In a complicated or large project, it's not unusual for a merge of two changesets to result in some headaches. Suppose there's a big source file that's been extensively edited by each side of a merge: this is almost inevitably going to result in conflicts, some of which can take a few tries to sort out.

Let's develop a simple case of this and see how to deal with it. We'll start off with a repository containing one file, and clone it twice.

```
$ hg init conflict
$ cd conflict
$ echo first > myfile.txt
$ hg ci -A -m first
adding myfile.txt
$ cd ..
$ hg clone conflict left
updating working directory
1 files updated, 0 files merged, 0 files removed, 0 files unresolved
$ hg clone conflict right
updating working directory
1 files updated, 0 files merged, 0 files removed, 0 files unresolved
```

In one clone, we'll modify the file in one way.

```
$ cd left
$ echo left >> myfile.txt
$ hg ci -m left
```

In another, we'll modify the file differently.

```
$ cd ../right
$ echo right >> myfile.txt
$ hg ci -m right
```

Next, we'll pull each set of changes into our original repo.

```
$ cd ../conflict
$ hg pull -u ../left
pulling from ../left
searching for changes
adding changesets
adding manifests
adding file changes
added 1 changesets with 1 changes to 1 files
1 files updated, 0 files merged, 0 files removed, 0 files unresolved
$ hg pull -u ../right
pulling from ../right
searching for changes
adding changesets
adding manifests
adding file changes
added 1 changesets with 1 changes to 1 files (+1 heads)
not updating, since new heads added
(run 'hg heads' to see heads, 'hg merge' to merge)
```

We expect our repository to now contain two heads.

```
$ hg heads
changeset:   2:ef015a2d8ff7
tag:         tip
parent:      0:7795ddfbad20
user:        Bryan O'Sullivan <bos@serpentine.com>
date:        Tue May 05 06:44:30 2009 +0000
summary:     right

changeset:   1:9c07968fae18
user:        Bryan O'Sullivan <bos@serpentine.com>
date:        Tue May 05 06:44:30 2009 +0000
summary:     left
```

Normally, if we run hg merge at this point, it will drop us into a GUI that will let us manually resolve the conflicting edits to *myfile.txt*. However, to simplify things for presentation here, we'd like the merge to fail immediately instead. Here's one way we can do so.

```
$ export HGMERGE=merge
```

We've told Mercurial's merge machinery to run the command false (which, as we desire, fails immediately) if it detects a merge that it can't sort out automatically.

If we now fire up hg merge, it should grind to a halt and report a failure.

```
$ hg merge
merging myfile.txt
merge: warning: conflicts during merge
merging myfile.txt failed!
0 files updated, 0 files merged, 0 files removed, 1 files unresolved
use 'hg resolve' to retry unresolved file merges
```

Even if we don't notice that the merge failed, Mercurial will prevent us from accidentally committing the result of a failed merge.

```
$ hg commit -m 'Attempt to commit a failed merge'
abort: unresolved merge conflicts (see hg resolve)
```

When `hg commit` fails in this case, it suggests that we use the unfamiliar `hg resolve` command. As usual, `hg help resolve` will print a helpful synopsis.

File Resolution States

When a merge occurs, most files will usually remain unmodified. For each file where Mercurial has to do something, it tracks the state of the file:

- A *resolved* file has been successfully merged, either automatically by Mercurial or manually with human intervention.
- An *unresolved* file was not merged successfully, and needs more attention.

If Mercurial sees *any* file in the unresolved state after a merge, it considers the merge to have failed. Fortunately, we do not need to restart the entire merge from scratch.

The `--list` or `-l` option to `hg resolve` prints out the state of each merged file.

```
$ hg resolve -l
U myfile.txt
```

In the output from `hg resolve`, a resolved file is marked with `R`, while an unresolved file is marked with `U`. If any files are listed with `U`, we know that an attempt to commit the results of the merge will fail.

Resolving a File Merge

We have several options to move a file from the unresolved into the resolved state. By far the most common is to rerun `hg resolve`. If we pass the names of individual files or directories, it will retry the merges of any unresolved files present in those locations. We can also pass the `--all` or `-a` option, which will retry the merges of *all* unresolved files.

Mercurial also lets us modify the resolution state of a file directly. We can manually mark a file as resolved using the `--mark` option, or as unresolved using the `--unmark` option. This allows us to clean up a particularly messy merge by hand, and to keep track of our progress with each file as we go.

More Useful Diffs

The default output of the `hg diff` command is backwards compatible with the regular `diff` command, but this has some drawbacks.

Consider the case where we use `hg rename` to rename a file:

```
$ hg rename a b
$ hg diff
diff -r be6d2cb7c776 a
--- a/a     Tue May 05 06:44:29 2009 +0000
+++ /dev/null       Thu Jan 01 00:00:00 1970 +0000
@@ -1,1 +0,0 @@
-a
diff -r be6d2cb7c776 b
--- /dev/null       Thu Jan 01 00:00:00 1970 +0000
+++ b/b     Tue May 05 06:44:29 2009 +0000
@@ -0,0 +1,1 @@
+a
```

The output of hg diff above obscures the fact that we simply renamed a file. The hg diff command accepts an option, --git or -g, to use a newer diff format that displays such information in a more readable form:

```
$ hg diff -g
diff --git a/a b/b
rename from a
rename to b
```

This option also helps with a case that can otherwise be confusing: a file that appears to be modified according to hg status, but for which hg diff prints nothing. This situation can arise if we change the file's execute permissions:

```
$ chmod +x a
$ hg st
M a
$ hg diff
```

The normal diff command pays no attention to file permissions, which is why hg diff prints nothing by default. If we supply it with the -g option, it tells us what really happened:

```
$ hg diff -g
diff --git a/a b/a
old mode 100644
new mode 100755
```

Which Files to Manage, and Which to Avoid

Revision control systems are generally best at managing text files that are written by humans, such as source code, where the files do not change much from one revision to the next. Some centralized revision control systems can also deal tolerably well with binary files, such as bitmap images.

For instance, a game development team will typically manage both its source code and all of its binary assets (e.g., geometry data, textures, map layouts) in a revision control system.

Because it is usually impossible to merge two conflicting modifications to a binary file, centralized systems often provide a file locking mechanism that allows a user to say "I am the only person who can edit this file."

Compared to a centralized system, a distributed revision control system changes some of the factors that guide decisions over which files to manage and how.

For instance, a distributed revision control system cannot, by its nature, offer a file locking facility. There is thus no built-in mechanism to prevent two people from making conflicting changes to a binary file. If you have a team where several people may be editing binary files frequently, it may not be a good idea to use Mercurial—or any other distributed revision control system—to manage those files.

When storing modifications to a file, Mercurial usually saves only the differences between the previous and current versions of the file. For most text files, this is extremely efficient. However, some files (particularly binary files) are laid out in such a way that even a small change to a file's logical content results in many or most of the bytes inside the file changing. For instance, compressed files are particularly susceptible to this. If the differences between each successive version of a file are always large, Mercurial will not be able to store the file's revision history very efficiently. This can affect both local storage needs and the amount of time it takes to clone a repository.

To get an idea of how this could affect you in practice, suppose you want to use Mercurial to manage an OpenOffice document. OpenOffice stores documents on disk as compressed zip files. Edit even a single letter of your document in OpenOffice, and almost every byte in the entire file will change when you save it. Now suppose that file is 2MB in size. Because most of the file changes every time you save, Mercurial will have to store all 2MB of the file every time you commit, even though from your perspective, perhaps only a few words are changing each time. A single frequently edited file that is not friendly to Mercurial's storage assumptions can easily have an outsized effect on the size of the repository.

Even worse, if both you and someone else edit the OpenOffice document you're working on, there is no useful way to merge your work. In fact, there isn't even a good way to tell what the differences are between your respective changes.

There are thus a few clear recommendations about specific kinds of files to be very careful with.

- Files that are very large and incompressible, e.g., ISO CD-ROM images, will by virtue of sheer size make clones over a network very slow.

- Files that change a lot from one revision to the next may be expensive to store if you edit them frequently, and conflicts due to concurrent edits may be difficult to resolve.

Backups and Mirroring

Since Mercurial maintains a complete copy of history in each clone, everyone who uses Mercurial to collaborate on a project can potentially act as a source of backups in the event of a catastrophe. If a central repository becomes unavailable, you can construct a replacement simply by cloning a copy of the repository from one contributor, and pulling any changes they may not have seen from others.

It is simple to use Mercurial to perform offsite backups and remote mirrors. Set up a periodic job (e.g., via the `cron` command) on a remote server to pull changes from your master repositories every hour. This will only be tricky in the unlikely case that the number of master repositories you maintain changes frequently, in which case you'll need to do a little scripting to refresh the list of repositories to back up.

If you perform traditional backups of your master repositories to tape or disk, and you want to back up a repository named *myrepo*, use `hg clone -U myrepo myrepo.bak` to create a clone of *myrepo* before you start your backups. The `-U` option doesn't check out a working directory after the clone completes, since that would be superfluous and make the backup take longer.

If you then back up *myrepo.bak* instead of *myrepo*, you will be guaranteed to have a consistent snapshot of your repository that won't be pushed to by an insomniac developer in mid-backup.

## CHAPTER 6

Collaborating with Other People

As a completely decentralized tool, Mercurial doesn't impose any policy on how people ought to work with each other. However, if you're new to distributed revision control, it helps to have some tools and examples in mind when you're thinking about possible workflow models.

Mercurial's Web Interface

Mercurial has a powerful web interface that provides several useful capabilities.

For interactive use, the web interface lets you browse a single repository or a collection of repositories. You can view the history of a repository, examine each change (comments and diffs), and view the contents of each directory and file. You can even get a view of history that gives a graphical view of the relationships between individual changes and merges.

Also for human consumption, the web interface provides Atom and RSS feeds of the changes in a repository. This lets you "subscribe" to a repository using your favorite feed reader, and be automatically notified of activity in that repository as soon as it happens. I find this capability much more convenient than the model of subscribing to a mailing list to which notifications are sent, as it requires no additional configuration on the part of whoever is serving the repository.

The web interface also lets remote users clone a repository, pull changes from it, and (when the server is configured to permit it) push changes back to it. Mercurial's HTTP tunneling protocol aggressively compresses data, so that it works efficiently even over low-bandwidth network connections.

The easiest way to get started with the web interface is to use your web browser to visit an existing repository, such as the master Mercurial repository at *http://www.selenic .com/repo/hg*.

If you're interested in providing a web interface to your own repositories, there are several good ways to do this.

The easiest and fastest way to get started in an informal environment is to use the hg serve command, which is best suited to short-term "lightweight" serving. See "Informal Sharing with hg serve" on page 85 for details of how to use this command.

For longer-lived repositories that you'd like to have permanently available, there are several public hosting services. Some are free to open source projects, while others offer paid commercial hosting. An up-to-date list is available at *http://www.selenic.com/mercurial/wiki/index.cgi/MercurialHosting*.

If you would prefer to host your own repositories, Mercurial has built-in support for several popular hosting technologies, most notably CGI (Common Gateway Interface) and WSGI (Web Services Gateway Interface). See "Serving Over HTTP Using CGI" on page 91 for details of CGI and WSGI configuration.

Collaboration Models

With a suitably flexible tool, making decisions about workflow is much more of a social engineering challenge than a technical one. Mercurial imposes few limitations on how you can structure the flow of work in a project, so it's up to you and your group to set up and live with a model that matches your own particular needs.

Factors to Keep in Mind

The most important aspect of any model that you must keep in mind is how well it matches the needs and capabilities of the people who will be using it. This might seem self-evident; even so, you can't afford to forget it even for a moment.

I once put together a workflow model that seemed to make perfect sense to me, but that caused a considerable amount of consternation and strife within my development team. In spite of my attempts to explain why we needed a complex set of branches, and how changes ought to flow between them, a few team members revolted. Even though they were smart people, they didn't want to pay attention to the constraints we were operating under, or face the consequences of those constraints in the details of the model that I was advocating.

Don't sweep foreseeable social or technical problems under the rug. Whatever scheme you put into effect, you should plan for mistakes and problem scenarios. Consider adding automated machinery to prevent, or quickly recover from, trouble that you can anticipate. As an example, if you intend to have a branch with not-for-release changes in it, you'd do well to think early about the possibility that someone might accidentally merge those changes into a release branch. You could avoid this particular problem by writing a hook that prevents changes from being merged from an inappropriate branch.

Informal Anarchy

I wouldn't suggest an "anything goes" approach as something sustainable, but it's a model that's easy to grasp, and it works perfectly well in a few unusual situations.

As one example, many projects have a loose-knit group of collaborators who rarely physically meet each other. Some groups like to overcome the isolation of working at a distance by organizing occasional "sprints." In a sprint, a number of people get together in a single location (a company's conference room, a hotel meeting room, that kind of place) and spend several days more or less locked in there, hacking intensely on a handful of projects.

A sprint or hacking session in a coffee shop is the perfect place to use the `hg serve` command, since `hg serve` does not require any fancy server infrastructure. You can get started with `hg serve` in moments, by reading "Informal Sharing with hg serve" on page 85. Then simply tell the person next to you that you're running a server, send the URL to them in an instant message, and you immediately have a quick-turnaround way to work together. They can type your URL into their web browser and quickly review your changes; they can pull a bug fix from you and verify it; or they can clone a branch containing a new feature and try it out.

The charm, and the problem, with doing things in an ad-hoc fashion like this is that only people who know about your changes, and where they are, can see them. Such an informal approach simply doesn't scale beyond a handful of people, because each individual needs to know about n different repositories to pull from.

A Single Central Repository

For smaller projects migrating from a centralized revision control tool, perhaps the easiest way to get started is to have changes flow through a single shared central repository. This is also the most common "building block" for more ambitious workflow schemes.

Contributors start by cloning a copy of this repository. They can pull changes from it whenever they need to, and some (perhaps all) developers have permission to push a change back when they're ready for other people to see it.

Under this model, it can still often make sense for people to pull changes directly from each other, without going through the central repository. Consider a case in which I have a tentative bug fix, but I am worried that if I were to publish it to the central repository, it might subsequently break everyone else's trees as they pull it. To reduce the potential for damage, I can ask you to clone my repository into a temporary repository of your own and test it. This lets us put off publishing the potentially unsafe change until it has had a little testing.

If a team is hosting its own repository in this kind of scenario, people will usually use the `ssh` protocol to securely push changes to the central repository, as documented in

"Using the Secure Shell Protocol" on page 86. It's also usual to publish a read-only copy of the repository over HTTP, as in "Serving Over HTTP Using CGI" on page 91. Publishing over HTTP satisfies the needs of people who don't have push access, and those who want to use web browsers to browse the repository's history.

A Hosted Central Repository

A wonderful thing about public hosting services like Bitbucket (*http://bitbucket.org/*) is that not only do they handle the fiddly server configuration details, such as user accounts, authentication, and secure wire protocols, they provide additional infrastructure to make this model work well.

For instance, a well-engineered hosting service will let people clone their own copies of a repository with a single click. This lets people work in separate spaces and share their changes when they're ready.

In addition, a good hosting service will let people communicate with each other, for instance to say "there are changes ready for you to review in this tree."

Working with Multiple Branches

Projects of any significant size naturally tend to make progress on several fronts simultaneously. In the case of software, it's common for a project to go through periodic official releases. A release might then go into "maintenance mode" for a while after its first publication; maintenance releases tend to contain only bug fixes, not new features. In parallel with these maintenance releases, one or more future releases may be under development. People normally use the word "branch" to refer to one of these many slightly different directions in which development is proceeding.

Mercurial is particularly well suited to managing a number of simultaneous, but not identical, branches. Each "development direction" can live in its own central repository, and you can merge changes from one to another as the need arises. Because repositories are independent of each other, unstable changes in a development branch will never affect a stable branch unless someone explicitly merges those changes into the stable branch.

Here's an example of how this can work in practice. Let's say you have one "main branch" on a central server.

```
$ hg init main
$ cd main
$ echo 'This is a boring feature.' > myfile
$ hg commit -A -m 'We have reached an important milestone!'
adding myfile
```

People clone it, make changes locally, test them, and push them back.

Once the main branch reaches a release milestone, you can use the `hg tag` command to give a permanent name to the milestone revision.

```
$ hg tag v1.0
$ hg tip
changeset:   1:50a91fd70908
tag:         tip
user:        Bryan O'Sullivan <bos@serpentine.com>
date:        Tue May 05 06:44:27 2009 +0000
summary:     Added tag v1.0 for changeset 1af137d00325

$ hg tags
tip                               1:50a91fd70908
v1.0                              0:1af137d00325
```

Let's say some ongoing development occurs on the main branch.

```
$ cd ../main
$ echo 'This is exciting and new!' >> myfile
$ hg commit -m 'Add a new feature'
$ cat myfile
This is a boring feature.
This is exciting and new!
```

Using the tag that was recorded at the milestone, people who clone that repository at any time in the future can use `hg update` to get a copy of the working directory exactly as it was when that tagged revision was committed.

```
$ cd ..
$ hg clone -U main main-old
$ cd main-old
$ hg update v1.0
1 files updated, 0 files merged, 0 files removed, 0 files unresolved
$ cat myfile
This is a boring feature.
```

In addition, immediately after the main branch is tagged, we can then clone the main branch on the server to a new "stable" branch, also on the server.

```
$ cd ..
$ hg clone -rv1.0 main stable
requesting all changes
adding changesets
adding manifests
adding file changes
added 1 changesets with 1 changes to 1 files
updating working directory
1 files updated, 0 files merged, 0 files removed, 0 files unresolved
```

If we need to make a change to the stable branch, we can then clone *that* repository, make our changes, commit, and push our changes back there.

```
$ hg clone stable stable-fix
updating working directory
1 files updated, 0 files merged, 0 files removed, 0 files unresolved
$ cd stable-fix
```

```
$ echo 'This is a fix to a boring feature.' > myfile
$ hg commit -m 'Fix a bug'
$ hg push
pushing to /tmp/branchingOreYcT/stable
searching for changes
adding changesets
adding manifests
adding file changes
added 1 changesets with 1 changes to 1 files
```

Because Mercurial repositories are independent, and Mercurial doesn't move changes around automatically, the stable and main branches are *isolated* from each other. The changes that we made on the main branch don't "leak" to the stable branch, and vice versa.

We'll often want all of our bug fixes on the stable branch to show up on the main branch, too. Rather than rewrite a bug fix on the main branch, we can simply pull and merge changes from the stable to the main branch, and Mercurial will bring those bug fixes in for us.

```
$ cd ../main
$ hg pull ../stable
pulling from ../stable
searching for changes
adding changesets
adding manifests
adding file changes
added 1 changesets with 1 changes to 1 files (+1 heads)
(run 'hg heads' to see heads, 'hg merge' to merge)
$ hg merge
merging myfile
0 files updated, 1 files merged, 0 files removed, 0 files unresolved
(branch merge, don't forget to commit)
$ hg commit -m 'Bring in bugfix from stable branch'
$ cat myfile
This is a fix to a boring feature.
This is exciting and new!
```

The main branch will still contain changes that are not on the stable branch, but it will also contain all of the bug fixes from the stable branch. The stable branch remains unaffected by these changes, since changes are only flowing from the stable to the main branch, and not the other way.

Feature Branches

For larger projects, an effective way to manage change is to break up a team into smaller groups. Each group has a shared branch of its own, cloned from a single "master" branch used by the entire project. People working on an individual branch are typically quite isolated from developments on other branches (see Figure 6-1).

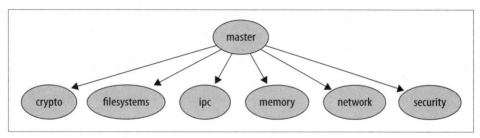

Figure 6-1. Feature branches

When a particular feature is deemed to be in suitable shape, someone on that feature team pulls and merges from the master branch into the feature branch, then pushes back up to the master branch.

The Release Train

Some projects are organized on a "train" basis: a release is scheduled to happen every few months, and whatever features are ready when the "train" is ready to leave are allowed in.

This model resembles working with feature branches. The difference is that when a feature branch misses a train, someone on the feature team pulls and merges the changes that went out on that train release into the feature branch, and the team continues its work on top of that release so that their feature can make the next release.

The Linux Kernel Model

The development of the Linux kernel has a shallow hierarchical structure, surrounded by a cloud of apparent chaos. Because most Linux developers use Git, a distributed revision control tool with capabilities similar to Mercurial, it's useful to describe the way work flows in that environment; if you like the ideas, the approach translates well across tools.

At the center of the community sits Linus Torvalds, the creator of Linux. He publishes a single source repository that is considered the "authoritative" current tree by the entire developer community. Anyone can clone Linus's tree, but he is very choosy about whose trees he pulls from.

Linus has a number of "trusted lieutenants." As a general rule, he pulls whatever changes they publish, in most cases without even reviewing those changes. Some of those lieutenants are generally agreed to be "maintainers," responsible for specific subsystems within the kernel. If a random kernel hacker wants to make a change to a subsystem that they want to end up in Linus's tree, they must find out who the subsystem's maintainer is, and ask that maintainer to take their change. If the maintainer reviews the changes and agrees to take them, the maintainer will pass them along to Linus in due course.

Individual lieutenants have their own approaches to reviewing, accepting, and publishing changes, and for deciding when to feed them to Linus. In addition, there are several well-known branches that people use for different purposes. For example, a few people maintain "stable" repositories of older versions of the kernel, to which they apply critical fixes as needed. Some maintainers publish multiple trees: one for experimental changes, one for changes that they are about to feed upstream, and so on. Others just publish a single tree.

This model has two notable features. The first is that it's "pull only." You have to ask, convince, or beg another developer to take a change from you, because there are almost no trees to which more than one person can push, and there's no way to push changes into a tree that someone else controls.

The second is that it's based on reputation and acclaim. If you're an unknown, Linus will probably ignore changes from you without even responding. But a subsystem maintainer will probably review them, and will likely take them if they pass their criteria for suitability. The more "good" changes you contribute to a maintainer, the more likely they are to trust your judgment and accept your changes. If you're well known and maintain a long-lived branch for something Linus hasn't yet accepted, people with similar interests may pull your changes regularly to keep up with your work.

Reputation and acclaim don't necessarily cross subsystem or "people" boundaries. If you're a respected but specialized storage hacker, and you try to fix a networking bug, that change will receive a level of scrutiny from a network maintainer comparable to a change from a complete stranger.

To people who come from more orderly project backgrounds, the comparatively chaotic Linux kernel development process often seems completely insane. It's subject to the whims of individuals; people make sweeping changes whenever they deem it appropriate; and the pace of development is astounding. And yet Linux is a highly successful, well-regarded piece of software.

Pull-Only Versus Shared-Push Collaboration

A perpetual source of heat in the open source community is whether a development model in which people only ever pull changes from others is "better than" one in which multiple people can push changes to a shared repository.

Typically, the backers of the shared-push model use tools that actively enforce this approach. If you're using a centralized revision control tool such as Subversion, there's no way to make a choice over which model you'll use: the tool gives you shared-push, and if you want to do anything else, you'll have to roll your own approach on top (such as applying a patch by hand).

A good distributed revision control tool will support both models. You and your collaborators can then structure how you work together based on your own needs and preferences, not on what contortions your tools force you into.

Where Collaboration Meets Branch Management

Once you and your team set up some shared repositories and start propagating changes back and forth between local and shared repos, you begin to face a related but slightly different challenge: that of managing the multiple directions in which your team may be moving at once. Even though this subject is intimately related to how your team collaborates, it's dense enough to merit treatment of its own, in Chapter 8.

The Technical Side of Sharing

The remainder of this chapter is devoted to the question of sharing changes with your collaborators.

Informal Sharing with hg serve

Mercurial's `hg serve` command is wonderfully suited to small, tight-knit, and fast-paced group environments. It also provides a great way to get a feel for using Mercurial commands over a network.

Run `hg serve` inside a repository, and in under a second it will bring up a specialized HTTP server; this will accept connections from any client, and serve up data for that repository until you terminate it. Anyone who knows the URL of the server you just started, and can talk to your computer over the network, can then use a web browser or Mercurial to read data from that repository. A URL for a `hg serve` instance running on a laptop is likely to look something like `http://my-laptop.local:8000/`.

The `hg serve` command is *not* a general-purpose web server. It can do only two things:

- Allow people to browse the history of the repository it's serving, from their normal web browsers.

- Speak Mercurial's wire protocol, so that people can `hg clone` or `hg pull` changes from that repository.

In particular, `hg serve` won't allow remote users to *modify* your repository. It's intended for read-only use.

If you're getting started with Mercurial, there's nothing to prevent you from using `hg serve` to serve up a repository on your own computer, then use commands like `hg clone`, `hg incoming`, and so on to talk to that server as if the repository were hosted remotely. This can help you to quickly get acquainted with using commands on network-hosted repositories.

A Few Things to Keep in Mind

Because it provides unauthenticated read access to all clients, you should only use hg serve in an environment where you either don't care, or have complete control over, who can access your network and pull data from your repository.

The hg serve command knows nothing about any firewall software you might have installed on your system or network. It cannot detect or control your firewall software. If other people are unable to talk to a running hg serve instance, the second thing you should do (*after* you make sure that they're using the correct URL) is check your firewall configuration.

By default, hg serve listens for incoming connections on port 8000. If another process is already listening on the port you want to use, you can specify a different port to listen on using the -p option.

Normally, when hg serve starts, it prints no output, which can be a bit unnerving. If you'd like to confirm that it is indeed running correctly, and find out what URL you should send to your collaborators, start it with the -v option.

Using the Secure Shell Protocol

You can pull and push changes securely over a network connection using the Secure Shell (ssh) protocol. To use this successfully, you may have to do a little bit of configuration on the client or server sides.

If you're not familiar with ssh, it's the name of both a command and a network protocol that let you securely communicate with another computer. To use it with Mercurial, you'll be setting up one or more user accounts on a server so that remote users can log in and execute commands.

(If you *are* familiar with ssh, you'll probably find some of the material that follows to be elementary in nature.)

How to Read and Write ssh URLs

An ssh URL tends to look like this:

```
ssh://bos@hg.serpentine.com:22/hg/hgbook
```

1. The ssh:// part tells Mercurial to use the ssh protocol.
2. The bos@ component indicates what username to log into the server as. You can leave this out if the remote username is the same as your local username.
3. The hg.serpentine.com gives the hostname of the server to log into.
4. The :22 identifies the port number to connect to the server on. The default port is 22, so you only need to specify a colon and port number if you're *not* using port 22.
5. The remainder of the URL is the local path to the repository on the server.

There's plenty of scope for confusion with the path component of ssh URLs, as there is no standard way for tools to interpret it. Some programs behave differently than others when dealing with these paths. This isn't an ideal situation, but it's unlikely to change. Please read the following paragraphs carefully.

Mercurial treats the path to a repository on the server as relative to the remote user's home directory. For example, if user foo on the server has a home directory of */home/ foo*, then an ssh URL that contains a path component of *bar* in fact refers to the directory */home/foo/bar*.

If you want to specify a path relative to another user's home directory, you can use a path that starts with a tilde character followed by the user's name (let's say other user), like this.

```
ssh://server/~otheruser/hg/repo
```

And if you really want to specify an *absolute* path on the server, begin the path component with two slashes, as in this example.

```
ssh://server//absolute/path
```

Finding an ssh Client for Your System

Almost every Unix-like system comes with OpenSSH preinstalled. If you're using such a system, run which ssh to find out if the ssh command is installed (it's usually in */usr/ bin*). In the unlikely event that it isn't present, take a look at your system documentation to figure out how to install it.

On Windows, the TortoiseHg package is bundled with a version of Simon Tatham's excellent plink command, and you should not need to do any further configuration.

Generating a Key Pair

To avoid the need to repetitively type a password every time you need to use your ssh client, I recommend generating a key pair.

Key pairs are not mandatory
Mercurial knows nothing about ssh authentication or key pairs. You can, if you like, safely ignore this section and the one that follows until you grow tired of repeatedly typing ssh passwords.

- On a Unix-like system, the ssh-keygen command will do the trick.

  On Windows, if you're using TortoiseHg, you may need to download a command named puttygen from the PuTTY website (*http://www.chiark.greenend.org.uk/ ~sgtatham/putty*) to generate a key pair. See the puttygen documentation (*http://*

the.earth.li/~sgtatham/putty/0.60/htmldoc/Chapter8.html#pubkey-puttygen) for details of how to use the command.

When you generate a key pair, it's usually *highly* advisable to protect it with a passphrase. (The only time that you might not want to do this is when you're using the ssh protocol for automated tasks on a secure network.)

Simply generating a key pair isn't enough, however. You'll need to add the public key to the set of authorized keys for whatever user you're logging in remotely as. For servers using OpenSSH (the vast majority), this will mean adding the public key to a list in a file called *authorized_keys* in their *.ssh* directory.

On a Unix-like system, your public key will have a *.pub* extension. If you're using puttygen on Windows, you can save the public key to a file of your choosing, or paste it from the window it's displayed in straight into the *authorized_keys* file.

Using an Authentication Agent

An authentication agent is a daemon that stores passphrases in memory (so it will forget passphrases if you log out and log back in again). An ssh client will notice if it's running, and query it for a passphrase. If there's no authentication agent running, or the agent doesn't store the necessary passphrase, you'll have to type your passphrase every time Mercurial tries to communicate with a server on your behalf (e.g., whenever you pull or push changes).

The downside of storing passphrases in an agent is that it's possible for a well-prepared attacker to recover the plain text of your passphrases, in some cases even if your system has been power-cycled. You should make your own judgment as to whether this is an acceptable risk. It certainly saves a lot of repeated typing.

- On Unix-like systems, the agent is called ssh-agent, and it's often run automatically for you when you log in. You'll need to use the ssh-add command to add passphrases to the agent's store.

- On Windows, if you're using TortoiseHg, the pageant command acts as the agent. As with puttygen, you'll need to download pageant (*http://www.chiark.green end.org.uk/%7Esgtatham/putty/download.html*) from the PuTTY website and read its documentation (*http://the.earth.li/~sgtatham/putty/0.60/htmldoc/Chapter9 .html#pageant*). The pageant command adds an icon to your system tray that will let you manage stored passphrases.

Configuring the Server Side Properly

Because ssh can be fiddly to set up if you're new to it, a variety of things can go wrong. Add Mercurial on top, and there's plenty more scope for head-scratching. Most of these potential problems occur on the server side, not the client side. The good news is that once you've gotten a configuration working, it will usually continue to work indefinitely.

Before you try using Mercurial to talk to an ssh server, it's best to make sure that you can use the normal `ssh` or `putty` command to talk to the server first. If you run into problems with using these commands directly, Mercurial surely won't work. Worse, it will obscure the underlying problem. Any time you want to debug ssh-related Mercurial problems, you should drop back to making sure that plain ssh client commands work first, *before* you worry about whether there's a problem with Mercurial.

The first thing to be sure of on the server side is that you can actually log in from another machine at all. If you can't use `ssh` or `putty` to log in, the error message you get may give you a few hints as to what's wrong. The most common problems are as follows:

- If you get a "connection refused" error, either there isn't an ssh daemon running on the server at all, or it's inaccessible due to firewall configuration.

- If you get a "no route to host" error, you either have an incorrect address for the server or a seriously locked-down firewall that won't admit its existence at all.

- If you get a "permission denied" error, you may have mistyped the username on the server, or you could have mistyped your key's passphrase or the remote user's password.

In summary, if you're having trouble talking to the server's ssh daemon, first make sure that one is running at all. On many systems it will be installed, but disabled, by default. Once you're done with this step, you should then check that the server's firewall is configured to allow incoming connections on the port the ssh daemon is listening on (usually 22). Don't worry about more exotic possibilities for misconfiguration until you've checked these two first.

If you're using an authentication agent on the client side to store passphrases for your keys, you ought to be able to log into the server without being prompted for a passphrase or a password. If you're prompted for a passphrase, there are a few possible culprits:

- You might have forgotten to use `ssh-add` or `pageant` to store the passphrase.

- You might have stored the passphrase for the wrong key.

If you're being prompted for the remote user's password, there are a few other possible problems to check:

- Either the user's home directory or his *.ssh* directory might have excessively liberal permissions. As a result, the ssh daemon will not trust or read his *authorized_keys* file. For example, a group-writable home or *.ssh* directory will often cause this symptom.

- The user's *authorized_keys* file may have a problem. If anyone other than the user owns or can write to that file, the ssh daemon will not trust or read it.

In an ideal world, you should be able to run the following command successfully, and it should print exactly one line of output, the current date and time.

```
ssh myserver date
```

If, on your server, you have login scripts that print banners or other junk even when running non-interactive commands like this, you should fix them before you continue, so that they only print output if they're run interactively. Otherwise these banners will at least clutter up Mercurial's output. Worse, they could potentially cause problems with running Mercurial commands remotely. Mercurial tries to detect and ignore banners in non-interactive ssh sessions, but it is not foolproof. (If you're editing your login scripts on your server, the usual way to see if a login script is running in an interactive shell is to check the return code from the command `tty -s`.)

Once you've verified that plain old ssh is working with your server, the next step is to ensure that Mercurial runs on the server. The following command should run successfully:

```
ssh myserver hg version
```

If you see an error message instead of normal `hg version` output, this is usually because you haven't installed Mercurial to */usr/bin*. Don't worry if this is the case; you don't need to do that. But you should check for a few possible problems:

- Is Mercurial really installed on the server at all? I know this sounds trivial, but it's worth checking!
- Maybe your shell's search path (usually set via the `PATH` environment variable) is simply misconfigured.
- Perhaps your `PATH` environment variable is only being set to point to the location of the `hg` executable if the login session is interactive. This can happen if you're setting the path in the wrong shell login script. See your shell's documentation for details.
- The `PYTHONPATH` environment variable may need to contain the path to the Mercurial Python modules. It might not be set at all; it could be incorrect; or it may be set only if the login is interactive.

If you can run `hg version` over an ssh connection, well done! You've got the server and client sorted out. You should now be able to use Mercurial to access repositories hosted by that username on that server. If you run into problems with Mercurial and ssh at this point, try using the `--debug` option to get a clearer picture of what's going on.

Using Compression with ssh

Mercurial does not compress data when it uses the ssh protocol, because the ssh protocol can transparently compress data. However, the default behavior of ssh clients is *not* to request compression.

Over any network other than a fast LAN (even a wireless network), using compression is likely to significantly speed up Mercurial's network operations. For example, over a WAN, someone measured compression as reducing the amount of time required to clone a particularly large repository from 51 minutes to 17 minutes.

Both `ssh` and `plink` accept a `-C` option, which turns on compression. You can easily edit your ~/*.hgrc* to enable compression for all of Mercurial's uses of the ssh protocol. Here is how to do so for regular `ssh` on Unix-like systems, for example.

```
[ui]
ssh = ssh -C
```

If you use `ssh` on a Unix-like system, you can configure it to always use compression when talking to your server. To do this, edit your *.ssh/config* file (which may not yet exist) as follows.

```
Host hg
  Compression yes
  HostName hg.example.com
```

This defines a hostname alias, `hg`. When you use that hostname on the `ssh` command line or in a Mercurial `ssh`-protocol URL, it will cause `ssh` to connect to `hg.exam ple.com` and use compression. This gives you both a shorter name to type and compression, each of which is a good thing in its own right.

Serving Over HTTP Using CGI

The simplest way to host one or more repositories in a permanent way is to use a web server and Mercurial's CGI support.

Depending on how ambitious you are, configuring Mercurial's CGI interface can take anything from a few moments to several hours.

We'll begin with the simplest of examples, and work our way towards a more complex configuration. Even for the most basic case, you're almost certainly going to need to read and modify your web server's configuration.

High pain tolerance required

Configuring a web server is a complex, fiddly, and highly system-dependent activity. I can't possibly give you instructions that will cover anything like all of the cases you will encounter. Please use your discretion and judgment in following the sections below. Be prepared to make plenty of mistakes, and to spend a lot of time reading your server's error logs.

If you don't have a strong stomach for tweaking configurations over and over, or a compelling need to host your own services, you might want to try one of the public hosting services that I mentioned earlier.

Web Server Configuration Checklist

Before you continue, do take a few moments to check a few aspects of your system's setup.

1. Do you have a web server installed at all? Mac OS X and some Linux distributions ship with Apache, but many other systems may not have a web server installed.
2. If you have a web server installed, is it actually running? On most systems, even if one is present, it will be disabled by default.
3. Is your server configured to allow you to run CGI programs in the directory where you plan to do so? Most servers default to explicitly disabling the ability to run CGI programs.

If you don't have a web server installed, and don't have substantial experience configuring Apache, you should consider using the lighttpd web server instead of Apache. Apache has a well-deserved reputation for baroque and confusing configuration. While lighttpd is less capable in some ways than Apache, most of these capabilities are not relevant to serving Mercurial repositories. And lighttpd is undeniably *much* easier to get started with than Apache.

Basic CGI Configuration

On Unix-like systems, it's common for users to have a subdirectory named something like *public_html* in their home directory, from which they can serve up web pages. A file named *foo* in this directory will be accessible at a URL of the form *http://www.example.com/username/foo*.

To get started, find the *hgweb.cgi* script that should be present in your Mercurial installation. If you can't quickly find a local copy on your system, simply download one from the master Mercurial repository at *http://www.selenic.com/repo/hg/raw-file/tip/hgweb.cgi*.

You'll need to copy this script into your *public_html* directory, and ensure that it's executable.

```
cp .../hgweb.cgi ~/public_html
chmod 755 ~/public_html/hgweb.cgi
```

The 755 argument to chmod is a little more general than just making the script executable: it ensures that the script is executable by anyone, and that "group" and "other" write permissions are *not* set. If you were to leave those write permissions enabled, Apache's suexec subsystem would likely refuse to execute the script. In fact, suexec also insists that the *directory* in which the script resides must not be writable by others.

```
chmod 755 ~/public_html
```

What could possibly go wrong?

Once you've copied the CGI script into place, go into a web browser and try to open the URL *http://myhostname/~myuser/hgweb.cgi*, *but* brace yourself for instant failure. There's a high probability that trying to visit this URL will fail, and there are many possible reasons for this. In fact, you're likely to stumble over almost every one of the possible errors below, so please read carefully. The following are all of the problems I ran into on a system running Fedora 7, with a fresh installation of Apache, and a user account that I created specifically to perform this exercise.

Your web server may have per-user directories disabled. If you're using Apache, search your config file for a `UserDir` directive. If there's none present, per-user directories will be disabled. If one exists, but its value is `disabled`, then per-user directories will be disabled. Otherwise, the string after `UserDir` gives the name of the subdirectory that Apache will look in under your home directory, for example *public_html*.

Your file access permissions may be too restrictive. The web server must be able to traverse your home directory and directories under your *public_html* directory, and read files under the latter too. Here's a quick recipe to help you to make your permissions more appropriate.

```
chmod 755 ~
find ~/public_html -type d -print0 | xargs -0r chmod 755
find ~/public_html -type f -print0 | xargs -0r chmod 644
```

The other possibility with permissions is that you might get a completely empty window when you try to load the script. In this case, it's likely that your access permissions are too permissive. Apache's `suexec` subsystem won't execute a script that's group- or world-writable, for example.

Your web server may be configured to disallow execution of CGI programs in your per-user web directory. Here's Apache's default per-user configuration from my Fedora system.

```
<Directory /home/*/public_html>
  AllowOverride FileInfo AuthConfig Limit
  Options MultiViews Indexes SymLinksIfOwnerMatch IncludesNoExec
  <Limit GET POST OPTIONS>
    Order allow,deny
    Allow from all
  </Limit>
  <LimitExcept GET POST OPTIONS>
    Order deny,allow Deny from all
  </LimitExcept>
</Directory>
```

If you find a similar-looking `Directory` group in your Apache configuration, the directive to look at inside it is `Options`. Add `ExecCGI` to the end of this list if it's missing, and restart the web server.

If you find that Apache serves you the text of the CGI script instead of executing it, you may need to either uncomment (if already present) or add a directive like this.

```
AddHandler cgi-script .cgi
```

The next possibility is that you might be served with a colorful Python backtrace claiming that it can't import a mercurial-related module. This is actually progress! The server is now capable of executing your CGI script. This error is only likely to occur if you're running a private installation of Mercurial, instead of a systemwide version. Remember that the web server runs the CGI program without any of the environment variables that you take for granted in an interactive session. If this error happens to you, edit your copy of *hgweb.cgi* and follow the directions inside it to correctly set your PYTHON PATH environment variable.

Finally, you are *certain* to be served with another colorful Python backtrace: this one will complain that it can't find */path/to/repository*. Edit your *hgweb.cgi* script and re-place the */path/to/repository* string with the complete path to the repository you want to serve up.

At this point, when you try to reload the page, you should be presented with a nice HTML view of your repository's history. Whew!

Configuring lighttpd

To be exhaustive in my experiments, I tried configuring the increasingly popular lighttpd web server to serve the same repository as I described with Apache above. I had already overcome all of the problems I outlined with Apache, many of which are not server-specific. As a result, I was fairly sure that my file and directory permissions were good, and that my *hgweb.cgi* script was properly edited.

Once I had Apache running, getting lighttpd to serve the repository was a snap (in other words, even if you're trying to use lighttpd, you should read the Apache section). I first had to edit the mod_access section of its config file to enable mod_cgi and mod_user dir, both of which were disabled by default on my system. I then added a few lines to the end of the config file, to configure these modules.

```
userdir.path = "public_html"
cgi.assign = (".cgi" => "" )
```

With this done, lighttpd ran immediately for me. If I had configured lighttpd before Apache, I'd almost certainly have run into many of the same system-level configuration problems as I did with Apache. However, I found lighttpd to be noticeably easier to configure than Apache, even though I've used Apache for over a decade, and this was my first exposure to lighttpd.

Sharing Multiple Repositories with One CGI Script

The *hgweb.cgi* script only lets you publish a single repository, which is an annoying restriction. If you want to publish more than one without wracking yourself with

---

multiple copies of the same script, each with a different name, a better choice is to use the *hgwebdir.cgi* script.

The procedure to configure *hgwebdir.cgi* is only a little more involved than for *hgweb.cgi*. First, you must obtain a copy of the script. If you don't have one handy, you can download a copy from the master Mercurial repository at *http://www.selenic.com/ repo/hg/raw-file/tip/hgwebdir.cgi*.

You'll need to copy this script into your *public_html* directory, and ensure that it's executable.

```
cp .../hgwebdir.cgi ~/public_html
chmod 755 ~/public_html ~/public_html/hgwebdir.cgi
```

With basic configuration out of the way, try to visit `http://myhostname/~myuser/hgweb dir.cgi` in your browser. It should display an empty list of repositories. If you get a blank window or error message, try walking through the list of potential problems described in "What could possibly go wrong?" on page 93.

The *hgwebdir.cgi* script relies on an external configuration file. By default, it searches for a file named *hgweb.config* in the same directory as itself. You'll need to create this file, and make it world-readable. The format of the file is similar to a Windows "ini" file, as understood by Python's `ConfigParser` module (*http://docs.python.org/library/ configparser.html*).

The easiest way to configure *hgwebdir.cgi* is with a section named `collections`. This will automatically publish *every* repository under the directories you name. The section should look like this:

```
[collections]
/my/root = /my/root
```

Mercurial interprets this by looking at the directory name on the right-hand side of the equals sign, finding repositories in that directory hierarchy, and using the text on the left-hand side to strip off matching text from the names it will actually list in the web interface. The remaining component of a path after this stripping has occurred is called a "virtual path."

Given the example above, if we have a repository whose local path is */my/root/this/ repo*, the CGI script will strip the leading */my/root* from the name, and publish the repository with a virtual path of *this/repo*. If the base URL for our CGI script is `http:// myhostname/~myuser/hgwebdir.cgi`, the complete URL for that repository will be `http://myhostname/~myuser/hgwebdir.cgi/this/repo`.

If we replace */my/root* on the left-hand side of this example with */my*, then *hgweb dir.cgi* will only strip off */my* from the repository name, and will give us a virtual path of *root/this/repo* instead of *this/repo*.

The *hgwebdir.cgi* script will recursively search each directory listed in the `collections` section of its configuration file, but it will *not* recurse into the repositories it finds.

The collections mechanism makes it easy to publish many repositories in a "fire and forget" manner. You only need to set up the CGI script and configuration file one time. Afterwards, you can publish or unpublish a repository at any time by simply moving it into, or out of, the directory hierarchy in which you've configured *hgwebdir.cgi* to look.

Explicitly specifying which repositories to publish

In addition to the `collections` mechanism, the *hgwebdir.cgi* script allows you to publish a specific list of repositories. To do so, create a `paths` section, with contents of the following form.

```
[paths]
repo1 = /my/path/to/some/repo
repo2 = /some/path/to/another
```

In this case, the virtual path (the component that will appear in a URL) is on the left-hand side of each definition, while the path to the repository is on the right. Notice that there does not need to be any relationship between the virtual path you choose and the location of a repository in your filesystem.

If you wish, you can use both the `collections` and `paths` mechanisms simultaneously in a single configuration file.

Beware duplicate virtual paths

If several repositories have the same virtual path, *hgwebdir.cgi* will not report an error. Instead, it will behave unpredictably.

Downloading Source Archives

Mercurial's web interface lets users download an archive of any revision. This archive will contain a snapshot of the working directory as of that revision, but it will not contain a copy of the repository data.

By default, this feature is not enabled. To enable it, you'll need to add an `allow_archive` item to the `web` section of your *~/.hgrc*; see below for details.

Web Configuration Options

Mercurial's web interfaces (the `hg serve` command, and the *hgweb.cgi* and *hgweb dir.cgi* scripts) have a number of configuration options that you can set. These belong in a section named `web`.

- `allow_archive`: Determines which (if any) archive download mechanisms Mercurial supports. If you enable this feature, users of the web interface will be able to download an archive of whatever revision of a repository they are viewing. To enable the archive feature, this item must take the form of a sequence of words drawn from the following list:

—bz2: A `tar` archive, compressed using `bzip2` compression. This has the best compression ratio, but uses the most CPU time on the server.

—gz: A `tar` archive, compressed using `gzip` compression.

—zip: A `zip` archive, compressed using LZW compression. This format has the worst compression ratio, but is widely used in the Windows world.

If you provide an empty list, or don't have an `allow_archive` entry at all, this feature will be disabled. Here is an example of how to enable all three supported formats.

```
[web]
allow_archive = bz2 gz zip
```

- `allowpull`: Boolean. Determines whether the web interface allows remote users to `hg pull` and `hg clone` this repository over HTTP. If set to `no` or `false`, only the "human-oriented" portion of the web interface is available.

- `contact`: String. A free-form (but preferably brief) string identifying the person or group in charge of the repository. This often contains the name and email address of a person or mailing list. It often makes sense to place this entry in a repository's own *.hg/hgrc* file, but it can make sense to use in a global *~/.hgrc* if every repository has a single maintainer.

- `maxchanges`: Integer. The default maximum number of changesets to display in a single page of output.

- `maxfiles`: Integer. The default maximum number of modified files to display in a single page of output.

- `stripes`: Integer. If the web interface displays alternating "stripes" to make it easier to visually align rows when you are looking at a table, this number controls the number of rows in each stripe.

- `style`: Controls the template Mercurial uses to display the web interface. Mercurial ships with several web templates:

—`coal` is monochromatic.

—`gitweb` emulates the visual style of Git's web interface.

—`monoblue` uses solid blues and grays.

—`paper` is the default.

—`spartan` was the default for a long time.

You can also specify a custom template of your own; see Chapter 11 for details. Here, you can see how to enable the `gitweb` style.

```
[web]
style = gitweb
```

- `templates`: Path. The directory in which to search for template files. By default, Mercurial searches in the directory in which it was installed.

If you are using *hgwebdir.cgi*, you can place a few configuration items in a `web` section of the *hgweb.config* file instead of a *~/.hgrc* file, for convenience. These items are `motd` and `style`.

Options specific to an individual repository

A few `web` configuration items ought to be placed in a repository's local *.hg/hgrc*, rather than a user's or global *~/.hgrc*.

- `description`: String. A free-form (but preferably brief) string that describes the contents or purpose of the repository.
- `name`: String. The name to use for the repository in the web interface. This overrides the default name, which is the last component of the repository's path.

Options specific to the hg serve command

Some of the items in the `web` section of a *~/.hgrc* file are only for use with the `hg serve` command.

- `accesslog`: Path. The name of a file into which to write an access log. By default, the `hg serve` command writes this information to standard output, not to a file. Log entries are written in the standard "combined" file format used by almost all web servers.
- `address`: String. The local address on which the server should listen for incoming connections. By default, the server listens on all addresses.
- `errorlog`: Path. The name of a file into which to write an error log. By default, the `hg serve` command writes this information to standard error, not to a file.
- `ipv6`: Boolean. Whether to use the IPv6 protocol. By default, IPv6 is not used.
- `port`: Integer. The TCP port number on which the server should listen. The default port number used is 8000.

Choosing the right ~/.hgrc file to add web items to

It is important to remember that a web server like Apache or `lighttpd` will run under a user ID that is different from yours. CGI scripts run by your server, such as *hgweb.cgi*, will usually also run under that user ID.

If you add `web` items to your own personal *~/.hgrc* file, CGI scripts won't read that *~/.hgrc* file. Those settings will thus only affect the behavior of the `hg serve` command when you run it. To cause CGI scripts to see your settings, either create a *~/.hgrc* file in the home directory of the user ID that runs your web server, or add those settings to a system-wide *hgrc* file.

System-Wide Configuration

On Unix-like systems shared by multiple users (such as a server to which people publish changes), it often makes sense to set up some global default behaviors, such as what theme to use in web interfaces.

If a file named */etc/mercurial/hgrc* exists, Mercurial will read it at startup time and apply any configuration settings it finds in that file. It will also look for files ending in a *.rc* extension in a directory named */etc/mercurial/hgrc.d*, and apply any configuration settings it finds in each of those files.

Making Mercurial More Trusting

One situation in which a global *hgrc* can be useful is if users are pulling changes owned by other users. By default, Mercurial will not trust most of the configuration items in a *.hg/hgrc* file inside a repository that is owned by a different user. If we clone or pull changes from such a repository, Mercurial will print a warning stating that it does not trust their *.hg/hgrc*.

If everyone in a particular Unix group is on the same team and *should* trust each other's configuration settings, or we want to trust particular users, we can override Mercurial's skeptical defaults by creating a system-wide *hgrc* file such as the following:

```
# Save this as e.g. /etc/mercurial/hgrc.d/trust.rc
[trusted]
# Trust all entries in any hgrc file owned by the "editors" or
# "www-data" groups.
groups = editors, www-data

# Trust entries in hgrc files owned by the following users.
users = apache, bobo
```

## CHAPTER 7

Filenames and Pattern Matching

Mercurial provides mechanisms that let you work with file names in a consistent and expressive way.

Simple File Naming

Mercurial uses a unified piece of machinery "under the hood" to handle filenames. Every command behaves uniformly with respect to filenames. The way in which commands work with filenames is as follows.

If you explicitly name real files on the command line, Mercurial works with exactly those files, as you would expect.

```
$ hg add COPYING README examples/simple.py
```

When you provide a directory name, Mercurial will interpret this as "operate on every file in this directory and its subdirectories." Mercurial traverses the files and subdirectories in a directory in alphabetical order. When it encounters a subdirectory, it will traverse that subdirectory before continuing with the current directory.

```
$ hg status src
? src/main.py
? src/watcher/_watcher.c
? src/watcher/watcher.py
? src/xyzzy.txt
```

Running Commands Without Any Filenames

Mercurial's commands that work with filenames have useful default behaviors when you invoke them without providing any filenames or patterns. What kind of behavior you should expect depends on what the command does. Here are a few rules of thumb you can use to predict what a command is likely to do if you don't give it any names to work with.

- Most commands will operate on the entire working directory. This is what the `hg add` command does, for example.
- If the command has effects that are difficult or impossible to reverse, it will force you to explicitly provide at least one name or pattern (see below). This protects you from accidentally deleting files by running `hg remove` with no arguments, for example.

It's easy to work around these default behaviors if they don't suit you. If a command normally operates on the whole working directory, you can invoke it on just the current directory and its subdirectories by giving it the name ".".

```
$ cd src
$ hg add -n
adding ../MANIFEST.in
adding ../examples/performant.py
adding ../setup.py
adding main.py
adding watcher/_watcher.c
adding watcher/watcher.py
adding xyzzy.txt
$ hg add -n .
adding main.py
adding watcher/_watcher.c
adding watcher/watcher.py
adding xyzzy.txt
```

Along the same lines, some commands normally print filenames relative to the root of the repository, even if you're invoking them from a subdirectory. Such a command will print filenames relative to your subdirectory if you give it explicit names. Here, we're going to run `hg status` from a subdirectory, and get it to operate on the entire working directory while printing filenames relative to our subdirectory, by passing it the output of the `hg root` command.

```
$ hg status
A COPYING
A README
A examples/simple.py
? MANIFEST.in
? examples/performant.py
? setup.py
? src/main.py
? src/watcher/_watcher.c
? src/watcher/watcher.py
? src/xyzzy.txt
$ hg status `hg root`
A ../COPYING
A ../README
A ../examples/simple.py
? ../MANIFEST.in
? ../examples/performant.py
? ../setup.py
? main.py
? watcher/_watcher.c
```

```
? watcher/watcher.py
? xyzzy.txt
```

Telling You What's Going On

The `hg` `add` example in the preceding section illustrates something else that's helpful about Mercurial commands. If a command operates on a file that you didn't name explicitly on the command line, it will usually print the name of the file, so that you will not be surprised what's going on.

The principle here is of *least surprise*. If you've exactly named a file on the command line, there's no point in repeating it back to you. If Mercurial is acting on a file *implicitly*, e.g., because you provided no names, or a directory, or a pattern (see below), it is safest to tell you what files it's operating on.

For commands that behave this way, you can silence them using the `-q` option. You can also get them to print the name of every file, even those you've named explicitly, using the `-v` option.

Using Patterns to Identify Files

In addition to working with file and directory names, Mercurial lets you use *patterns* to identify files. Mercurial's pattern handling is expressive.

On Unix-like systems (Linux, Mac OS, etc.), the job of matching filenames to patterns normally falls to the shell. On these systems, you must explicitly tell Mercurial that a name is a pattern. On Windows, the shell does not expand patterns, so Mercurial will automatically identify names that are patterns, and expand them for you.

To provide a pattern in place of a regular name on the command line, the mechanism is simple:

```
syntax:patternbody
```

That is, a pattern is identified by a short text string that says what kind of pattern this is, followed by a colon, followed by the actual pattern.

Mercurial supports two kinds of pattern syntax. The most frequently used is called `glob`; this is the same kind of pattern matching used by the Unix shell, and should be familiar to Windows command prompt users, too.

When Mercurial does automatic pattern matching on Windows, it uses `glob` syntax. You can thus omit the glob: prefix on Windows, but it's safe to use it, too.

The `re` syntax is more powerful; it lets you specify patterns using regular expressions, also known as regexps.

By the way, in the examples that follow, notice that I'm careful to wrap all of my patterns in quote characters, so that they won't get expanded by the shell before Mercurial sees them.

Shell-Style Glob Patterns

This is an overview of the kinds of patterns you can use when you're matching on glob patterns.

The * character matches any string within a single directory.

```
$ hg add 'glob:*.py'
adding main.py
```

The ** pattern matches any string and crosses directory boundaries. It's not a standard Unix glob token, but it's accepted by several popular Unix shells, and is very useful.

```
$ cd ..
$ hg status 'glob:**.py'
A examples/simple.py
A src/main.py
? examples/performant.py
? setup.py
? src/watcher/watcher.py
```

The ? pattern matches any single character.

```
$ hg status 'glob:**.?'
? src/watcher/_watcher.c
```

The [character begins a *character class*. This matches any single character within the class. The class ends with a] character. A class may contain multiple *ranges* of the form a-f, which is shorthand for abcdef.

```
$ hg status 'glob:**[nr-t]'
? MANIFEST.in
? src/xyzzy.txt
```

If the first character after the [in a character class is a !, it *negates* the class, making it match any single character *not* in the class.

A { begins a group of subpatterns, where the whole group matches if any subpattern in the group matches. The , character separates subpatterns, and } ends the group.

```
$ hg status 'glob:*.{in,py}'
? MANIFEST.in
? setup.py
```

Watch out!

Don't forget that if you want to match a pattern in any directory, you should not be using the * match-any token, as this will only match within one directory. Instead, use the ** token. This small example illustrates the difference between the two.

```
$ hg status 'glob:*.py'
? setup.py
$ hg status 'glob:**.py'
A examples/simple.py
A src/main.py
? examples/performant.py
? setup.py
? src/watcher/watcher.py
```

Regular Expression Matching with Re Patterns

Mercurial accepts the same regular expression syntax as the Python programming language (it uses Python's regexp engine internally). This is based on the Perl language's regexp syntax, which is the most popular dialect in use (it's also used in Java, for example).

I won't discuss Mercurial's regexp dialect in any detail here, as regexps are not often used. Perl-style regexps are in any case already exhaustively documented on a multitude of websites, and in many books. Instead, I will focus here on a few things you should know if you find yourself needing to use regexps with Mercurial.

A regexp is matched against an entire filename, relative to the root of the repository. In other words, even if you're already in subdirectory *foo*, if you want to match files under this directory, your pattern must start with foo/.

One thing to note, if you're familiar with Perl-style regexps, is that Mercurial's are *rooted*. That is, a regexp starts matching against the beginning of a string; it doesn't look for a match anywhere within the string. To match anywhere in a string, start your pattern with .*.

Filtering Files

Not only does Mercurial give you a variety of ways to specify files, it lets you further winnow those files using *filters*. Commands that work with filenames accept two filtering options:

- -I, or --include, lets you specify a pattern that filenames must match in order to be processed.
- -X, or --exclude, gives you a way to *avoid* processing files if they match this pattern.

You can provide multiple -I and -X options on the command line, and intermix them as you please. Mercurial interprets the patterns you provide using glob syntax by default (but you can use regexps if you need to).

You can read a -I filter as "process only the files that match this filter."

```
$ hg status -I '*.in'
? MANIFEST.in
```

The -X filter is best read as "process only the files that don't match this pattern."

```
$ hg status -X '**.py' src
? src/watcher/_watcher.c
? src/xyzzy.txt
```

Permanently Ignoring Unwanted Files and Directories

When you create a new repository, chances are that over time it will grow to contain files that ought to *not* be managed by Mercurial, and which you don't want to see listed every time you run hg status. For instance, "build products" are files that are created as part of a build but that should not be managed by a revision control system. The most common build products are output files produced by software tools such as compilers. As another example, many text editors litter a directory with lock files, temporary working files, and backup files, which it also makes no sense to manage.

To have Mercurial permanently ignore such files, create a file named *.hgignore* in the root of your repository. You should hg add this file so that it gets tracked with the rest of your repository contents, since your collaborators will probably find it useful too.

By default, the *.hgignore* file should contain a list of regular expressions, one per line. Empty lines are skipped. Most people prefer to describe the files they want to ignore using the glob syntax that we described above, so a typical *.hgignore* file will start with this directive:

```
syntax: glob
```

This tells Mercurial to interpret the lines that follow as glob patterns, not regular expressions.

Here is a typical-looking *.hgignore* file.

```
syntax: glob
# This line is a comment, and will be skipped.
# Empty lines are skipped too.

# Backup files left behind by the Emacs editor.
*~

# Lock files used by the Emacs editor.
# Notice that the "#" character is quoted with a backslash.
# This prevents it from being interpreted as starting a comment.
.\#*

# Temporary files used by the vim editor.
.*.swp

# A hidden file created by the Mac OS X Finder.
.DS_Store
```

Case Sensitivity

If you're working in a mixed development environment that contains both Linux (or other Unix) systems and Macs or Windows systems, you should keep in the back of your mind the knowledge that they treat the *case* ("N" versus "n") of filenames in incompatible ways. This is not very likely to affect you, and it's easy to deal with if it does, but it could surprise you if you don't know about it.

Operating systems and filesystems differ in the way they handle the case of characters in file and directory names. There are three common ways to handle case in names:

- Completely case insensitive. Uppercase and lowercase versions of a letter are treated as identical, both when creating a file and during subsequent accesses. This is common on older DOS-based systems.
- Case preserving, but insensitive. When a file or directory is created, the case of its name is stored, and can be retrieved and displayed by the operating system. When an existing file is being looked up, its case is ignored. This is the standard arrangement on Windows and Mac OS. The names *foo* and *FoO* identify the same file. This treatment of uppercase and lowercase letters as interchangeable is also referred to as *case folding*.
- Case sensitive. The case in a name is significant at all times. The names *foo* and *FoO* identify different files. This is the way Linux and Unix systems normally work.

On Unix-like systems, it is possible to have any or all of the above ways of handling case in action at once. For example, if you use a USB thumb drive formatted with a FAT32 filesystem on a Linux system, Linux will handle names on that filesystem in a case preserving, but insensitive, way.

Safe, Portable Repository Storage

Mercurial's repository storage mechanism is *case safe*. It translates filenames so that they can be safely stored on both case-sensitive and case-insensitive filesystems. This means that you can use normal file copying tools to transfer a Mercurial repository onto, for example, a USB thumb drive, and safely move that drive and repository back and forth between a Mac, a PC running Windows, and a Linux box.

Detecting Case Conflicts

When operating in the working directory, Mercurial honors the naming policy of the filesystem where the working directory is located. If the filesystem is case preserving, but insensitive, Mercurial will treat names that differ only in case as the same.

An important aspect of this approach is that it is possible to commit a changeset on a case-sensitive (typically Linux or Unix) filesystem that will cause trouble for users on case-insensitive (usually Windows and Mac OS) filesystems. If a Linux user commits changes to two files, one named *myfile.c* and the other named *MyFile.C*, they will be stored correctly in the repository. And in the working directories of other Linux users, they will be correctly represented as separate files.

If a Windows or Mac user pulls this change, they will not initially have a problem, because Mercurial's repository storage mechanism is case safe. However, once the user tries to `hg update` the working directory to that changeset, or `hg merge` with that changeset, Mercurial will spot the conflict between the two filenames that the filesystem would treat as the same, and forbid the update or merge from occurring.

Fixing a Case Conflict

If you are using Windows or a Mac in a mixed environment where some of your collaborators are using Linux or Unix, and Mercurial reports a case-folding conflict when you try to `hg update` or `hg merge`, the procedure to fix the problem is simple.

Just find a nearby Linux or Unix box, clone the problem repository onto it, and use Mercurial's `hg rename` command to change the names of any offending files or directories so that they will no longer cause case-folding conflicts. Commit this change, `hg pull` or `hg push` it across to your Windows or Mac OS system, and `hg update` to the revision with the non-conflicting names.

The changeset with case-conflicting names will remain in your project's history, and you still won't be able to `hg update` your working directory to that changeset on a Windows or Mac OS system, but you can continue development unimpeded.

## CHAPTER 8

Managing Releases and Branchy Development

Mercurial provides several mechanisms for you to manage a project that is progressing on multiple fronts at once. To understand these mechanisms, let's first take a brief look at a fairly normal software project structure.

Many software projects issue periodic "major" releases that contain substantial new features. In parallel, they may issue "minor" releases. These are usually identical to the major releases off which they're based, but with a few bugs fixed.

In this chapter, we'll start by talking about how to keep records of project milestones such as releases. We'll then continue on to talk about the flow of work between different phases of a project, and how Mercurial can help you to isolate and manage this work.

Giving a Persistent Name to a Revision

Once you decide that you'd like to call a particular revision a "release," it's a good idea to record the identity of that revision. This will let you reproduce that release at a later date, for whatever purpose you might need at the time (reproducing a bug, porting to a new platform, etc.).

```
$ hg init mytag
$ cd mytag
$ echo hello > myfile
$ hg commit -A -m 'Initial commit'
adding myfile
```

Mercurial lets you give a permanent name to any revision using the `hg tag` command. Not surprisingly, these names are called "tags."

```
$ hg tag v1.0
```

A tag is nothing more than a "symbolic name" for a revision. Tags exist purely for your convenience, so that you have a handy, permanent way to refer to a revision; Mercurial doesn't interpret the tag names in any way. Neither does Mercurial place any restrictions on the name of a tag, beyond a few that are necessary to ensure that a tag can be parsed unambiguously. A tag name cannot contain any of the following characters:

- Colon (ASCII 58, :)
- Carriage return (ASCII 13, \r)
- Newline (ASCII 10, \n)

You can use the `hg tags` command to display the tags present in your repository. In the output, each tagged revision is identified first by its name, then by revision number, and finally by the unique hash of the revision.

```
$ hg tags
tip                          1:ccd961c70ae0
v1.0                         0:c78e12f9da76
```

Notice that `tip` is listed in the output of `hg tags`. The `tip` tag is a special "floating" tag, which always identifies the newest revision in the repository.

In the output of the `hg tags` command, tags are listed in reverse order by revision number. This usually means that recent tags are listed before older tags. It also means that `tip` is always going to be the first tag listed in the output of `hg tags`.

When you run `hg log`, if it displays a revision that has tags associated with it, it will print those tags.

```
$ hg log
changeset:   1:ccd961c70ae0
tag:         tip
user:        Bryan O'Sullivan <bos@serpentine.com>
date:        Tue May 05 06:44:45 2009 +0000
summary:     Added tag v1.0 for changeset c78e12f9da76

changeset:   0:c78e12f9da76
tag:         v1.0
user:        Bryan O'Sullivan <bos@serpentine.com>
date:        Tue May 05 06:44:45 2009 +0000
summary:     Initial commit
```

Any time you need to provide a revision ID to a Mercurial command, the command will accept a tag name in its place. Internally, Mercurial will translate your tag name into the corresponding revision ID, then use that.

```
$ echo goodbye > myfile2
$ hg commit -A -m 'Second commit'
adding myfile2
$ hg log -r v1.0
changeset:   0:c78e12f9da76
tag:         v1.0
user:        Bryan O'Sullivan <bos@serpentine.com>
date:        Tue May 05 06:44:45 2009 +0000
summary:     Initial commit
```

There's no limit on the number of tags you can have in a repository, or on the number of tags that a single revision can have. As a practical matter, it's not a great idea to have "too many" (a number that will vary from project to project), simply because tags are supposed to help you to find revisions. If you have lots of tags, the ease of using them to identify revisions diminishes rapidly.

For example, if your project has milestones as frequent as every few days, it's perfectly reasonable to tag each one of those. But if you have a continuous build system that makes sure every revision can be built cleanly, you'd be introducing a lot of noise if you were to tag every clean build. Instead, you could tag failed builds (on the assumption that they're rare!), or simply not use tags to track buildability.

If you want to remove a tag that you no longer want, use `hg tag --remove`.

```
$ hg tag --remove v1.0
$ hg tags
tip                              3:6a30b02be96a
```

You can also modify a tag at any time, so that it identifies a different revision, by simply issuing a new `hg tag` command. You'll have to use the `-f` option to tell Mercurial that you *really* want to update the tag.

```
$ hg tag -r 1 v1.1
$ hg tags
tip                              4:2f612e0b083a
v1.1                             1:ccd961c70ae0
$ hg tag -r 2 v1.1
abort: tag 'v1.1' already exists (use -f to force)
$ hg tag -f -r 2 v1.1
$ hg tags
tip                              5:dd9e7a899c13
v1.1                             2:9ac23a7cc526
```

There will still be a permanent record of the previous identity of the tag, but Mercurial will no longer use it. There's thus no penalty to tagging the wrong revision; all you have to do is turn around and tag the correct revision once you discover your error.

Mercurial stores tags in a normal revision-controlled file in your repository. If you've created any tags, you'll find them in a file in the root of your repository named *.hgtags*. When you run the `hg tag` command, Mercurial modifies this file, then automatically commits the change to it. This means that every time you run `hg tag`, you'll see a corresponding changeset in the output of `hg log`.

```
$ hg tip
changeset:   5:dd9e7a899c13
tag:         tip
user:        Bryan O'Sullivan <bos@serpentine.com>
date:        Tue May 05 06:44:45 2009 +0000
summary:     Added tag v1.1 for changeset 9ac23a7cc526
```

Handling Tag Conflicts During a Merge

You won't often need to care about the *.hgtags* file, but it sometimes makes its presence known during a merge. The format of the file is simple: it consists of a series of lines. Each line starts with a changeset hash, followed by a space, followed by the name of a tag.

If you're resolving a conflict in the *.hgtags* file during a merge, there's one twist to modifying the *.hgtags* file: when Mercurial is parsing the tags in a repository, it *never* reads the working copy of the *.hgtags* file. Instead, it reads the *most recently committed* revision of the file.

An unfortunate consequence of this design is that you can't actually verify that your merged *.hgtags* file is correct until *after* you've committed a change. So if you find yourself resolving a conflict on *.hgtags* during a merge, be sure to run hg tags after you commit. If it finds an error in the *.hgtags* file, it will report the location of the error, which you can then fix and commit. You should then run hg tags again, just to be sure that your fix is correct.

Tags and Cloning

You may have noticed that the hg clone command has a -r option that lets you clone an exact copy of the repository as of a particular changeset. The new clone will not contain any project history that comes after the revision you specified. This has an interaction with tags that can surprise the unwary.

Recall that a tag is stored as a revision to the *.hgtags* file. When you create a tag, the changeset in which it is recorded refers to an older changeset. When you run hg clone -r foo to clone a repository as of tag foo, the new clone *will not contain any revision newer than the one the tag refers to, including the revision where the tag was created*. The result is that you'll get exactly the right subset of the project's history in the new repository, but *not* the tag you might have expected.

When Permanent Tags Are Too Much

Since Mercurial's tags are revision controlled and carried around with a project's history, everyone you work with will see the tags you create. But giving names to revisions has uses beyond simply noting that revision 4237e45506ee is really v2.0.2. If you're trying to track down a subtle bug, you might want a tag to remind you of something like "Anne saw the symptoms with this revision."

For cases like this, what you might want to use are *local* tags. You can create a local tag with the -l option to the hg tag command. This will store the tag in a file called *.hg/localtags*. Unlike *.hgtags*, *.hg/localtags* is not revision controlled. Any tags you create using -l remain strictly local to the repository you're currently working in.

The Flow of Changes: Big Picture Versus Little Picture

To return to the outline I sketched at the beginning of the chapter, let's think about a project that has multiple concurrent pieces of work under development at once.

There might be a push for a new "main" release; a new minor bug fix release to the last main release; and an unexpected "hot fix" to an old release that is now in maintenance mode.

The usual way people refer to these different concurrent directions of development is as "branches." However, we've already seen numerous times that Mercurial treats *all of history* as a series of branches and merges. Really, what we have here are two ideas that are peripherally related, but which happen to share a name.

- "Big picture" branches represent the sweep of a project's evolution; people give them names, and talk about them in conversation.
- "Little picture" branches are artefacts of the day-to-day activity of developing and merging changes. They expose the narrative of how the code was developed.

Managing Big-Picture Branches in Repositories

The easiest way to isolate a big-picture branch in Mercurial is in a dedicated repository. If you have an existing shared repository—let's call it myproject—that reaches a "1.0" milestone, you can start to prepare for future maintenance releases on top of version 1.0 by tagging the revision from which you prepared the 1.0 release.

```
$ cd myproject
$ hg tag v1.0
```

You can then clone a new shared myproject-1.0.1 repository as of that tag.

```
$ cd ..
$ hg clone myproject myproject-1.0.1
updating working directory
2 files updated, 0 files merged, 0 files removed, 0 files unresolved
```

Afterwards, if someone needs to work on a bug fix that ought to go into an upcoming 1.0.1 minor release, they clone the myproject-1.0.1 repository, make their changes, and push them back.

```
$ hg clone myproject-1.0.1 my-1.0.1-bugfix
updating working directory
2 files updated, 0 files merged, 0 files removed, 0 files unresolved
$ cd my-1.0.1-bugfix
$ echo 'I fixed a bug using only echo!' >> myfile
$ hg commit -m 'Important fix for 1.0.1'
$ hg push
pushing to /tmp/branch-repo8ztZpS/myproject-1.0.1
searching for changes
adding changesets
adding manifests
```

```
adding file changes
added 1 changesets with 1 changes to 1 files
```

Meanwhile, development for the next major release can continue, isolated and unabated, in the myproject repository.

```
$ cd ..
$ hg clone myproject my-feature
updating working directory
2 files updated, 0 files merged, 0 files removed, 0 files unresolved
$ cd my-feature
$ echo 'This sure is an exciting new feature!' > mynewfile
$ hg commit -A -m 'New feature'
adding mynewfile
$ hg push
pushing to /tmp/branch-repo8ztZpS/myproject
searching for changes
adding changesets
adding manifests
adding file changes
added 1 changesets with 1 changes to 1 files
```

Don't Repeat Yourself: Merging Across Branches

In many cases, if you have a bug to fix on a maintenance branch, the chances are good that the bug exists on your project's main branch (and possibly other maintenance branches, too). It's a rare developer who wants to fix the same bug multiple times, so let's look at a few ways that Mercurial can help you to manage these bug fixes without duplicating your work.

In the simplest instance, all you need to do is pull changes from your maintenance branch into your local clone of the target branch.

```
$ cd ..
$ hg clone myproject myproject-merge
updating working directory
3 files updated, 0 files merged, 0 files removed, 0 files unresolved
$ cd myproject-merge
$ hg pull ../myproject-1.0.1
pulling from ../myproject-1.0.1
searching for changes
adding changesets
adding manifests
adding file changes
added 1 changesets with 1 changes to 1 files (+1 heads)
(run 'hg heads' to see heads, 'hg merge' to merge)
```

You'll then need to merge the heads of the two branches, and push back to the main branch.

```
$ hg merge
1 files updated, 0 files merged, 0 files removed, 0 files unresolved
(branch merge, don't forget to commit)
$ hg commit -m 'Merge bugfix from 1.0.1 branch'
```

```
$ hg push
pushing to /tmp/branch-repo8ztZpS/myproject
searching for changes
adding changesets
adding manifests
adding file changes
added 2 changesets with 1 changes to 1 files
```

Naming Branches Within One Repository

In most instances, isolating branches in repositories is the right approach. Its simplicity makes it easy to understand, so it's hard to make mistakes. There's a one-to-one relationship between branches you're working in and directories on your system. This lets you use normal (non-Mercurial-aware) tools to work on files within a branch/repository.

If you're more in the "power user" category (*and* your collaborators are too), there is an alternative way of handling branches that you can consider. I've already mentioned the human-level distinction between "little picture" and "big picture" branches. While Mercurial works with multiple small-picture branches in a repository all the time (for example after you pull changes in, but before you merge them), it can *also* work with multiple big-picture branches.

The key to working this way is that Mercurial lets you assign a persistent *name* to a branch. There always exists a branch named default. Even before you start naming branches yourself, you can find traces of the default branch if you look for them.

As an example, when you run the hg commit command, and it pops up your editor so that you can enter a commit message, look for a line that contains the text HG: branch default at the bottom. This is telling you that your commit will occur on the branch named default.

To start working with named branches, use the hg branches command. This command lists the named branches already present in your repository, telling you which changeset is the tip of each.

```
$ hg tip
changeset:   0:9a972e4b5a97
tag:         tip
user:        Bryan O'Sullivan <bos@serpentine.com>
date:        Tue May 05 06:44:25 2009 +0000
summary:     Initial commit

$ hg branches
default                        0:9a972e4b5a97
```

Since you haven't created any named branches yet, the only one that exists is default.

To find out what the "current" branch is, run the hg branch command, giving it no arguments. This tells you what branch the parent of the current changeset is on.

```
$ hg branch
default
```

To create a new branch, run the hg branch command again. This time, give it one argument: the name of the branch you want to create.

```
$ hg branch foo
marked working directory as branch foo
$ hg branch
foo
```

After you've created a branch, you might wonder what effect the hg branch command has had. What do the hg status and hg tip commands report?

```
$ hg status
$ hg tip
changeset:   0:9a972e4b5a97
tag:         tip
user:        Bryan O'Sullivan <bos@serpentine.com>
date:        Tue May 05 06:44:25 2009 +0000
summary:     Initial commit
```

Nothing has changed in the working directory, and there's been no new history created. As this suggests, running the hg branch command has no permanent effect; it only tells Mercurial what branch name to use the *next* time you commit a changeset.

When you commit a change, Mercurial records the name of the branch on which you committed. Once you've switched from the default branch to another and committed, you'll see the name of the new branch show up in the output of hg log, hg tip, and other commands that display the same kind of output.

```
$ echo 'hello again' >> myfile
$ hg commit -m 'Second commit'
$ hg tip
changeset:   1:8928355fee43
branch:      foo
tag:         tip
user:        Bryan O'Sullivan <bos@serpentine.com>
date:        Tue May 05 06:44:25 2009 +0000
summary:     Second commit
```

The hg log-like commands will print the branch name of every changeset that's not on the default branch. As a result, if you never use named branches, you'll never see this information.

Once you've named a branch and committed a change with that name, every subsequent commit that descends from that change will inherit the same branch name. You can change the name of a branch at any time, using the hg branch command.

```
$ hg branch
foo
$ hg branch bar
marked working directory as branch bar
$ echo new file > newfile
$ hg commit -A -m 'Third commit'
```

```
adding newfile
$ hg tip
changeset:    2:f32855c6764f
branch:       bar
tag:          tip
user:         Bryan O'Sullivan <bos@serpentine.com>
date:         Tue May 05 06:44:25 2009 +0000
summary:      Third commit
```

In practice, this is something you won't do very often, as branch names tend to have fairly long lifetimes. (This isn't a rule, just an observation.)

Dealing with Multiple Named Branches in a Repository

If you have more than one named branch in a repository, Mercurial will remember the branch that your working directory is on when you start a command like hg update or hg pull -u. It will update the working directory to the tip of this branch, no matter what the "repo-wide" tip is. To update to a revision that's on a different named branch, you may need to use the -C option to hg update.

This behavior is a little subtle, so let's see it in action. First, let's remind ourselves what branch we're currently on, and what branches are in our repository.

```
$ hg parents
changeset:    2:f32855c6764f
branch:       bar
tag:          tip
user:         Bryan O'Sullivan <bos@serpentine.com>
date:         Tue May 05 06:44:25 2009 +0000
summary:      Third commit

$ hg branches
bar                            2:f32855c6764f
foo                            1:8928355fee43 (inactive)
default                        0:9a972e4b5a97 (inactive)
```

We're on the bar branch, but there also exists an older hg foo branch.

We can hg update back and forth between the tips of the foo and bar branches without needing to use the -C option, because this only involves going backwards and forwards linearly through our change history.

```
$ hg update foo
0 files updated, 0 files merged, 1 files removed, 0 files unresolved
$ hg parents
changeset:    1:8928355fee43
branch:       foo
user:         Bryan O'Sullivan <bos@serpentine.com>
date:         Tue May 05 06:44:25 2009 +0000
summary:      Second commit

$ hg update bar
1 files updated, 0 files merged, 0 files removed, 0 files unresolved
```

```
$ hg parents
changeset:   2:f32855c6764f
branch:      bar
tag:         tip
user:        Bryan O'Sullivan <bos@serpentine.com>
date:        Tue May 05 06:44:25 2009 +0000
summary:     Third commit
```

If we go back to the foo branch and then run hg update, it will keep us on foo, not move us to the tip of bar.

```
$ hg update foo
0 files updated, 0 files merged, 1 files removed, 0 files unresolved
$ hg update
0 files updated, 0 files merged, 0 files removed, 0 files unresolved
```

Committing a new change on the foo branch introduces a new head.

```
$ echo something > somefile
$ hg commit -A -m 'New file'
adding somefile
created new head
$ hg heads
changeset:   3:2e55e6a73143
branch:      foo
tag:         tip
parent:      1:8928355fee43
user:        Bryan O'Sullivan <bos@serpentine.com>
date:        Tue May 05 06:44:26 2009 +0000
summary:     New file

changeset:   2:f32855c6764f
branch:      bar
user:        Bryan O'Sullivan <bos@serpentine.com>
date:        Tue May 05 06:44:25 2009 +0000
summary:     Third commit
```

Branch Names and Merging

As you've probably noticed, merges in Mercurial are not symmetrical. Let's say our repository has two heads, 17 and 23. If I hg update to 17 and then hg merge with 23, Mercurial records 17 as the first parent of the merge, and 23 as the second. Whereas if I hg update to 23 and then hg merge with 17, it records 23 as the first parent, and 17 as the second.

This affects Mercurial's choice of branch name when you merge. After a merge, Mercurial will retain the branch name of the first parent when you commit the result of the merge. If your first parent's branch name is foo, and you merge with bar, the branch name will still be foo after you merge.

It's not unusual for a repository to contain multiple heads, each with the same branch name. Let's say I'm working on the foo branch, and so are you. We commit different changes; I pull your changes; I now have two heads, each claiming to be on the foo branch. The result of a merge will be a single head on the foo branch, as you might hope.

But if I'm working on the bar branch, and I merge work from the foo branch, the result will remain on the bar branch.

```
$ hg branch
bar
$ hg merge foo
1 files updated, 0 files merged, 0 files removed, 0 files unresolved
(branch merge, don't forget to commit)
$ hg commit -m 'Merge'
$ hg tip
changeset:   4:00d606298226
branch:      bar
tag:         tip
parent:      2:f32855c6764f
parent:      3:2e55e6a73143
user:        Bryan O'Sullivan <bos@serpentine.com>
date:        Tue May 05 06:44:26 2009 +0000
summary:     Merge
```

To give a more concrete example, if I'm working on the bleeding-edge branch, and I want to bring in the latest fixes from the stable branch, Mercurial will choose the "right" (bleeding-edge) branch name when I pull and merge from stable.

Branch Naming Is Generally Useful

You shouldn't think of named branches as applicable only to situations where you have multiple long-lived branches cohabiting in a single repository. They're very useful even in the one-branch-per-repository case.

In the simplest case, giving a name to each branch gives you a permanent record of which branch a changeset originated on. This gives you more context when you're trying to follow the history of a long-lived branchy project.

If you're working with shared repositories, you can set up a pretxnchangegroup hook on each that will block incoming changes that have the "wrong" branch name. This provides a simple, but effective, defense against people accidentally pushing changes from a "bleeding edge" branch to a "stable" branch. Such a hook might look like this inside the shared repo's /.hgrc.

```
[hooks]
pretxnchangegroup.branch = hg heads --template '{branches} ' | grep mybranch
```

## CHAPTER 9

Finding and Fixing Mistakes

To err might be human, but to really handle the consequences well takes a top-notch revision control system. In this chapter, we'll discuss some of the techniques you can use when you find that a problem has crept into your project. Mercurial has some highly capable features that will help you to isolate the sources of problems, and to handle them appropriately.

Erasing Local History

The Accidental Commit

I have an occasional but persistent problem of typing rather more quickly than I can think, which sometimes results in me committing a changeset that is either incomplete or plain wrong. In my case, the usual kind of incomplete changeset is one in which I've created a new source file, but forgotten to hg add it. A "plain wrong" changeset is not as common, but no less annoying.

Rolling Back a Transaction

In "Safe Operation" on page 47, I mentioned that Mercurial treats each modification of a repository as a *transaction*. Every time you commit a changeset or pull changes from another repository, Mercurial remembers what you did. You can undo, or *roll back*, exactly one of these actions using the hg rollback command. (See "Rolling Back Is Useless Once You've Pushed" on page 123 for an important caveat about the use of this command.)

Here's a mistake that I often find myself making: committing a change in which I've created a new file, but forgotten to hg add it.

```
$ hg status
M a
$ echo b > b
$ hg commit -m 'Add file b'
```

Looking at the output of hg status after the commit immediately confirms the error.

```
$ hg status
? b
$ hg tip
changeset:   1:c6a8d372cddf
tag:         tip
user:        Bryan O'Sullivan <bos@serpentine.com>
date:        Tue May 05 06:44:44 2009 +0000
summary:     Add file b
```

The commit captured the changes to the file *a*, but not the new file *b*. If I were to push this changeset to a repository that I shared with a colleague, the chances are high that something in *a* would refer to *b*, which would not be present in their repository when they pulled my changes. I would thus become the object of some indignation.

However, luck is with me—I've caught my error before I pushed the changeset. I use the hg rollback command, and Mercurial makes that last changeset vanish.

```
$ hg rollback
rolling back last transaction
$ hg tip
changeset:   0:b80eb7d60f97
tag:         tip
user:        Bryan O'Sullivan <bos@serpentine.com>
date:        Tue May 05 06:44:44 2009 +0000
summary:     First commit

$ hg status
M a
? b
```

Notice that the changeset is no longer present in the repository's history, and the working directory once again thinks that the file *a* is modified. The commit and rollback have left the working directory exactly as it was prior to the commit; the changeset has been completely erased. I can now safely hg add the file *b*, and rerun my commit.

```
$ hg add b
$ hg commit -m 'Add file b, this time for real'
```

The Erroneous Pull

It's common practice with Mercurial to maintain separate development branches of a project in different repositories. Your development team might have one shared repository for your project's "0.9" release, and another, containing different changes, for the "1.0" release.

Given this, you can imagine that the consequences could be messy if you had a local "0.9" repository, and accidentally pulled changes from the shared "1.0" repository into it. At worst, you could be paying insufficient attention, and push those changes into the shared "0.9" tree, confusing your entire team (but don't worry, we'll return to this horror scenario later). However, it's more likely that you'll notice immediately, because

Mercurial will display the URL it's pulling from, or you will see it pull a suspiciously large number of changes into the repository.

The `hg rollback` command will work nicely to expunge all of the changesets that you just pulled. Mercurial groups all changes from one `hg pull` into a single transaction, so one `hg rollback` is all you need to undo this mistake.

Rolling Back Is Useless Once You've Pushed

The value of the `hg rollback` command drops to zero once you've pushed your changes to another repository. Rolling back a change makes it disappear entirely, but *only* in the repository in which you performed the `hg rollback`. Because a rollback eliminates history, there's no way for the disappearance of a change to propagate between repositories.

If you've pushed a change to another repository—particularly if it's a shared repository—it has essentially "escaped into the wild," and you'll have to recover from your mistake in a different way. If you push a changeset somewhere, then roll it back, then pull from the repository you pushed to, the changeset you thought you'd gotten rid of will simply reappear in your repository.

(If you absolutely know for sure that the change you want to roll back is the most recent change in the repository that you pushed to, *and* you know that nobody else could have pulled it from that repository, you can roll back the changeset there, too, but you really should not expect this to work reliably. Sooner or later a change really will make it into a repository that you don't directly control [or have forgotten about], and come back to bite you.)

You Can Only Roll Back Once

Mercurial stores exactly one transaction in its transaction log; that transaction is the most recent one that occurred in the repository. This means that you can only roll back one transaction. If you expect to be able to roll back one transaction and then its predecessor, this is not the behavior you will get.

```
$ hg rollback
rolling back last transaction
$ hg rollback
no rollback information available
```

Once you've rolled back one transaction in a repository, you can't roll back again in that repository until you perform another commit or pull.

Reverting the Mistaken Change

If you make a modification to a file, and decide that you really didn't want to change the file at all, and you haven't yet committed your changes, the `hg revert` command is the one you'll need. It looks at the changeset that's the parent of the working directory, and restores the contents of the file to their state as of that changeset. (That's a long-winded way of saying that, in the normal case, it undoes your modifications.)

Let's illustrate how the `hg` `revert` command works with yet another small example. We'll begin by modifying a file that Mercurial is already tracking.

```
$ cat file
original content
$ echo unwanted change >> file
$ hg diff file
diff -r 68bfacc0125f file
--- a/file      Tue May 05 06:44:36 2009 +0000
+++ b/file      Tue May 05 06:44:36 2009 +0000
@@ -1,1 +1,2 @@
 original content
+unwanted change
```

If we don't want that change, we can simply `hg` `revert` the file.

```
$ hg status
M file
$ hg revert file
$ cat file
original content
```

The `hg` `revert` command provides us with an extra degree of safety by saving our modified file with a *.orig* extension.

```
$ hg status
? file.orig
$ cat file.orig
original content
unwanted change
```

Be careful with .orig files

It's extremely unlikely that you are using Mercurial to manage files with *.orig* extensions or that you even care about the contents of such files. Just in case, though, it's useful to remember that `hg` `revert` will unconditionally overwrite an existing file with a *.orig* extension. For instance, if you already have a file named *foo.orig* when you revert *foo*, the contents of *foo.orig* will be clobbered.

Here is a summary of the cases that the `hg` `revert` command can deal with. We will discuss each of these in more detail in the section that follows.

- If you modify a file, it will restore the file to its unmodified state.
- If you `hg` `add` a file, it will undo the "added" state of the file, but leave the file itself untouched.
- If you delete a file without telling Mercurial, it will restore the file to its unmodified contents.

- If you use the `hg remove` command to remove a file, it will undo the "removed" state of the file, and restore the file to its unmodified contents.

File Management Errors

The `hg revert` command is useful for more than just modified files. It lets you reverse the results of all of Mercurial's file management commands—`hg add`, `hg remove`, and so on.

If you `hg add` a file, then decide that in fact you don't want Mercurial to track it, use `hg revert` to undo the add. Don't worry; Mercurial will not modify the file in any way. It will just "unmark" the file.

```
$ echo oops > oops
$ hg add oops
$ hg status oops
A oops
$ hg revert oops
$ hg status
? oops
```

Similarly, if you ask Mercurial to `hg remove` a file, you can use `hg revert` to restore it to the contents it had as of the parent of the working directory.

```
$ hg remove file
$ hg status
R file
$ hg revert file
$ hg status
$ ls file
file
```

This works just as well for a file that you deleted by hand, without telling Mercurial (recall that in Mercurial terminology, this kind of file is called "missing").

```
$ rm file
$ hg status
! file
$ hg revert file
$ ls file
file
```

If you revert a `hg copy`, the copied-to file remains in your working directory afterwards, untracked. Since a copy doesn't affect the copied-from file in any way, Mercurial doesn't do anything with the copied-from file.

```
$ hg copy file new-file
$ hg revert new-file
$ hg status
? new-file
```

Dealing with Committed Changes

Consider a case where you have committed a change *a*, and another change *b* on top of it, and you then realize that change *a* was incorrect. Mercurial lets you "back out" an entire changeset automatically, and building blocks that let you reverse part of a changeset by hand.

Before you read this section, here's something to keep in mind: the `hg backout` command undoes the effect of a change by *adding* to your repository's history, not by modifying or erasing it. It's the right tool to use if you're fixing bugs, but not if you're trying to undo some change that has catastrophic consequences. To deal with those, see "Changes That Should Never Have Been" on page 132.

Backing Out a Changeset

The `hg backout` command lets you "undo" the effects of an entire changeset in an automated fashion. Because Mercurial's history is immutable, this command does *not* get rid of the changeset you want to undo. Instead, it creates a new changeset that *reverses* the effect of the to-be-undone changeset.

The operation of the `hg backout` command is a little intricate, so let's illustrate it with some examples. First, we'll create a repository with some simple changes.

```
$ hg init myrepo
$ cd myrepo
$ echo first change >> myfile
$ hg add myfile
$ hg commit -m 'first change'
$ echo second change >> myfile
$ hg commit -m 'second change'
```

The `hg backout` command takes a single changeset ID as its argument; this is the changeset to back out. Normally, `hg backout` will drop you into a text editor to write a commit message, so you can record why you're backing the change out. In this example, we provide a commit message on the command line using the -m option.

Backing Out the Tip Changeset

We're going to start by backing out the last changeset we committed.

```
$ hg backout -m 'back out second change' tip
reverting myfile
changeset 2:d4c21ae7349f backs out changeset 1:60b1c4c78499
$ cat myfile
first change
```

You can see that the second line from *myfile* is no longer present. Taking a look at the output of `hg log` gives us an idea of what the `hg backout` command has done.

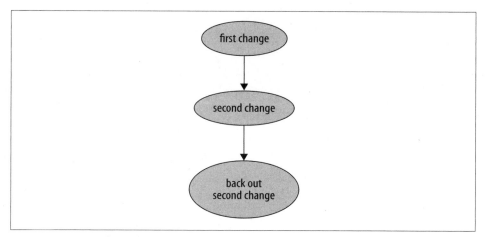

Figure 9-1. Backing out a change using the hg backout command

```
$ hg log --style compact
2[tip]   d4c21ae7349f   2009-05-05 06:44 +0000   bos
  back out second change

1   60b1c4c78499   2009-05-05 06:44 +0000   bos
  second change

0   fea7474d43c3   2009-05-05 06:44 +0000   bos
  first change
```

Notice that the new changeset that hg backout has created is a child of the changeset we backed out. It's easier to see this in Figure 9-1, which presents a graphical view of the change history. As you can see, the history is nice and linear.

Backing Out a Non-Tip Change

If you want to back out a change other than the last one you committed, pass the --merge option to the hg backout command.

```
$ cd ..
$ hg clone -r1 myrepo non-tip-repo
requesting all changes
adding changesets
adding manifests
adding file changes
added 2 changesets with 2 changes to 1 files
updating working directory
1 files updated, 0 files merged, 0 files removed, 0 files unresolved
$ cd non-tip-repo
```

This makes backing out any changeset a "one-shot" operation that's usually simple and fast.

```
$ echo third change >> myfile
$ hg commit -m 'third change'
```

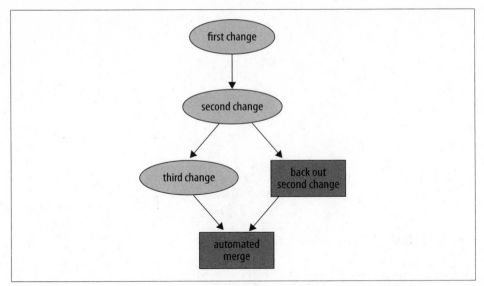

Figure 9-2. Automated backout of a non-tip change using the hg backout command

```
$ hg backout --merge -m 'back out second change' 1
reverting myfile
created new head
changeset 3:d4c21ae7349f backs out changeset 1:60b1c4c78499
merging with changeset 3:d4c21ae7349f
merging myfile
0 files updated, 1 files merged, 0 files removed, 0 files unresolved
(branch merge, don't forget to commit)
```

If you take a look at the contents of *myfile* after the backout finishes, you'll see that the first and third changes are present, but the second is not.

```
$ cat myfile
first change
third change
```

As the graphical history in Figure 9-2 illustrates, Mercurial still commits one change in this kind of situation (the box-shaped node represents the ones that Mercurial commits automatically), but the revision graph now looks different. Before Mercurial begins the backout process, it first remembers what the current parent of the working directory is. It then backs out the target changeset, and commits that as a changeset. Finally, it merges back to the previous parent of the working directory, but notice that it *does not commit* the result of the merge. The repository now contains two heads, and the working directory is in a merge state.

The result is that you end up "back where you were," only with some extra history that undoes the effect of the changeset you wanted to back out.

You might wonder why Mercurial does not commit the result of the merge that it performed. The reason lies in Mercurial behaving conservatively: a merge naturally has more scope for error than simply undoing the effect of the tip changeset, so your work will be safest if you first inspect (and test!) the result of the merge, *then* commit it.

Always use the --merge option

In fact, since the `--merge` option will do the "right thing" whether or not the changeset you're backing out is the tip (i.e., it won't try to merge if it's backing out the tip, since there's no need), you should *always* use this option when you run the `hg backout` command.

Gaining More Control of the Backout Process

While I've recommended that you always use the `--merge` option when backing out a change, the `hg backout` command lets you decide how to merge a backout changeset. Taking control of the backout process by hand is something you will rarely need to do, but it can be useful to understand what the `hg backout` command is doing for you automatically. To illustrate this, let's clone our first repository, but omit the backout change that it contains.

```
$ cd ..
$ hg clone -r1 myrepo newrepo
requesting all changes
adding changesets
adding manifests
adding file changes
added 2 changesets with 2 changes to 1 files
updating working directory
1 files updated, 0 files merged, 0 files removed, 0 files unresolved
$ cd newrepo
```

As with our earlier example, we'll commit a third changeset, then back out its parent, and see what happens.

```
$ echo third change >> myfile
$ hg commit -m 'third change'
$ hg backout -m 'back out second change' 1
reverting myfile
created new head
changeset 3:b47000db73c8 backs out changeset 1:60b1c4c78499
the backout changeset is a new head - do not forget to merge
(use "backout --merge" if you want to auto-merge)
```

Our new changeset is again a descendant of the changeset we backed out; it's thus a new head, *not* a descendant of the changeset that was the tip. The `hg backout` command was quite explicit in telling us this.

```
$ hg log --style compact
3[tip]:1   b47000db73c8   2009-05-05 06:44 +0000   bos
  back out second change

2   b0ecc05c2a5d   2009-05-05 06:44 +0000   bos
  third change
```

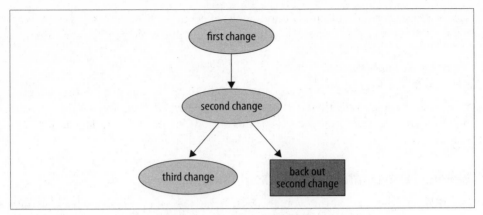

Figure 9-3. Backing out a change using the hg backout command

```
1   60b1c4c78499   2009-05-05 06:44 +0000   bos
    second change

0   fea7474d43c3   2009-05-05 06:44 +0000   bos
    first change
```

Again, it's easier to see what has happened by looking at a graph of the revision history, in Figure 9-3. This makes it clear that when we use hg backout to back out a change other than the tip, Mercurial adds a new head to the repository (the change it committed is box-shaped).

After the hg backout command has completed, it leaves the new "backout" changeset as the parent of the working directory.

```
$ hg parents
changeset:   2:b0ecc05c2a5d
user:        Bryan O'Sullivan <bos@serpentine.com>
date:        Tue May 05 06:44:22 2009 +0000
summary:     third change
```

Now we have two isolated sets of changes.

```
$ hg heads
changeset:   3:b47000db73c8
tag:         tip
parent:      1:60b1c4c78499
user:        Bryan O'Sullivan <bos@serpentine.com>
date:        Tue May 05 06:44:22 2009 +0000
summary:     back out second change

changeset:   2:b0ecc05c2a5d
user:        Bryan O'Sullivan <bos@serpentine.com>
date:        Tue May 05 06:44:22 2009 +0000
summary:     third change
```

Let's think about what we expect to see as the contents of *myfile* now. The first change should be present, because we've never backed it out. The second change should be

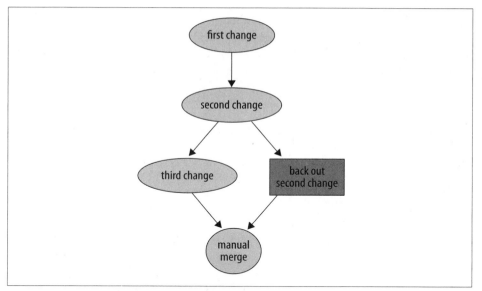

Figure 9-4. Manually merging a backout change

missing, as that's the change we backed out. Since the history graph shows the third change as a separate head, we *don't* expect to see the third change present in *myfile*.

```
$ cat myfile
first change
```

To get the third change back into the file, we just do a normal merge of our two heads.

```
$ hg merge
abort: outstanding uncommitted changes
$ hg commit -m 'merged backout with previous tip'
$ cat myfile
first change
```

Afterwards, the graphical history of our repository looks like Figure 9-4.

Why hg backout Works As It Does

Here's a brief description of how the hg backout command works.

1. It ensures that the working directory is "clean," i.e., that the output of hg status would be empty.

2. It remembers the current parent of the working directory. Let's call this changeset orig.

3. It does the equivalent of a hg update to sync the working directory to the changeset you want to back out. Let's call this changeset backout.

4. It finds the parent of that changeset. Let's call that changeset parent.

5. For each file that the backout changeset affected, it does the equivalent of a hg revert -r parent on that file, to restore it to the contents it had before that changeset was committed.

6. It commits the result as a new changeset. This changeset has backout as its parent.

7. If you specify --merge on the command line, it merges with orig, and commits the result of the merge.

An alternative way to implement the hg backout command would be to hg export the to-be-backed-out changeset as a diff, then use the --reverse option to the patch command to reverse the effect of the change without fiddling with the working directory. This sounds much simpler, but it would not work nearly as well.

The reason that hg backout does an update, a commit, a merge, and another commit is to give the merge machinery the best chance to do a good job when dealing with all the changes *between* the change you're backing out and the current tip.

If you're backing out a changeset that's 100 revisions back in your project's history, the chances that the patch command will be able to apply a reverse diff cleanly are not good, because intervening changes are likely to have "broken the context" that patch uses to determine whether it can apply a patch (if this sounds like gibberish, see "Understanding Patches" on page 186 for a discussion of the patch command). Also, Mercurial's merge machinery will handle files and directories being renamed, permission changes, and modifications to binary files, none of which patch can deal with.

Changes That Should Never Have Been

Most of the time, the hg backout command is exactly what you need if you want to undo the effects of a change. It leaves a permanent record of exactly what you did, both when committing the original changeset and when you cleaned up after it.

On rare occasions, though, you may find that you've committed a change that really should not be present in the repository at all. For example, it would be very unusual, and usually considered a mistake, to commit a software project's object files as well as its source files. Object files have almost no intrinsic value, and they're *big*, so they increase the size of the repository and the amount of time it takes to clone or pull changes.

Before I discuss the options that you have if you commit a "brown paper bag" change (the kind that's so bad that you want to pull a brown paper bag over your head), let me first discuss some approaches that probably won't work.

Since Mercurial treats history as accumulative—every change builds on top of all changes that preceded it—you generally can't just make disastrous changes disappear. The one exception is when you've just committed a change, and it hasn't been pushed or pulled into another repository. That's when you can safely use the hg rollback command, as detailed in "Rolling Back a Transaction" on page 121.

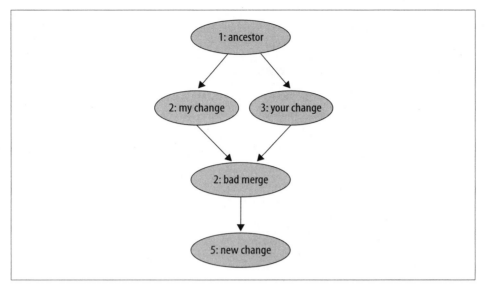

Figure 9-5. A bad merge

After you've pushed a bad change to another repository, you *could* still use `hg rollback` to make your local copy of the change disappear, but it won't have the consequences you want. The change will still be present in the remote repository, so it will reappear in your local repository the next time you pull.

If a situation like this arises, and you know which repositories your bad change has propagated into, you can *try* to get rid of the change from *every one* of those repositories. This is, of course, not a satisfactory solution: if you miss even a single repository while you're expunging, the change is still "in the wild" and could propagate further.

If you've committed one or more changes *after* the change that you'd like to see disappear, your options are further reduced. Mercurial doesn't provide a way to "punch a hole" in history, leaving changesets intact.

Backing Out a Merge

Since merges are often complicated, it is not unheard of for a merge to be mangled badly, but committed erroneously. Mercurial provides an important safeguard against bad merges by refusing to commit unresolved files, but human ingenuity guarantees that it is still possible to mess a merge up and commit it.

Given a bad merge that has been committed, usually the best way to approach it is to simply try to repair the damage by hand. A complete disaster that cannot be easily fixed up by hand ought to be very rare, but the `hg backout` command may help in making the cleanup easier. It offers a `--parent` option, which lets you specify which parent to revert to when backing out a merge.

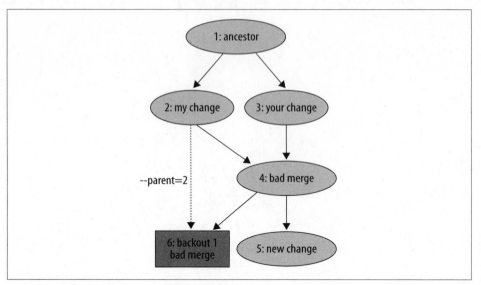

Figure 9-6. Backing out the merge, favoring one parent

Suppose we have a revision graph like that in Figure 9-5. What we'd like is to *redo* the merge of revisions 2 and 3.

One way to do so would be as follows.

1. Call `hg backout --rev=4 --parent=2`. This tells `hg backout` to back out revision 4, which is the bad merge, and when deciding which revision to prefer, to choose parent 2, one of the parents of the merge. The effect can be seen in Figure 9-6.

2. Call `hg backout --rev=4 --parent=3`. This tells `hg backout` to back out revision 4 again, but this time to choose parent 3, the other parent of the merge. The result is visible in Figure 9-7, in which the repository now contains three heads.

3. Redo the bad merge by merging the two backout heads, which reduces the number of heads in the repository to two, as can be seen in Figure 9-8.

4. Merge with the commit that was made after the bad merge, as shown in Figure 9-9.

Protect Yourself from "Escaped" Changes

If you've committed some changes to your local repository and they've been pushed or pulled somewhere else, this isn't necessarily a disaster. You can protect yourself ahead of time against some classes of bad changeset. This is particularly easy if your team usually pulls changes from a central repository.

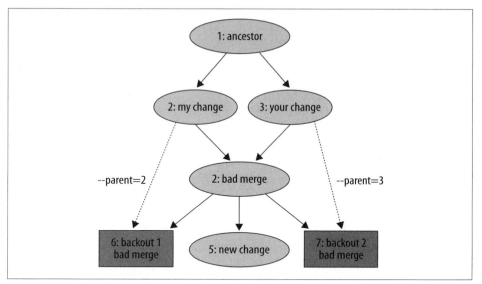

Figure 9-7. Backing out the merge, favoring the other parent

By configuring some hooks on that repository to validate incoming changesets (see Chapter 10), you can automatically prevent some kinds of bad changeset from being pushed to the central repository at all. With such a configuration in place, some kinds of bad changeset will naturally tend to "die out" because they can't propagate into the central repository. Better yet, this happens without any need for explicit intervention.

For instance, an incoming change hook that verifies that a changeset will actually compile can prevent people from inadvertently "breaking the build."

What to Do About Sensitive Changes That Escape

Even a carefully run project can suffer an unfortunate event such as the committing and uncontrolled propagation of a file that contains important passwords.

If something like this happens to you, and the information that gets accidentally propagated is truly sensitive, your first step should be to mitigate the effect of the leak without trying to control the leak itself. If you are not 100% certain that you know exactly who could have seen the changes, you should immediately change passwords, cancel credit cards, or find some other way to make sure that the information that has leaked is no longer useful. In other words, assume that the change has propagated far and wide, and that there's nothing more you can do.

You might hope that there would be mechanisms you could use to either figure out who has seen a change or to erase the change permanently everywhere, but there are good reasons why these are not possible.

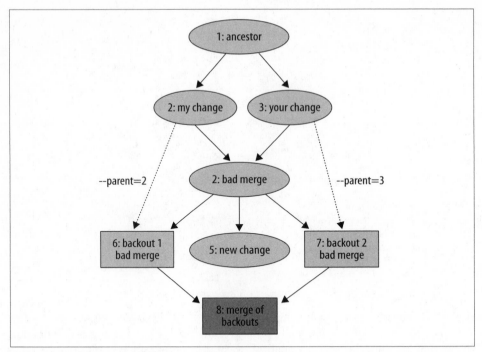

Figure 9-8. Merging the backouts

Mercurial does not provide an audit trail of who has pulled changes from a repository, because it is usually either impossible to record such information or trivial to spoof it. In a multi-user or networked environment, you should thus be extremely skeptical of yourself if you think that you have identified every place that a sensitive changeset has propagated to. Don't forget that people can and will send bundles by email, have their backup software save data offsite, carry repositories on USB sticks, and find other completely innocent ways to confound your attempts to track down every copy of a problematic change.

Mercurial also does not provide a way to make a file or changeset completely disappear from history, because there is no way to enforce its disappearance; someone could easily modify their copy of Mercurial to ignore such directives. In addition, even if Mercurial provided such a capability, someone who simply hadn't pulled a "make this file disappear" changeset wouldn't be affected by it, nor would web crawlers visiting at the wrong time, disk backups, or other mechanisms. Indeed, no distributed revision control system can make data reliably vanish. Providing the illusion of such control could easily give a false sense of security, and would be worse than not providing it at all.

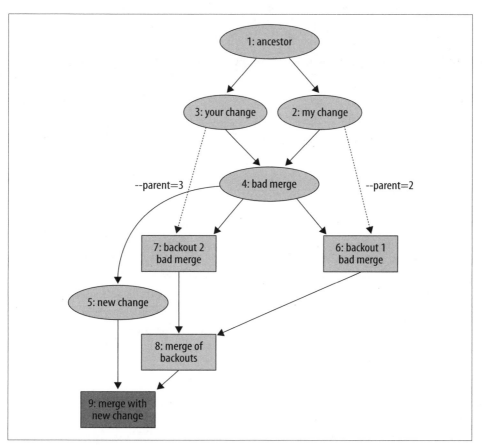

Figure 9-9. Merging the backouts

Finding the Source of a Bug

While it's all very well to be able to back out a changeset that introduced a bug, this requires that you know which changeset to back out. Mercurial provides an invaluable command, called hg bisect, that helps you to automate this process and accomplish it very efficiently.

The idea behind the hg bisect command is that a changeset has introduced some change of behavior that you can identify with a simple pass/fail test. You don't know which piece of code introduced the change, but you know how to test for the presence of the bug. The hg bisect command uses your test to direct its search for the changeset that introduced the code that caused the bug.

Here are a few scenarios to help you understand how you might apply this command.

- The most recent version of your software has a bug that you remember wasn't present a few weeks ago, but you don't know when it was introduced. Here, your binary test checks for the presence of that bug.

- You fixed a bug in a rush, and now it's time to close the entry in your team's bug database. The bug database requires a changeset ID when you close an entry, but you don't remember which changeset you fixed the bug in. Once again, your binary test checks for the presence of the bug.

- Your software works correctly, but runs 15% slower than the last time you measured it. You want to know which changeset introduced the performance regression. In this case, your binary test measures the performance of your software, to see whether it's "fast" or "slow."

- The sizes of the components of your project that you ship exploded recently, and you suspect that something changed in the way you build your project.

From these examples, it should be clear that the hg bisect command is not useful only for finding the sources of bugs. You can use it to find any "emergent property" of a repository (anything that you can't find from a simple text search of the files in the tree) for which you can write a binary test.

We'll introduce a little bit of terminology here, just to make it clear which parts of the search process are your responsibility, and which are Mercurial's. A *test* is something that *you* run when hg bisect chooses a changeset. A *probe* is what hg bisect runs to tell whether a revision is good. Finally, we'll use the word "bisect," as both a noun and a verb, to stand in for the phrase "search using the hg bisect command."

One simple way to automate the searching process would be simply to probe every changeset. However, this scales poorly. If it took ten minutes to test a single changeset and you had 10,000 changesets in your repository, the exhaustive approach would take on average 35 *days* to find the changeset that introduced a bug. Even if you knew that the bug was introduced by one of the last 500 changesets and limited your search to those, you'd still be looking at over 40 hours to find the changeset that introduced your bug.

What the hg bisect command does is use its knowledge of the "shape" of your project's revision history to perform a search in time proportional to the *logarithm* of the number of changesets to check (the kind of search it performs is called a dichotomic search). With this approach, searching through 10,000 changesets will take less than three hours, even at ten minutes per test (the search will require about 14 tests). Limit your search to the last hundred changesets, and it will take only about an hour (roughly seven tests).

The hg bisect command is aware of the "branchy" nature of a Mercurial project's revision history, so it has no problems dealing with branches, merges, or multiple heads in a repository. It can prune entire branches of history with a single probe, which is how it operates so efficiently.

Using the hg bisect Command

Here's an example of hg bisect in action.

 In versions 0.9.5 and earlier of Mercurial, hg bisect was not a core command: it was distributed with Mercurial as an extension. This section describes the built-in command, not the old extension.

Let's create a repository, so that we can try out the hg bisect command in isolation.

```
$ hg init mybug
$ cd mybug
```

We'll simulate a project that has a bug in it in a simple-minded way: create trivial changes in a loop, and nominate one specific change that will have the "bug." This loop creates 35 changesets, each adding a single file to the repository. We'll represent our "bug" with a file that contains the text "i have a gub".

```
$ buggy_change=22
$ for (( i = 0; i < 35; i++ )); do
>   if [[ $i = $buggy_change ]]; then
>     echo 'i have a gub' > myfile$i
>     hg commit -q -A -m 'buggy changeset'
>   else
>     echo 'nothing to see here, move along' > myfile$i
>     hg commit -q -A -m 'normal changeset'
>   fi
> done
```

The next thing that we'd like to do is figure out how to use the hg bisect command. We can use Mercurial's normal built-in help mechanism for this.

```
$ hg help bisect
hg bisect [-gbsr] [-c CMD] [REV]

subdivision search of changesets

    This command helps to find changesets which introduce problems.
    To use, mark the earliest changeset you know exhibits the problem
    as bad, then mark the latest changeset which is free from the
    problem as good. Bisect will update your working directory to a
    revision for testing (unless the --noupdate option is specified).
    Once you have performed tests, mark the working directory as bad
    or good and bisect will either update to another candidate changeset
    or announce that it has found the bad revision.

    As a shortcut, you can also use the revision argument to mark a
    revision as good or bad without checking it out first.

    If you supply a command it will be used for automatic bisection. Its exit
    status will be used as flag to mark revision as bad or good. In case exit
    status is 0 the revision is marked as good, 125 - skipped, 127 (command not
    found) - bisection will be aborted and any other status bigger than 0 will
```

```
       mark revision as bad.

    options:

     -r --reset      reset bisect state
     -g --good       mark changeset good
     -b --bad        mark changeset bad
     -s --skip       skip testing changeset
     -c --command    use command to check changeset state
     -U --noupdate   do not update to target

    use "hg -v help bisect" to show global options
```

The hg bisect command works in steps. Each step proceeds as follows.

1. You run your binary test.
   - If the test succeeded, you tell hg bisect by running the hg bisect --good command.
   - If it failed, run the hg bisect --bad command.
2. The command uses your information to decide which changeset to test next.
3. It updates the working directory to that changeset, and the process begins again.

The process ends when hg bisect identifies a unique changeset that marks the point where your test transitioned from "succeeding" to "failing."

To start the search, we must run the hg bisect --reset command.

```
$ hg bisect --reset
```

In our case, the binary test we use is simple: we check to see if any file in the repository contains the string "i have a gub". If it does, this changeset contains the change that caused the bug. By convention, a changeset that has the property we're searching for is "bad," while one that doesn't is "good."

Most of the time, the revision to which the working directory is synced (usually the tip) already exhibits the problem introduced by the buggy change, so we'll mark it as "bad."

```
$ hg bisect --bad
```

Our next task is to nominate a changeset that we know *doesn't* have the bug; the hg bisect command will "bracket" its search between the first pair of good and bad changesets. In our case, we know that revision 10 didn't have the bug. (I'll talk more about choosing the first "good" changeset later.)

```
$ hg bisect --good 10
Testing changeset 22:c4a8a1b1985d (24 changesets remaining, ~4 tests)
0 files updated, 0 files merged, 12 files removed, 0 files unresolved
```

Notice that this command printed some output:

- It told us how many changesets it must consider before it can identify the one that introduced the bug, and how many tests that will require.

- It updated the working directory to the next changeset to test, and told us which changeset it's testing.

We now run our test in the working directory. We use the `grep` command to see if our "bad" file is present in the working directory. If it is, this revision is bad; if not, this revision is good.

```
$ if grep -q 'i have a gub' *
> then
>    result=bad
> else
>    result=good
> fi
$ echo this revision is $result
this revision is bad
$ hg bisect --$result
Testing changeset 16:e1f9bd22c281 (12 changesets remaining, ~3 tests)
0 files updated, 0 files merged, 6 files removed, 0 files unresolved
```

This test looks like a perfect candidate for automation, so let's turn it into a shell function.

```
$ mytest() {
>    if grep -q 'i have a gub' *
>    then
>      result=bad
>    else
>      result=good
>    fi
>    echo this revision is $result
>    hg bisect --$result
> }
```

We can now run an entire test step with a single command, `mytest`.

```
$ mytest
this revision is good
Testing changeset 19:faf233531e55 (6 changesets remaining, ~2 tests)
3 files updated, 0 files merged, 0 files removed, 0 files unresolved
```

A few more invocations of our canned test step command, and we're done.

```
$ mytest
this revision is good
Testing changeset 20:03fb7a882290 (3 changesets remaining, ~1 tests)
1 files updated, 0 files merged, 0 files removed, 0 files unresolved
$ mytest
this revision is good
Testing changeset 21:768bc298a8db (2 changesets remaining, ~1 tests)
1 files updated, 0 files merged, 0 files removed, 0 files unresolved
$ mytest
this revision is good
The first bad revision is:
changeset:   22:c4a8a1b1985d
user:        Bryan O'Sullivan <bos@serpentine.com>
```

```
date:       Tue May 05 06:44:23 2009 +0000
summary:    buggy changeset
```

Even though we had 40 changesets to search through, the `hg bisect` command let us find the changeset that introduced our "bug" with only five tests. Because the number of tests that the `hg bisect` command performs grows logarithmically with the number of changesets to search, the advantage that it has over the "brute force" search approach increases with every changeset you add.

Cleaning Up After Your Search

When you're finished using the `hg bisect` command in a repository, you can use the `hg bisect --reset` command to drop the information it was using to drive your search. The command doesn't use much space, so it doesn't matter if you forget to run this command. However, `hg bisect` won't let you start a new search in that repository until you do a `hg bisect --reset`.

```
$ hg bisect --reset
```

Tips for Finding Bugs Effectively

Give Consistent Input

The `hg bisect` command requires that you correctly report the result of every test you perform. If you tell it that a test failed when it really succeeded, it *might* be able to detect the inconsistency. If it can identify an inconsistency in your reports, it will tell you that a particular changeset is both good and bad. However, it can't do this perfectly; it's about as likely to report the wrong changeset as the source of the bug.

Automate As Much As Possible

When I started using the `hg bisect` command, I tried a few times to run my tests by hand, on the command line. This is an approach that I, at least, am not suited to. After a few tries, I found that I was making enough mistakes that I was having to restart my searches several times before finally getting correct results.

My initial problems with driving the `hg bisect` command by hand occurred even with simple searches on small repositories; if the problem you're looking for is more subtle, or the number of tests that `hg bisect` must perform increases, the likelihood of operator error ruining the search is much higher. Once I started automating my tests, I had much better results.

The key to automated testing is twofold:

- always test for the same symptom, and
- always feed consistent input to the `hg bisect` command.

In my tutorial example above, the `grep` command tests for the symptom, and the `if` statement takes the result of this check and ensures that we always feed the same input to the `hg bisect` command. The `mytest` function marries these together in a reproducible way, so that every test is uniform and consistent.

Check Your Results

Because the output of a `hg bisect` search is only as good as the input you give it, don't take the changeset it reports as the absolute truth. A simple way to cross-check its report is to manually run your test at each of the following changesets:

- The changeset that it reports as the first bad revision. Your test should still report this as bad.
- The parent of that changeset (either parent, if it's a merge). Your test should report this changeset as good.
- A child of that changeset. Your test should report this changeset as bad.

Beware Interference Between Bugs

It's possible that your search for one bug could be disrupted by the presence of another. For example, let's say your software crashes at revision 100, and worked correctly at revision 50. Unknown to you, someone else introduced a different crashing bug at revision 60, and fixed it at revision 80. This could distort your results in one of several ways.

It is possible that this other bug completely "masks" yours, which is to say that it occurs before your bug has a chance to manifest itself. If you can't avoid that other bug (for example, it prevents your project from building), and so can't tell whether your bug is present in a particular changeset, the `hg bisect` command cannot help you directly. Instead, you can mark a changeset as untested by running `hg bisect --skip`.

A different problem could arise if your test for a bug's presence is not specific enough. If you check for "my program crashes," then both your crashing bug and an unrelated crashing bug that masks it will look like the same thing, and mislead `hg bisect`.

Another useful situation in which to use `hg bisect --skip` is if you can't test a revision because your project was in a broken and hence untestable state at that revision, perhaps because someone checked in a change that prevented the project from building.

Bracket Your Search Lazily

Choosing the first "good" and "bad" changesets that will mark the end points of your search is often easy, but it bears a little discussion nevertheless. From the perspective of `hg bisect`, the "newest" changeset is conventionally "bad," and the older changeset is "good."

If you're having trouble remembering when a suitable "good" change was so that you can tell `hg bisect`, you could do worse than testing changesets at random. Just remember to eliminate contenders that can't possibly exhibit the bug (perhaps because the feature with the bug isn't present yet) and those where another problem masks the bug (as I discussed above).

Even if you end up "early" by thousands of changesets or months of history, you will only add a handful of tests to the total number that `hg bisect` must perform, thanks to its logarithmic behavior.

## CHAPTER 10

Handling Repository Events with Hooks

Mercurial offers a powerful mechanism to let you perform automated actions in response to events that occur in a repository. In some cases, you can even control Mercurial's response to those events.

The name Mercurial uses for one of these actions is a *hook*. Hooks are called "triggers" in some revision control systems, but the two names refer to the same idea.

An Overview of Hooks in Mercurial

Here is a brief list of the hooks that Mercurial supports. We will revisit each of these hooks in more detail later, in "Information for Writers of Hooks" on page 162.

Each of the hooks whose description begins with the word "Controlling" has the ability to determine whether an activity can proceed. If the hook succeeds, the activity may proceed; if it fails, the activity is either not permitted or undone, depending on the hook.

- `changegroup`: This is run after a group of changesets has been brought into the repository from elsewhere.
- `commit`: This is run after a new changeset has been created in the local repository.
- `incoming`: This is run once for each new changeset that is brought into the repository from elsewhere. Notice the difference from `changegroup`, which is run once per *group* of changesets brought in.
- `outgoing`: This is run after a group of changesets has been transmitted from this repository.
- `prechangegroup`: This is run before starting to bring a group of changesets into the repository.
- `precommit`: Controlling. This is run before starting a commit.

- **preoutgoing**: Controlling. This is run before starting to transmit a group of change-sets from this repository.

- **pretag**: Controlling. This is run before creating a tag.

- **pretxnchangegroup**: Controlling. This is run after a group of changesets has been brought into the local repository from another, but before the transaction completes that will make the changes permanent in the repository.

- **pretxncommit**: Controlling. This is run after a new changeset has been created in the local repository, but before the transaction completes that will make it permanent.

- **preupdate**: Controlling. This is run before starting an update or merge of the working directory.

- **tag**: This is run after a tag is created.

- **update**: This is run after an update or merge of the working directory has finished.

Hooks and Security

Hooks Are Run with Your Privileges

When you run a Mercurial command in a repository, and the command causes a hook to run, that hook runs on *your* system, under *your* user account, with *your* privilege level. Since hooks are arbitrary pieces of executable code, you should treat them with an appropriate level of suspicion. Do not install a hook unless you are confident that you know who created it and what it does.

In some cases, you may be exposed to hooks that you did not install yourself. If you work with Mercurial on an unfamiliar system, Mercurial will run hooks defined in that system's global *~/.hgrc* file.

If you are working with a repository owned by another user, Mercurial can run hooks defined in that user's repository, but it will still run them as "you." For example, if you hg pull from that repository, and its *.hg/hgrc* defines a local outgoing hook, that hook will run under your user account, even though you don't own that repository.

 This only applies if you are pulling from a repository on a local or net-work filesystem. If you're pulling over http or ssh, any outgoing hook will run under whatever account is executing the server process on the server.

To see what hooks are defined in a repository, use the hg showconfig hooks command. If you are working in one repository but talking to another that you do not own (e.g., using hg pull or hg incoming), remember that it is the other repository's hooks you should be checking, not your own.

Hooks Do Not Propagate

In Mercurial, hooks are not revision controlled, and do not propagate when you clone, or pull from, a repository. The reason for this is simple: a hook is a completely arbitrary piece of executable code. It runs under your user identity, with your privilege level, on your machine.

It would be extremely reckless for any distributed revision control system to implement revision-controlled hooks, as this would offer an easily exploitable way to subvert the accounts of users of the revision control system.

Since Mercurial does not propagate hooks, if you are collaborating with other people on a common project, you should not assume that they are using the same Mercurial hooks as you are, or that theirs are correctly configured. You should document the hooks you expect people to use.

In a corporate intranet, this is somewhat easier to control, as you can for example provide a "standard" installation of Mercurial on an NFS filesystem, and use a site-wide ~/.hgrc file to define hooks that all users will see. However, this too has its limits; see below.

Hooks Can Be Overridden

Mercurial allows you to override a hook definition by redefining the hook. You can disable it by setting its value to the empty string, or change its behavior as you wish.

If you deploy a system- or site-wide ~/.hgrc file that defines some hooks, you should thus understand that your users can disable or override those hooks.

Ensuring That Critical Hooks Are Run

Sometimes you may want to enforce a policy that you do not want others to be able to work around. For example, you may have a requirement that every changeset must pass a rigorous set of tests. Defining this requirement via a hook in a site-wide ~/.hgrc won't work for remote users on laptops, and of course local users can subvert it at will by overriding the hook.

Instead, you can set up your policies for use of Mercurial so that people are expected to propagate changes through a well-known "canonical" server that you have locked down and configured appropriately.

One way to do this is via a combination of social engineering and technology. Set up a restricted-access account; users can push changes over the network to repositories managed by this account, but they cannot log into the account and run normal shell commands. In this scenario, a user can commit a changeset that contains any old garbage they want.

When someone pushes a changeset to the server that everyone pulls from, the server will test the changeset before it accepts it as permanent, and reject it if it fails to pass the test suite. If people only pull changes from this filtering server, it will serve to ensure that all changes that people pull have been automatically vetted.

A Short Tutorial on Using Hooks

It is easy to write a Mercurial hook. Let's start with a hook that runs when you finish a hg commit, and simply prints the hash of the changeset you just created. The hook is called commit.

All hooks follow the pattern in this example.

```
$ hg init hook-test
$ cd hook-test
$ echo '[hooks]' >> .hg/hgrc
$ echo 'commit = echo committed $HG_NODE' >> .hg/hgrc
$ cat .hg/hgrc
[hooks]
commit = echo committed $HG_NODE
$ echo a > a
$ hg add a
$ hg commit -m 'testing commit hook'
committed ffec6cdc3a79c21f42d9e0c8fa460ea72c1748e5
```

You add an entry to the hooks section of your *~/.hgrc*. On the left is the name of the event to trigger on; on the right is the action to take. As you can see, you can run an arbitrary shell command in a hook. Mercurial passes extra information to the hook using environment variables (look for HG_NODE in the example).

Performing Multiple Actions Per Event

Quite often, you will want to define more than one hook for a particular kind of event, as shown below.

```
$ echo 'commit.when = echo -n "date of commit: "; date' >> .hg/hgrc
$ echo a >> a
$ hg commit -m 'i have two hooks'
committed e2b474b33334b9c332deeaa7a211f36b03266ac9
date of commit: Tue May  5 06:44:39 GMT 2009
```

Mercurial lets you do this by adding an *extension* to the end of a hook's name. You extend a hook's name by giving the name of the hook, followed by a full stop (the . character), followed by some more text of your choosing. For example, Mercurial will run both commit.foo and commit.bar when the commit event occurs.

To give a well-defined order of execution when there are multiple hooks defined for an event, Mercurial sorts hooks by extension, and executes the hook commands in this sorted order. In the above example, it will execute commit.bar before commit.foo, and commit before both.

It is a good idea to use a somewhat descriptive extension when you define a new hook. This will help you to remember what the hook was for. If the hook fails, you'll get an error message that contains the hook name and extension, so using a descriptive extension could give you an immediate hint as to why the hook failed (see "Controlling Whether an Activity Can Proceed" on page 149 for an example).

Controlling Whether an Activity Can Proceed

In our earlier examples, we used the `commit` hook, which is run after a commit has completed. This is one of several Mercurial hooks that run after an activity finishes. Such hooks have no way of influencing the activity itself.

Mercurial defines a number of events that occur before an activity starts, or after it starts but before it finishes. Hooks that trigger on these events have the added ability to choose whether the activity can continue, or will abort.

The `pretxncommit` hook runs after a commit has all but completed. In other words, the metadata representing the changeset has been written out to disk, but the transaction has not yet been allowed to complete. The `pretxncommit` hook has the ability to decide whether the transaction can complete, or must be rolled back.

If the `pretxncommit` hook exits with a status code of zero, the transaction is allowed to complete, the commit finishes, and the `commit` hook is run. If the `pretxncommit` hook exits with a non-zero status code, the transaction is rolled back, the metadata representing the changeset is erased, and the `commit` hook is not run.

```
$ cat check_bug_id
#!/bin/sh
# check that a commit comment mentions a numeric bug id
hg log -r $1 --template {desc} | grep -q "\<bug *[0-9]"
$ echo 'pretxncommit.bug_id_required = ./check_bug_id $HG_NODE' >> .hg/hgrc
$ echo a >> a
$ hg commit -m 'i am not mentioning a bug id'
transaction abort!
rollback completed
abort: pretxncommit.bug_id_required hook exited with status 1
$ hg commit -m 'i refer you to bug 666'
committed 8e23f09593369ce73361346d89e875e152432402
date of commit: Tue May  5 06:44:39 GMT 2009
```

The hook in the example above checks that a commit comment contains a bug ID. If it does, the commit can complete. If not, the commit is rolled back.

Writing Your Own Hooks

When you are writing a hook, you might find it useful to run Mercurial either with the `-v` option, or the `verbose` config item set to "true." When you do so, Mercurial will print a message before it calls each hook.

Choosing How Your Hook Should Run

You can write a hook either as a normal program—typically a shell script—or as a Python function that is executed within the Mercurial process.

Writing a hook as an external program has the advantage that it requires no knowledge of Mercurial's internals. You can call normal Mercurial commands to get any added information you need. The trade-off is that external hooks are slower than in-process hooks.

An in-process Python hook has complete access to the Mercurial API, and does not "shell out" to another process, so it is inherently faster than an external hook. It is also easier to obtain much of the information that a hook requires by using the Mercurial API than by running Mercurial commands.

If you are comfortable with Python or require high performance, writing your hooks in Python may be a good choice. However, when you have a straightforward hook to write and you don't need to care about performance (probably the majority of hooks), a shell script is perfectly fine.

Hook Parameters

Mercurial calls each hook with a set of well-defined parameters. In Python, a parameter is passed as a keyword argument to your hook function. For an external program, a parameter is passed as an environment variable.

Whether your hook is written in Python or as a shell script, the hook-specific parameter names and values will be the same. A boolean parameter will be represented as a boolean value in Python, but as the number 1 (for "true") or 0 (for "false") as an environment variable for an external hook. If a hook parameter is named foo, the keyword argument for a Python hook will also be named foo, while the environment variable for an external hook will be named HG_FOO.

Hook Return Values and Activity Control

A hook that executes successfully must exit with a status of zero if external, or return boolean "false" if in-process. Failure is indicated with a non-zero exit status from an external hook, or an in-process hook returning boolean "true." If an in-process hook raises an exception, the hook is considered to have failed.

For a hook that controls whether an activity can proceed, zero/false means "allow," while non-zero/true/exception means "deny."

Writing an External Hook

When you define an external hook in your ~/.hgrc and the hook is run, its value is passed to your shell, which interprets it. This means that you can use normal shell constructs in the body of the hook.

An executable hook is always run with its current directory set to a repository's root directory.

Each hook parameter is passed in as an environment variable; the name is upper cased, and prefixed with the string HG_.

With the exception of hook parameters, Mercurial does not set or modify any environment variables when running a hook. This is useful to remember if you are writing a site-wide hook that may be run by a number of different users with differing environment variables set. In multi-user situations, you should not rely on environment variables being set to the values you have in your environment when testing the hook.

Telling Mercurial to Use an In-Process Hook

The ~/.hgrc syntax for defining an in-process hook is slightly different than for an executable hook. The value of the hook must start with the text python:, and continue with the fully qualified name of a callable object to use as the hook's value.

The module in which a hook lives is automatically imported when a hook is run. As long as you have the module name and PYTHONPATH right, it should "just work."

The following ~/.hgrc example snippet illustrates the syntax and meaning of the notions we just described.

```
[hooks]
commit.example = python:mymodule.submodule.myhook
```

When Mercurial runs the commit.example hook, it imports mymodule.submodule, looks for the callable object named myhook, and calls it.

Writing an In-Process Hook

The simplest in-process hook does nothing, but illustrates the basic shape of the hook API:

```
def myhook(ui, repo, **kwargs):
    pass
```

The first argument to a Python hook is always a ui object. The second is a repository object; at the moment, it is always an instance of localrepository. Following these two arguments are other keyword arguments. Which ones are passed in depends on the hook being called, but a hook can ignore arguments it doesn't care about by dropping them into a keyword argument dict, as with **kwargs above.

Some Hook Examples

Writing Meaningful Commit Messages

It's hard to imagine a useful commit message being very short. The simple `pretxncom mit` hook of the example below will prevent you from committing a changeset with a message that is less than ten bytes long.

```
$ cat .hg/hgrc
[hooks]
pretxncommit.msglen = test `hg tip --template {desc} | wc -c` -ge 10
$ echo a > a
$ hg add a
$ hg commit -A -m 'too short'
transaction abort!
rollback completed
abort: pretxncommit.msglen hook exited with status 1
$ hg commit -A -m 'long enough'
```

Checking for Trailing Whitespace

An interesting use of a commit-related hook is to help you to write cleaner code. A simple example of "cleaner code" is the dictum that a change should not add any new lines of text that contain "trailing whitespace." Trailing whitespace is a series of space and tab characters at the end of a line of text. In most cases, trailing whitespace is unnecessary, invisible noise, but it is occasionally problematic, and people often prefer to get rid of it.

You can use either the `precommit` or `pretxncommit` hook to tell whether you have a trailing whitespace problem. If you use the `precommit` hook, the hook will not know which files you are committing, so it will have to check every modified file in the repository for trailing white space. If you want to commit a change to just the file *foo*, but the file *bar* contains trailing whitespace, doing a check in the `precommit` hook will prevent you from committing *foo* due to the problem with *bar*. This doesn't seem right.

Should you choose the `pretxncommit` hook, the check won't occur until just before the transaction for the commit completes. This will allow you to check for problems only in the exact files that are being committed. However, if you entered the commit message interactively and the hook fails, the transaction will roll back; you'll have to re-enter the commit message after you fix the trailing whitespace and run `hg commit` again.

```
$ cat .hg/hgrc
[hooks]
pretxncommit.whitespace = hg export tip | (! egrep -q '^\+.*[ \t]$')
$ echo 'a ' > a
$ hg commit -A -m 'test with trailing whitespace'
adding a
transaction abort!
rollback completed
```

```
abort: pretxncommit.whitespace hook exited with status 1
$ echo 'a' > a
$ hg commit -A -m 'drop trailing whitespace and try again'
```

In this example, we introduce a simple `pretxncommit` hook that checks for trailing whitespace. This hook is short, but not very helpful. It exits with an error status if a change adds a line with trailing whitespace to any file, but does not print any information that might help us to identify the offending file or line. It also has the nice property of not paying attention to unmodified lines; only lines that introduce new trailing whitespace cause problems.

```python
#!/usr/bin/env python
#
# save as .hg/check_whitespace.py and make executable

import re

def trailing_whitespace(difflines):
    #
    linenum, header = 0, False

    for line in difflines:
        if header:
            # remember the name of the file that this diff affects
            m = re.match(r'(?:---|\+\+\+) ([^\t]+)', line)
            if m and m.group(1) != '/dev/null':
                filename = m.group(1).split('/', 1)[-1]
            if line.startswith('+++ '):
                header = False
            continue
        if line.startswith('diff '):
            header = True
            continue
        # hunk header - save the line number
        m = re.match(r'@@ -\d+,\d+ \+(\d+),', line)
        if m:
            linenum = int(m.group(1))
            continue
        # hunk body - check for an added line with trailing whitespace
        m = re.match(r'\+.*\s$', line)
        if m:
            yield filename, linenum
        if line and line[0] in ' +':
            linenum += 1

if __name__ == '__main__':
    import os, sys

    added = 0
    for filename, linenum in trailing_whitespace(os.popen('hg export tip')):
        print >> sys.stderr, ('%s, line %d: trailing whitespace added' %
                              (filename, linenum))
        added += 1
    if added:
        # save the commit message so we don't need to retype it
```

```
os.system('hg tip --template "{desc}" > .hg/commit.save')
print >> sys.stderr, 'commit message saved to .hg/commit.save'
sys.exit(1)
```

The above version is much more complex, but also more useful. It parses a unified diff to see if any lines add trailing whitespace, and prints the name of the file and the line number of each such occurrence. Even better, if the change adds trailing whitespace, this hook saves the commit comment and prints the name of the saved file before exiting and telling Mercurial to roll the transaction back, so you can use the -1 filename option to hg commit to reuse the saved commit message once you've corrected the problem.

```
$ cat .hg/hgrc
[hooks]
pretxncommit.whitespace = .hg/check_whitespace.py
$ echo 'a ' >> a
$ hg commit -A -m 'add new line with trailing whitespace'
a, line 2: trailing whitespace added
commit message saved to .hg/commit.save
transaction abort!
rollback completed
abort: pretxncommit.whitespace hook exited with status 1
$ sed -i 's, *$,,' a
$ hg commit -A -m 'trimmed trailing whitespace'
a, line 2: trailing whitespace added
commit message saved to .hg/commit.save
transaction abort!
rollback completed
abort: pretxncommit.whitespace hook exited with status 1
```

As a final aside, note in the example above the use of sed's in-place editing feature to get rid of trailing whitespace from a file. This is concise and useful enough that I will reproduce it here (using perl for good measure).

```
perl -pi -e 's,\s+$,,' filename
```

Bundled Hooks

Mercurial ships with several bundled hooks. You can find them in the *hgext* directory of a Mercurial source tree. If you are using a Mercurial binary package, the hooks will be located in the *hgext* directory of wherever your package installer put Mercurial.

acl—Access Control for Parts of a Repository

The acl extension lets you control which remote users are allowed to push changesets to a networked server. You can protect any portion of a repository (including the entire repo), so that a specific remote user can push changes that do not affect the protected portion.

This extension implements access control based on the identity of the user performing a push, *not* on who committed the changesets they're pushing. It makes sense to use this hook only if you have a locked-down server environment that authenticates remote users, and you want to be sure that only specific users are allowed to push changes to that server.

Configuring the acl hook

In order to manage incoming changesets, the `acl` hook must be used as a `pretxnchangegroup` hook. This lets it see which files are modified by each incoming changeset, and roll back a group of changesets if they modify "forbidden" files. For example:

```
[hooks]
pretxnchangegroup.acl = python:hgext.acl.hook
```

The `acl` extension is configured using three sections.

The `acl` section has only one entry, `sources`, which lists the sources of incoming changesets that the hook should pay attention to. You don't normally need to configure this section.

- `serve`: Control incoming changesets that are arriving from a remote repository over http or ssh. This is the default value of `sources`, and usually the only setting you'll need for this configuration item.
- `pull`: Control incoming changesets that are arriving via a pull from a local repository.
- `push`: Control incoming changesets that are arriving via a push from a local repository.
- `bundle`: Control incoming changesets that are arriving from another repository via a bundle.

The `acl.allow` section controls the users that are allowed to add changesets to the repository. If this section is not present, all users that are not explicitly denied are allowed. If this section is present, all users that are not explicitly allowed are denied (so an empty section means that all users are denied).

The `acl.deny` section determines which users are denied from adding changesets to the repository. If this section is not present or is empty, no users are denied.

The syntaxes for the `acl.allow` and `acl.deny` sections are identical. On the left of each entry is a glob pattern that matches files or directories, relative to the root of the repository; on the right, a username.

In the following example, the user `docwriter` can only push changes to the *docs* subtree of the repository, while `intern` can push changes to any file or directory except *source/ sensitive*.

```
[acl.allow]
docs/** = docwriter
[acl.deny]
source/sensitive/** = intern
```

Testing and troubleshooting

If you want to test the `acl` hook, run it with Mercurial's debugging output enabled. Since you'll probably be running it on a server where it's not convenient (or sometimes impossible) to pass in the `--debug` option, don't forget that you can enable debugging output in your *~/.hgrc*:

```
[ui]
debug = true
```

With this enabled, the `acl` hook will print enough information to let you figure out why it is allowing or forbidding pushes from specific users.

bugzilla—Integration with Bugzilla

The `bugzilla` extension adds a comment to a Bugzilla bug whenever it finds a reference to that bug ID in a commit comment. You can install this hook on a shared server, so that any time a remote user pushes changes to this server, the hook gets run.

The hook adds a comment to the bug that looks like this (you can configure the contents of the comment—see below):

```
Changeset aad8b264143a, made by Joe User
    <joe.user@domain.com> in the frobnitz repository, refers
    to this bug. For complete details, see
    http://hg.domain.com/frobnitz?cmd=changeset;node=aad8b264143a
    Changeset description: Fix bug 10483 by guarding against some
    NULL pointers
```

The value of this hook is that it automates the process of updating a bug any time a changeset refers to it. If you configure the hook properly, it makes it easy for people to browse straight from a Bugzilla bug to a changeset that refers to that bug.

You can use the code in this hook as a starting point for some more exotic Bugzilla integration recipes. Here are a few possibilities:

- Require that every changeset pushed to the server have a valid bug ID in its commit comment. In this case, you'd want to configure the hook as a **pretxncommit** hook. This would allow the hook to reject changes that didn't contain bug IDs.

- Allow incoming changesets to automatically modify the *state* of a bug, as well as simply adding a comment. For example, the hook could recognize the string "fixed bug 31337" as indicating that it should update the state of bug 31337 to "requires testing."

Configuring the bugzilla hook

You should configure this hook in your server's *~/.hgrc* as an `incoming` hook, for example as follows:

```
[hooks]
incoming.bugzilla = python:hgext.bugzilla.hook
```

Because of the specialized nature of this hook, and because Bugzilla was not written with this kind of integration in mind, configuring this hook is a somewhat involved process.

Before you begin, you must install the MySQL bindings for Python on the host(s) where you'll be running the hook. If this is not available as a binary package for your system, you can download it from *http://sourceforge.net/projects/mysql-python*.

Configuration information for this hook lives in the `bugzilla` section of your *~/.hgrc*.

- `version`: The version of Bugzilla installed on the server. The database schema that Bugzilla uses changes occasionally, so this hook has to know exactly which schema to use.

- `host`: The hostname of the MySQL server that stores your Bugzilla data. The database must be configured to allow connections from whatever host you are running the `bugzilla` hook on.

- `user`: The username with which to connect to the MySQL server. The database must be configured to allow this user to connect from whatever host you are running the `bugzilla` hook on. This user must be able to access and modify Bugzilla tables. The default value of this item is `bugs`, which is the standard name of the Bugzilla user in a MySQL database.

- `password`: The MySQL password for the user you configured above. This is stored as plain text, so you should make sure that unauthorized users cannot read the *~/.hgrc* file where you store this information.

- `db`: The name of the Bugzilla database on the MySQL server. The default value of this item is `bugs`, which is the standard name of the MySQL database where Bugzilla stores its data.

- `notify`: If you want Bugzilla to send out a notification email to subscribers after this hook has added a comment to a bug, you will need this hook to run a command whenever it updates the database. The command to run depends on where you have installed Bugzilla, but it will typically look something like this, if you have Bugzilla installed in */var/www/html/bugzilla*:

```
cd /var/www/html/bugzilla &&
        ./processmail %s nobody@nowhere.com
```

The Bugzilla `processmail` program expects to be given a bug ID (the hook replaces %s with the bug ID) and an email address. It also expects to be able to write to some files in the directory that it runs in. If Bugzilla and this hook are not installed on the same machine, you will need to find a way to run **processmail** on the server where Bugzilla is installed.

Mapping committer names to Bugzilla usernames

By default, the `bugzilla` hook tries to use the email address of a changeset's committer as the Bugzilla username with which to update a bug. If this does not suit your needs, you can map committer email addresses to Bugzilla usernames using a `usermap` section.

Each item in the `usermap` section contains an email address on the left, and a Bugzilla username on the right:

```
[usermap]
jane.user@example.com = jane
```

You can either keep the `usermap` data in a normal ~/.hgrc, or tell the `bugzilla` hook to read the information from an external *usermap* file. In the latter case, you can store *usermap* data by itself in (for example) a user-modifiable repository. This makes it possible to let your users maintain their own `usermap` entries. The main ~/.hgrc file might look like this:

```
# regular hgrc file refers to external usermap file
[bugzilla]
usermap = /home/hg/repos/userdata/bugzilla-usermap.conf
```

while the *usermap* file that it refers to might look like this:

```
# bugzilla-usermap.conf - inside a hg repository
[usermap] stephanie@example.com = steph
```

Configuring the text that gets added to a bug

You can configure the text that this hook adds as a comment; you specify it in the form of a Mercurial template. Several ~/.hgrc entries (still in the `bugzilla` section) control this behavior.

- `strip`: The number of leading path elements to strip from a repository's pathname to construct a partial path for a URL. For example, if the repositories on your server live under */home/hg/repos*, and you have a repository whose path is */home/hg/repos/ app/tests*, then setting `strip` to 4 will give a partial path of *app/tests*. The hook will make this partial path available when expanding a template, as `webroot`.

- `template`: The text of the template to use. In addition to the usual changeset-related variables, this template can use `hgweb` (the value of the `hgweb` configuration item above) and `webroot` (the path constructed using `strip` above).

In addition, you can add a `baseurl` item to the `web` section of your ~/.hgrc. The `bugzilla` hook will make this available when expanding a template, as the base string to use when constructing a URL that will let users browse from a Bugzilla comment to view a changeset. For example:

```
[web]
baseurl = http://hg.domain.com/
```

Here is an example set of `bugzilla` hook config information:

```
[bugzilla]
host = bugzilla.example.com
password = mypassword version = 2.16
# server-side repos live in /home/hg/repos, so strip 4 leading
# separators
strip = 4
hgweb = http://hg.example.com/
usermap = /home/hg/repos/notify/bugzilla.conf
template = Changeset {node|short}, made by {author} in the {webroot}
  repo, refers to this bug.\n
  For complete details, see
  {hgweb}{webroot}?cmd=changeset;node={node|short}\n
  Changeset description:\n
  \t{desc|tabindent}
```

Testing and troubleshooting

The most common problems with configuring the bugzilla hook relate to running Bugzilla's *processmail* script and mapping committer names to usernames.

Recall from "Configuring the bugzilla hook" on page 156 that the user that runs the Mercurial process on the server is also the one that will run the *processmail* script. The *processmail* script sometimes causes Bugzilla to write to files in its configuration directory, and Bugzilla's configuration files are usually owned by the user that your web server runs under.

You can cause *processmail* to be run with the suitable user's identity using the sudo command. Here is an example entry for a *sudoers* file:

```
hg_user = (httpd_user)
NOPASSWD: /var/www/html/bugzilla/processmail-wrapper %s
```

This allows the hg_user to run a *processmail-wrapper* program under the identity of httpd_user.

This indirection through a wrapper script is necessary, because *processmail* expects to be run with its current directory set to wherever you installed Bugzilla; you can't specify that kind of constraint in a *sudoers* file. The contents of the wrapper script are simple:

```
#!/bin/sh
cd `dirname $0` && ./processmail "$1" nobody@example.com
```

It doesn't seem to matter what email address you pass to *processmail*.

If your usermap is not set up correctly, users will see an error message from the bugzilla hook when they push changes to the server. The error message will look like this:

```
cannot find bugzilla user id for john.q.public@example.com
```

What this means is that the committer's address, john.q.public@example.com, is not a valid Bugzilla username, nor does it have an entry in your usermap that maps it to a valid Bugzilla username.

notify—Send Email Notifications

Although Mercurial's built-in web server provides RSS feeds of changes in every repository, many people prefer to receive change notifications via email. The `notify` hook lets you send out notifications to a set of email addresses whenever changesets arrive that those subscribers are interested in.

As with the `bugzilla` hook, the `notify` hook is template driven, so you can customize the contents of the notification messages that it sends.

By default, the `notify` hook includes a diff of every changeset that it sends out; you can limit the size of the diff, or turn this feature off entirely. It is useful for letting subscribers review changes immediately, rather than clicking to follow a URL.

Configuring the notify hook

You can set up the `notify` hook to send one email message per incoming changeset, or one per incoming group of changesets (all those that arrived in a single pull or push).

```
[hooks]
# send one email per group of changes
changegroup.notify = python:hgext.notify.hook
# send one email per change
incoming.notify = python:hgext.notify.hook
```

Configuration information for this hook lives in the `notify` section of the *~/.hgrc* file.

- `test`: By default, this hook does not send out email at all; instead, it prints the message that it *would* send. Set this item to `false` to allow email to be sent. The reason that sending of email is turned off by default is that it takes several tries to configure this extension exactly as you would like, and it would be bad form to spam subscribers with a number of "broken" notifications while you debug your configuration.

- `config`: The path to a configuration file that contains subscription information. This is kept separate from the main *~/.hgrc* so that you can maintain it in a repository of its own. People can then clone that repository, update their subscriptions, and push the changes back to your server.

- `strip`: The number of leading path separator characters to strip from a repository's path, when deciding whether a repository has subscribers. For example, if the repositories on your server live in */home/hg/repos*, and `notify` is considering a repository named */home/hg/repos/shared/test*, setting `strip` to 4 will cause `notify` to trim the path it considers down to *shared/test*, and it will match subscribers against that.

- `template`: The template text to use when sending messages. This specifies both the contents of the message header and its body.

- `maxdiff`: The maximum number of lines of diff data to append to the end of a message. If a diff is longer than this, it is truncated. By default, this is set to 300. Set this to 0 to omit diffs from notification emails.

- **sources**: A list of sources of changesets to consider. This lets you limit `notify` to only sending out email about changes that remote users pushed into this repository via a server, for example. See "Sources of changesets" on page 163 for the sources you can specify here.

If you set the `baseurl` item in the `web` section, you can use it in a template; it will be available as `webroot`.

Here is an example set of `notify` configuration information:

```
[notify]
# really send email
test = false
# subscriber data lives in the notify repo
config = /home/hg/repos/notify/notify.conf
# repos live in /home/hg/repos on server, so strip 4 "/" chars
strip = 4
template = X-Hg-Repo: {webroot}\n
  Subject: {webroot}: {desc|firstline|strip}\n
  From: {author}
  \n\n
  changeset {node|short} in {root}
  \n\ndetails:
  {baseurl}{webroot}?cmd=changeset;node={node|short}
  description: {desc|tabindent|strip}

[web]
baseurl =
http://hg.example.com/
```

This will produce a message that looks like the following:

```
X-Hg-Repo: tests/slave
Subject: tests/slave: Handle error case when slave has no buffers
Date: Wed,  2 Aug 2006 15:25:46 -0700 (PDT)

changeset 3cba9bfe74b5 in /home/hg/repos/tests/slave

details:
http://hg.example.com/tests/slave?cmd=changeset;node=3cba9bfe74b5

description: Handle error case when slave has no buffers

diffs (54 lines):
diff -r 9d95df7cf2ad -r 3cba9bfe74b5 include/tests.h
--- a/include/tests.h      Wed Aug 02 15:19:52 2006 -0700
+++ b/include/tests.h      Wed Aug 02 15:25:26 2006 -0700
@@ -212,6 +212,15 @@ static __inline__
void test_headers(void *h)
[...snip...]
```

Testing and troubleshooting

Do not forget that by default, the `notify` extension *will not send any mail* until you explicitly configure it to do so, by setting `test` to `false`. Until you do that, it simply prints the message it *would* send.

Information for Writers of Hooks

In-Process Hook Execution

An in-process hook is called with arguments of the following form:

```
def myhook(ui, repo, **kwargs): pass
```

The `ui` parameter is a `ui` object. The `repo` parameter is a `localrepository` object. The names and values of the `**kwargs` parameters depend on the hook being invoked, with the following common features:

- If a parameter is named `node` or `parentN`, it will contain a hexadecimal changeset ID. The empty string is used to represent "null changeset ID" instead of a string of zeros.
- If a parameter is named `url`, it will contain the URL of a remote repository, if that can be determined.
- Boolean-valued parameters are represented as Python `bool` objects.

An in-process hook is called without a change to the process's working directory (unlike external hooks, which are run in the root of the repository). It must not change the process's working directory, or it will cause any calls it makes into the Mercurial API to fail.

If a hook returns a boolean "false" value, it is considered to have succeeded. If it returns a boolean "true" value or raises an exception, it is considered to have failed. A useful way to think of the calling convention is "tell me if you fail."

Note that changeset IDs are passed into Python hooks as hexadecimal strings, not the binary hashes that Mercurial's APIs normally use. To convert a hash from hex to binary, use the `bin` function.

External Hook Execution

An external hook is passed to the shell of the user running Mercurial. Features of that shell, such as variable substitution and command redirection, are available. The hook is run in the root directory of the repository (unlike in-process hooks, which are run in the same directory that Mercurial was run in).

Hook parameters are passed to the hook as environment variables. Each environment variable's name is converted to uppercase and prefixed with the string `HG_`. For example, if the name of a parameter is node, the name of the environment variable representing that parameter will be HG_NODE.

A boolean parameter is represented as the string 1 for true, 0 for false. If an environment variable is named HG_NODE, HG_PARENT1, or HG_PARENT2, it contains a changeset ID represented as a hexadecimal string. The empty string is used to represent "null changeset ID" instead of a string of zeros. If an environment variable is named HG_URL, it will contain the URL of a remote repository, if that can be determined.

If a hook exits with a status of zero, it is considered to have succeeded. If it exits with a non-zero status, it is considered to have failed.

Finding Out Where Changesets Come From

A hook that involves the transfer of changesets between a local repository and another may be able to find out information about the "far side." Mercurial knows *how* changes are being transferred, and in many cases *where* they are being transferred to or from.

Sources of changesets

Mercurial will tell a hook what means are, or were, used to transfer changesets between repositories. This is provided by Mercurial in a Python parameter named source, or an environment variable named HG_SOURCE.

- serve: Changesets are transferred to or from a remote repository over http or ssh.
- pull: Changesets are being transferred via a pull from one repository into another.
- push: Changesets are being transferred via a push from one repository into another.
- bundle: Changesets are being transferred to or from a bundle.

Where changes are going—remote repository URLs

When possible, Mercurial will tell a hook the location of the "far side" of an activity that transfers changeset data between repositories. This is provided by Mercurial in a Python parameter named url, or an environment variable named HG_URL.

This information is not always known. If a hook is invoked in a repository that is being served via http or ssh, Mercurial cannot tell where the remote repository is, but it may know where the client is connecting from. In such cases, the URL will take one of the following forms:

- remote:ssh:1.2.3.4—remote ssh client, at the IP address 1.2.3.4.
- remote:http:1.2.3.4—remote http client, at the IP address 1.2.3.4. If the client is using SSL, this will be of the form remote:https:1.2.3.4.
- Empty—no information could be discovered about the remote client.

Hook Reference

changegroup—After Remote Changesets Added

This hook is run after a group of pre-existing changesets has been added to the repository, for example via `hg pull` or `hg unbundle`. This hook is run once per operation that added one or more changesets. This is in contrast to the `incoming` hook, which is run once per changeset, regardless of whether the changesets arrived in a group.

Some possible uses for this hook include kicking off an automated build or test of the added changesets, updating a bug database, or notifying subscribers that a repository contains new changes.

Parameters to this hook:

- `node`: A changeset ID. The changeset ID of the first changeset in the group that was added. All changesets between this and `tip`, inclusive, were added by a single `hg pull`, `hg push`, or `hg unbundle`.
- `source`: A string. The source of these changes. See "Sources of changesets" on page 163 for details.
- `url`: A URL. The location of the remote repository, if known. See "Where changes are going—remote repository URLs" on page 163 for more information.

See also: `incoming` ("incoming—After One Remote Changeset Is Added" on page 165), `prechangegroup` ("prechangegroup—Before Starting to Add Remote Changesets" on page 166), `pretxnchangegroup` ("pretxnchangegroup—Before Completing Addition of Remote Changesets" on page 167)

commit—After a New Changeset Is Created

This hook is run after a new changeset has been created.

Parameters to this hook:

- `node`: A changeset ID. The changeset ID of the newly committed changeset.
- `parent1`: A changeset ID. The changeset ID of the first parent of the newly committed changeset.
- `parent2`: A changeset ID. The changeset ID of the second parent of the newly committed changeset.

See also: `precommit` ("precommit—Before Starting to Commit a Changeset" on page 166), `pretxncommit` ("pretxncommit—Before Completing Commit of New Changeset" on page 168)

incoming—After One Remote Changeset Is Added

This hook is run after a pre-existing changeset has been added to the repository, for example via a `hg push`. If a group of changesets was added in a single operation, this hook is called once for each added changeset.

You can use this hook for the same purposes as the `changegroup` hook ("changegroup —After Remote Changesets Added" on page 164); it's simply more convenient sometimes to run a hook once per group of changesets, while other times it's handier once per changeset.

Parameters to this hook:

- `node`: A changeset ID. The ID of the newly added changeset.
- `source`: A string. The source of these changes. See "Sources of changesets" on page 163 for details.
- `url`: A URL. The location of the remote repository, if known. See "Where changes are going—remote repository URLs" on page 163 for more information.

See also: `changegroup` ("changegroup—After Remote Changesets Added" on page 164), `prechangegroup` ("prechangegroup—Before Starting to Add Remote Changesets" on page 166), `pretxnchangegroup` ("pretxnchangegroup—Before Completing Addition of Remote Changesets" on page 167)

outgoing—After Changesets Are Propagated

This hook is run after a group of changesets has been propagated out of this repository, for example by a `hg push` or `hg bundle` command.

One possible use for this hook is to notify administrators that changes have been pulled.

Parameters to this hook:

- `node`: A changeset ID. The changeset ID of the first changeset of the group that was sent.
- `source`: A string. The source of the operation (see "Sources of changesets" on page 163). If a remote client pulled changes from this repository, `source` will be `serve`. If the client that obtained changes from this repository was local, `source` will be `bundle`, `pull`, or `push`, depending on the operation the client performed.
- `url`: A URL. The location of the remote repository, if known. See "Where changes are going—remote repository URLs" on page 163 for more information.

See also: `preoutgoing` ("preoutgoing—Before Starting to Propagate Changesets" on page 167)

prechangegroup—Before Starting to Add Remote Changesets

This controlling hook is run before Mercurial begins to add a group of changesets from another repository.

This hook does not have any information about the changesets to be added, because it is run before transmission of those changesets is allowed to begin. If this hook fails, the changesets will not be transmitted.

One use for this hook is to prevent external changes from being added to a repository. For example, you could use this to "freeze" a server-hosted branch temporarily or permanently so that users cannot push to it, while still allowing a local administrator to modify the repository.

Parameters to this hook:

- `source`: A string. The source of these changes. See "Sources of changesets" on page 163 for details.
- `url`: A URL. The location of the remote repository, if known. See "Where changes are going—remote repository URLs" on page 163 for more information.

See also: `changegroup` ("changegroup—After Remote Changesets Added" on page 164), `incoming` ("incoming—After One Remote Changeset Is Added" on page 165), `pretxnchangegroup` ("pretxnchangegroup—Before Completing Addition of Remote Changesets" on page 167)

precommit—Before Starting to Commit a Changeset

This hook is run before Mercurial begins to commit a new changeset. It is run before Mercurial has any of the metadata for the commit, such as the files to be committed, the commit message, or the commit date.

One use for this hook is to disable the ability to commit new changesets, while still allowing incoming changesets. Another is to run a build or test, and only allow the commit to begin if the build or test succeeds.

Parameters to this hook:

- `parent1`: A changeset ID. The changeset ID of the first parent of the working directory.
- `parent2`: A changeset ID. The changeset ID of the second parent of the working directory.

If the commit proceeds, the parents of the working directory will become the parents of the new changeset.

See also: `commit` ("commit—After a New Changeset Is Created" on page 164), `pretxncommit` ("pretxncommit—Before Completing Commit of New Changeset" on page 168)

preoutgoing—Before Starting to Propagate Changesets

This hook is invoked before Mercurial knows the identities of the changesets to be transmitted.

One use for this hook is to prevent changes from being transmitted to another repository.

Parameters to this hook:

- source: A string. The source of the operation that is attempting to obtain changes from this repository (see "Sources of changesets" on page 163). See the documentation for the source parameter to the outgoing hook (in "outgoing—After Changesets Are Propagated" on page 165) for possible values of this parameter.
- url: A URL. The location of the remote repository, if known. See "Where changes are going—remote repository URLs" on page 163 for more information.

See also: outgoing ("outgoing—After Changesets Are Propagated" on page 165)

pretag—Before Tagging a Changeset

This controlling hook is run before a tag is created. If the hook succeeds, creation of the tag proceeds. If the hook fails, the tag is not created.

Parameters to this hook:

- local: A boolean. Whether the tag is local to this repository instance (i.e., stored in *.hg/localtags*) or managed by Mercurial (stored in *.hgtags*).
- node: A changeset ID. The ID of the changeset to be tagged.
- tag: A string. The name of the tag to be created.

If the tag to be created is revision-controlled, the precommit and pretxncommit hooks ("commit—After a New Changeset Is Created" on page 164 and "pretxncommit—Before Completing Commit of New Changeset" on page 168) will also be run.

See also: tag ("tag—After Tagging a Changeset" on page 169)

pretxnchangegroup—Before Completing Addition of Remote Changesets

This controlling hook is run before a transaction—that manages the addition of a group of new changesets from outside the repository—completes. If the hook succeeds, the transaction completes, and all of the changesets become permanent within this repository. If the hook fails, the transaction is rolled back, and the data for the changesets is erased.

This hook can access the metadata associated with the almost-added changesets, but it should not do anything permanent with this data. It must also not modify the working directory.

While this hook is running, if other Mercurial processes access this repository, they will be able to see the almost-added changesets as if they were permanent. This may lead to race conditions if you do not take steps to avoid them.

This hook can be used to automatically vet a group of changesets. If the hook fails, all of the changesets are "rejected" when the transaction rolls back.

Parameters to this hook:

- node: A changeset ID. The changeset ID of the first changeset in the group that was added. All changesets between this and `tip`, inclusive, were added by a single `hg pull`, `hg push`, or `hg unbundle`.
- source: A string. The source of these changes. See "Sources of changesets" on page 163 for details.
- url: A URL. The location of the remote repository, if known. See "Where changes are going—remote repository URLs" on page 163 for more information.

See also: `changegroup` ("changegroup—After Remote Changesets Added" on page 164), `incoming` ("incoming—After One Remote Changeset Is Added" on page 165), `prechangegroup` ("prechangegroup—Before Starting to Add Remote Changesets" on page 166)

pretxncommit—Before Completing Commit of New Changeset

This controlling hook is run before a transaction—that manages a new commit—completes. If the hook succeeds, the transaction completes and the changeset becomes permanent within this repository. If the hook fails, the transaction is rolled back, and the commit data is erased.

This hook can access the metadata associated with the almost-new changeset, but it should not do anything permanent with this data. It also must not modify the working directory.

While this hook is running, if other Mercurial processes access this repository, they will be able to see the almost-new changeset as if it were permanent. This may lead to race conditions if you do not take steps to avoid them.

Parameters to this hook:

- node: A changeset ID. The changeset ID of the newly committed changeset.
- parent1: A changeset ID. The changeset ID of the first parent of the newly committed changeset.
- parent2: A changeset ID. The changeset ID of the second parent of the newly committed changeset.

See also: `precommit` ("precommit—Before Starting to Commit a Changeset" on page 166)

preupdate—Before Updating or Merging Working Directory

This controlling hook is run before an update or merge of the working directory begins. It is run only if Mercurial's normal pre-update checks determine that the update or merge can proceed. If the hook succeeds, the update or merge may proceed; if it fails, the update or merge does not start.

Parameters to this hook:

- `parent1`: A changeset ID. The ID of the parent that the working directory is to be updated to. If the working directory is being merged, it will not change this parent.
- `parent2`: A changeset ID. Only set if the working directory is being merged. The ID of the revision that the working directory is being merged with.

See also: `update` ("update—After Updating or Merging Working Directory" on page 169)

tag—After Tagging a Changeset

This hook is run after a tag has been created.

Parameters to this hook:

- `local`: A boolean. Whether the new tag is local to this repository instance (i.e., stored in *.hg/localtags*) or managed by Mercurial (stored in *.hgtags*).
- `node`: A changeset ID. The ID of the changeset that was tagged.
- `tag`: A string. The name of the tag that was created.

If the created tag is revision-controlled, the `commit` hook (see "commit—After a New Changeset Is Created" on page 164) is run before this hook.

See also: `pretag` ("pretag—Before Tagging a Changeset" on page 167)

update—After Updating or Merging Working Directory

This hook is run after an update or merge of the working directory completes. Since a merge can fail (if the external `hgmerge` command fails to resolve conflicts in a file), this hook communicates whether the update or merge completed cleanly.

- `error`: A boolean. Indicates whether the update or merge completed successfully.
- `parent1`: A changeset ID. The ID of the parent that the working directory was updated to. If the working directory was merged, it will not have changed this parent.
- `parent2`: A changeset ID. Only set if the working directory was merged. The ID of the revision that the working directory was merged with.

See also: preupdate ("preupdate—Before Updating or Merging Working Directory" on page 169)

## CHAPTER 11

Customizing the Output of Mercurial

Mercurial provides a powerful mechanism to let you control how it displays information. The mechanism is based on templates. You can use templates to generate specific output for a single command, or to customize the entire appearance of the built-in web interface.

Using Precanned Output Styles

Packaged with Mercurial are some output styles that you can use immediately. A style is simply a precanned template that someone wrote and installed somewhere that Mercurial can find.

Before we take a look at Mercurial's bundled styles, let's review its normal output.

```
$ hg log -r1
changeset:   1:59ae2fd35d8a
tag:         mytag
user:        Bryan O'Sullivan <bos@serpentine.com>
date:        Tue May 05 06:44:45 2009 +0000
summary:     added line to end of <<hello>> file.
```

This is somewhat informative, but it takes up a lot of space—five lines of output per changeset. The compact style reduces this to three lines, presented in a sparse manner.

```
$ hg log --style compact
3[tip]   4b984b80759d   2009-05-05 06:44 +0000   bos
  Added tag v0.1 for changeset cefd14841d41

2[v0.1]   cefd14841d41   2009-05-05 06:44 +0000   bos
  Added tag mytag for changeset 59ae2fd35d8a

1[mytag]   59ae2fd35d8a   2009-05-05 06:44 +0000   bos
  added line to end of <<hello>> file.

0   6ed500684dd0   2009-05-05 06:44 +0000   bos
  added hello
```

The changelog style hints at the expressive power of Mercurial's templating engine. This style attempts to follow the GNU Project's changelog guidelines (*http://www.gnu .org/software/guile/changelogs/guile-changelogs_3.html*).

```
$ hg log --style changelog
2009-05-05  Bryan O'Sullivan  <bos@serpentine.com>

    * .hgtags:
    Added tag v0.1 for changeset cefd14841d41
    [4b984b80759d] [tip]

    * .hgtags:
    Added tag mytag for changeset 59ae2fd35d8a
    [cefd14841d41] [v0.1]

    * goodbye, hello:
    added line to end of <<hello>> file.

    in addition, added a file with the helpful name (at least i hope
    that some might consider it so) of goodbye.
    [59ae2fd35d8a] [mytag]

    * hello:
    added hello
    [6ed500684dd0]
```

You will not be shocked to learn that Mercurial's default output style is named `default`.

Setting a Default Style

You can modify the output style that Mercurial uses for every command by editing your *~/.hgrc* file and naming the style you would prefer to use.

```
[ui]
style = compact
```

If you write a style of your own, you can use it by either providing the path to your style file, or copying your style file into a location where Mercurial can find it (typically the `templates` subdirectory of your Mercurial install directory).

Commands That Support Styles and Templates

All of Mercurial's "log-like" commands let you use styles and templates: `hg incoming`, `hg log`, `hg outgoing`, and `hg tip`.

As of this writing, these are the only commands that support styles and templates. Since these are the most important commands that need customizable output, there has been little pressure from the Mercurial user community to add style and template support to other commands.

The Basics of Templating

At its simplest, a Mercurial template is a piece of text. Some of the text never changes, while other parts are *expanded*, or replaced with new text, when necessary.

Before we continue, let's look again at a simple example of Mercurial's normal output.

```
$ hg log -r1
changeset:   1:59ae2fd35d8a
tag:         mytag
user:        Bryan O'Sullivan <bos@serpentine.com>
date:        Tue May 05 06:44:45 2009 +0000
summary:     added line to end of <<hello>> file.
```

Now, let's run the same command, but using a template to change its output.

```
$ hg log -r1 --template 'i saw a changeset\n'
i saw a changeset
```

The example above illustrates the simplest possible template; it's just a piece of static text, printed once for each changeset. The `--template` option to the `hg log` command tells Mercurial to use the given text as the template when printing each changeset.

Notice that the template string above ends with the text \n. This is an *escape sequence*, telling Mercurial to print a newline at the end of each template item. If you omit this newline, Mercurial will run each piece of output together. See "Escape Sequences" on page 175 for more details.

A template that prints a fixed string of text all the time isn't very useful; let's try something a bit more complex.

```
$ hg log --template 'i saw a changeset: {desc}\n'
i saw a changeset: Added tag v0.1 for changeset cefd14841d41
i saw a changeset: Added tag mytag for changeset 59ae2fd35d8a
i saw a changeset: added line to end of <<hello>> file.

in addition, added a file with the helpful name (at least i hope that some
might consider it so)
of goodbye. i saw a changeset: added hello
```

As you can see, the string {desc} in the template has been replaced in the output with the description of each changeset. Every time Mercurial finds text enclosed in curly braces ({ and }), it will try to replace the braces and text with the expansion of whatever is inside. To print a literal curly brace, you must escape it, as described in "Escape Sequences" on page 175.

Common Template Keywords

You can start writing simple templates immediately using the keywords below:

- `author`: String. The unmodified author of the changeset.

- branches: String. The name of the branch on which the changeset was committed. Will be empty if the branch name was `default`.

- date: Date information. The date when the changeset was committed. This is *not* human-readable; you must pass it through a filter that will render it appropriately. See "Filtering Keywords to Change Their Results" on page 175 for more information on filters. The date is expressed as a pair of numbers. The first number is a Unix UTC timestamp (seconds since January 1, 1970); the second is the offset of the committer's timezone from UTC, in seconds.

- desc: String. The text of the changeset description.

- files: List of strings. All files modified, added, or removed by this changeset.

- file_adds: List of strings. Files added by this changeset.

- file_dels: List of strings. Files removed by this changeset.

- node: String. The changeset identification hash, as a 40-character hexadecimal string.

- parents: List of strings. The parents of the changeset.

- rev: Integer. The repository-local changeset revision number.

- tags: List of strings. Any tags associated with the changeset.

A few simple experiments will show us what to expect when we use these keywords; you can see the results below.

```
$ hg log -r1 --template 'author: {author}\n'
author: Bryan O'Sullivan <bos@serpentine.com>
$ hg log -r1 --template 'desc:\n{desc}\n'
desc:
added line to end of <<hello>> file.

in addition, added a file with the helpful name (at least i hope that some
might consider it so)
of goodbye.
$ hg log -r1 --template 'files: {files}\n'
files: goodbye hello
$ hg log -r1 --template 'file_adds: {file_adds}\n'
file_adds: goodbye
$ hg log -r1 --template 'file_dels: {file_dels}\n'
file_dels:
$ hg log -r1 --template 'node: {node}\n'
node: 59ae2fd35d8a09c1532bf5ecd9035b4ac6db2cda
$ hg log -r1 --template 'parents: {parents}\n'
parents:
$ hg log -r1 --template 'rev: {rev}\n'
rev: 1
$ hg log -r1 --template 'tags: {tags}\n'
tags: mytag
```

As noted above, the date keyword does not produce human-readable output, so we must treat it specially. This involves using a *filter*; see "Filtering Keywords to Change Their Results" on page 175.

```
$ hg log -r1 --template 'date: {date}\n'
date: 1241505885.00
$ hg log -r1 --template 'date: {date|isodate}\n'
date: 2009-05-05 06:44 +0000
```

Escape Sequences

Mercurial's templating engine recognizes the most commonly used escape sequences
in strings. When it sees a backslash (\) character, it looks at the following character and
substitutes the two characters with a single replacement, as described below:

- \: Backslash, \, ASCII 134.
- \n: Newline, ASCII 12.
- \r: Carriage return, ASCII 15.
- \t: Tab, ASCII 11.
- \v: Vertical tab, ASCII 13.
- \{: Open curly brace, {, ASCII 173.
- \}: Close curly brace, }, ASCII 175.

As indicated above, if you want the expansion of a template to contain a literal \, {, or
{ character, you must escape it.

Filtering Keywords to Change Their Results

Some of the results of template expansion are not immediately easy to use. Mercurial
lets you specify an optional chain of *filters* to modify the result of expanding a keyword.
You have already seen a common filter, isodate, in action above, to make a date readable.

Below is a list of the most commonly used filters that Mercurial supports. While some
filters can be applied to any text, others can only be used in specific circumstances. The
name of each filter is followed first by an indication of where it can be used, then a
description of its effect.

- addbreaks: Any text. Add an XHTML <br/> tag before the end of every line except
  the last. For example, foo\nbar becomes foo
\nbar.
- age: date keyword. Render the age of the date, relative to the current time. Yields
  a string like 10 minutes.
- basename: Any text, but most useful for the files keyword and its relatives. Treat
  the text as a path, and return the basename. For example, foo/bar/baz becomes baz.
- date: date keyword. Render a date in a similar format to the Unix date command,
  but with timezone included. Yields a string like Mon Sep 04 15:13:13 2006 -0700.

- **domain**: Any text, but most useful for the `author` keyword. Find the first string that looks like an email address, and extract just the domain component. For example, Bryan O'Sullivan <bos@serpentine.com> becomes serpentine.com.
- **email**: Any text, but most useful for the `author` keyword. Extract the first string that looks like an email address. For example, Bryan O'Sullivan <bos@serpentine.com> becomes bos@serpentine.com.
- **escape**: Any text. Replace the special XML/XHTML characters &, <, and > with XML entities.
- **fill68**: Any text. Wrap the text to fit in 68 columns. This is useful before you pass text through the `tabindent` filter, and still want it to fit in an 80-column fixed-font window.
- **fill76**: Any text. Wrap the text to fit in 76 columns.
- **firstline**: Any text. Yields the first line of text, without any trailing newlines.
- **hgdate**: `date` keyword. Render the date as a pair of readable numbers. Yields a string like 1157407993 25200.
- **isodate**: `date` keyword. Render the date as a text string in ISO 8601 format. Yields a string like 2006-09-04 15:13:13 -0700.
- **obfuscate**: Any text, but most useful for the `author` keyword. Yields the input text rendered as a sequence of XML entities. This helps to defeat some particularly stupid screen-scraping email harvesting spambots.
- **person**: Any text, but most useful for the `author` keyword. Yields the text before an email address. For example, Bryan O'Sullivan <bos@serpentine.com> becomes Bryan O'Sullivan.
- **rfc822date**: `date` keyword. Render a date using the same format used in email headers. Yields a string like Mon, 04 Sep 2006 15:13:13 -0700.
- **short**: Changeset hash. Yields the short form of a changeset hash, i.e., a 12-character hexadecimal string.
- **shortdate**: `date` keyword. Render the year, month, and day of the date. Yields a string like 2006-09-04.
- **strip**: Any text. Strip all leading and trailing whitespace from the string.
- **tabindent**: Any text. Yields the text, with every line except the first starting with a tab character.
- **urlescape**: Any text. Escape all characters that are considered "special" by URL parsers. For example, `foo bar` becomes `foo%20bar`.
- **user**: Any text, but most useful for the `author` keyword. Return the "user" portion of an email address. For example, Bryan O'Sullivan <bos@serpentine.com> becomes bos.

```
$ hg log -r1 --template '{author}\n'
Bryan O'Sullivan <bos@serpentine.com>
$ hg log -r1 --template '{author|domain}\n'
```

```
serpentine.com
$ hg log -r1 --template '{author|email}\n'
bos@serpentine.com
$ hg log -r1 --template '{author|obfuscate}\n' | cut -c-76
&#66;&#114;&#121;&#97;&#110;&#32;&#79;&#39;&#83;&#117;&#108;&#108;&#105;&#11
$ hg log -r1 --template '{author|person}\n'
Bryan O'Sullivan
$ hg log -r1 --template '{author|user}\n'
bos
$ hg log -r1 --template 'looks almost right, but actually garbage: {date}\n'
looks almost right, but actually garbage: 1241505885.00
$ hg log -r1 --template '{date|age}\n'
1 second
$ hg log -r1 --template '{date|date}\n'
Tue May 05 06:44:45 2009 +0000
$ hg log -r1 --template '{date|hgdate}\n'
1241505885 0
$ hg log -r1 --template '{date|isodate}\n'
2009-05-05 06:44 +0000
$ hg log -r1 --template '{date|rfc822date}\n'
Tue, 05 May 2009 06:44:45 +0000
$ hg log -r1 --template '{date|shortdate}\n'
2009-05-05
$ hg log -r1 --template '{desc}\n' | cut -c-76
added line to end of <<hello>> file.

in addition, added a file with the helpful name (at least i hope that some m
$ hg log -r1 --template '{desc|addbreaks}\n' | cut -c-76
added line to end of <<hello>> file.<br/>
<br/>
in addition, added a file with the helpful name (at least i hope that some m
$ hg log -r1 --template '{desc|escape}\n' | cut -c-76
added line to end of &lt;&lt;hello&gt;&gt; file.

in addition, added a file with the helpful name (at least i hope that some m
$ hg log -r1 --template '{desc|fill68}\n'
added line to end of <<hello>> file.

in addition, added a file with the helpful name (at least i hope
that some might consider it so) of goodbye.
$ hg log -r1 --template '{desc|fill76}\n'
added line to end of <<hello>> file.

in addition, added a file with the helpful name (at least i hope that some
might consider it so) of goodbye.
$ hg log -r1 --template '{desc|firstline}\n'
added line to end of <<hello>> file.
$ hg log -r1 --template '{desc|strip}\n' | cut -c-76
added line to end of <<hello>> file.

in addition, added a file with the helpful name (at least i hope that some m
$ hg log -r1 --template '{desc|tabindent}\n' | expand | cut -c-76
added line to end of <<hello>> file.

        in addition, added a file with the helpful name (at least i hope tha
```

```
$ hg log -r1 --template '{node}\n'
59ae2fd35d8a09c1532bf5ecd9035b4ac6db2cda
$ hg log -r1 --template '{node|short}\n'
59ae2fd35d8a
```

 If you try to apply a filter to a piece of data that it cannot process, Mercurial will fail and print a Python exception. For example, trying to run the output of the desc keyword into the isodate filter is not a good idea.

Combining Filters

It is easy to combine filters to yield output in the form you would like. The following chain of filters tidies up a description, then makes sure that it fits cleanly into 68 columns, then indents it by a further 8 characters (at least on Unix-like systems, where a tab is conventionally 8 characters wide).

```
$ hg log -r1 --template 'description:\n\t{desc|strip|fill68|tabindent}\n'
description:
        added line to end of <<hello>> file.

        in addition, added a file with the helpful name (at least i hope
        that some might consider it so) of goodbye.
```

Note the use of \t (a tab character) in the template to force the first line to be indented; this is necessary since tabindent indents all lines *except* the first.

Keep in mind that the order of filters in a chain is significant. The first filter is applied to the result of the keyword; the second to the result of the first filter; and so on. For example, using fill68|tabindent gives very different results from tabindent|fill68.

From Templates to Styles

A command-line template provides a quick and simple way to format some output. Templates can become verbose, though, and it's useful to be able to give a template a name. A *style file* is a template with a name, stored in a file.

More than that, using a style file unlocks the power of Mercurial's templating engine in ways that are not possible using the command-line --template option.

The Simplest of Style Files

Our simple style file contains just one line:

```
$ echo 'changeset = "rev: {rev}\n"' > rev
$ hg log -l1 --style ./rev
rev: 3
```

This tells Mercurial, "if you're printing a changeset, use the text on the right as the template."

Style File Syntax

The syntax rules for a style file are simple:

- The file is processed one line at a time.
- Leading and trailing whitespace is ignored.
- Empty lines are skipped.
- If a line starts with either of the characters # or ;, the entire line is treated as a comment, and skipped as if empty.
- A line starts with a keyword. This must start with an alphabetic character or underscore, and can subsequently contain any alphanumeric character or underscore (in regexp notation, a keyword must match [A-Za-z_][A-Za-z0-9_]*).
- The next element must be an = character, which can be preceded or followed by an arbitrary amount of whitespace.
- If the rest of the line starts and ends with matching quote characters (either single or double quotes), it is treated as a template body.
- If the rest of the line *does not* start with a quote character, it is treated as the name of a file; the contents of this file will be read and used as a template body.

Style Files by Example

To illustrate how to write a style file, we will construct a few by example. Rather than provide a complete style file and walk through it, we'll mirror the usual process of developing a style file by starting with something very simple, and walking through a series of successively more complete examples.

Identifying Mistakes in Style Files

If Mercurial encounters a problem in a style file you are working on, it prints a terse error message that, once you figure out what it means, is actually quite useful.

```
$ cat broken.style
changeset =
```

Notice that *broken.style* attempts to define a changeset keyword, but forgets to give any content for it. When instructed to use this style file, Mercurial promptly complains.

```
$ hg log -r1 --style broken.style
abort: broken.style:1: parse error
```

This error message looks intimidating, but it is not too hard to follow:

- The first component is simply Mercurial's way of saying "I am giving up":

      __abort__: broken.style:1: parse error

- Next comes the name of the style file that contains the error:

```
abort: ___broken.style___:1: parse error
```

- Following the filename is the line number where the error was encountered:

```
abort: broken.style:___1___: parse error
```

- Finally, a description of what went wrong:

```
abort: broken.style:1: ___parse error___
```

The description of the problem is not always clear (as in this case), but even when it is cryptic, it is almost always trivial to visually inspect the offending line in the style file and see what is wrong.

Uniquely Identifying a Repository

If you would like to be able to identify a Mercurial repository fairly uniquely using a short string as an identifier, you can use the first revision in the repository.

```
$ hg log -r0 --template '{node}'
c190a4d6b8ed776cf4103dd4ed9260cc3b79ba27
```

This is likely to be unique, and so it is useful in many cases. There are a few caveats:

- It will not work in a completely empty repository, because such a repository does not have a revision zero.
- Neither will it work in the (extremely rare) case where a repository is a merge of two or more formerly independent repositories, and you still have those repositories around.

Here are some uses to which you could put this identifier:

- As a key into a table for a database that manages repositories on a server.
- As half of a {repository ID, revision ID} tuple. Save this information away when you run an automated build or other activity, so that you can "replay" the build later if necessary.

Listing Files on Multiple Lines

Suppose we want to list the files changed by a changeset, one per line, with a little indentation before each filename.

```
$ cat > multiline << EOF
> changeset = "Changed in {node|short}:\n{files}"
> file = "  {file}\n"
> EOF
$ hg log --style multiline
Changed in f55a274d193b:
  .bashrc
  .hgrc
  test.c
```

Mimicking Subversion's Output

Let's try to emulate the default output format used by another revision control tool, Subversion.

```
$ svn log -r9653
------------------------------------------------------------------------
r9653 | sean.hefty | 2006-09-27 14:39:55 -0700 (Wed, 27 Sep 2006) | 5 lines

On reporting a route error, also include the status for the error,
rather than indicating a status of 0 when an error has occurred.

Signed-off-by: Sean Hefty <sean.hefty@intel.com>

------------------------------------------------------------------------
```

Since Subversion's output style is fairly simple, it is easy to copy-and-paste a hunk of its output into a file, and replace the text produced above by Subversion with the template values we'd like to see expanded.

```
$ cat svn.template
r{rev} | {author|user} | {date|isodate} ({date|rfc822date})

{desc|strip|fill76}

------------------------------------------------------------------------
```

There are a few small ways in which this template deviates from the output produced by Subversion:

- Subversion prints a "readable" date (the Wed, 27 Sep 2006 in the example output above) in parentheses. Mercurial's templating engine does not provide a way to display a date in this format without also printing the time and timezone.

- We emulate Subversion's printing of separator lines full of - characters by ending the template with such a line. We use the templating engine's **header** keyword to print a separator line as the first line of output (see below), thus achieving similar output to Subversion.

- Subversion's output includes a count in the header of the number of lines in the commit message. We cannot replicate this in Mercurial; the templating engine does not currently provide a filter that counts the number of lines the template generates.

It took me no more than a minute or two of work to replace literal text from an example of Subversion's output with some keywords and filters to give the template above. The style file simply refers to the template.

```
$ cat svn.style
header = '------------------------------------------------------------------------\n\n'
changeset = svn.template
```

We could have included the text of the template file directly in the style file by enclosing it in quotes and replacing the newlines with \n sequences, but it would have made the style file too difficult to read. Readability is a good guide when you're trying to decide whether some text belongs in a style file, or in a template file that the style file points to. If the style file will look too big or cluttered if you insert a literal piece of text, drop it into a template instead.

## CHAPTER 12

Managing Changes with Mercurial Queues

The Patch Management Problem

Here is a common scenario: you need to install a software package from source, but you find a bug that you must fix in the source before you can start using the package. You make your changes, forget about the package for a while, and a few months later you need to upgrade to a newer version of the package. If the newer version of the package still has the bug, you must extract your fix from the older source tree and apply it against the newer version. This is a tedious task, and it's easy to make mistakes.

This is a simple case of the "patch management" problem. You have an "upstream" source tree that you can't change; you need to make some local changes on top of the upstream tree; and you'd like to be able to keep those changes separate, so that you can apply them to newer versions of the upstream source.

The patch management problem arises in many situations. Probably the most visible is when a user of an open source software project contributes a bug fix or new feature to the project's maintainers in the form of a patch.

Distributors of operating systems that include open source software often need to make changes to the packages they distribute so that they will build properly in their environments.

When you have few changes to maintain, it is easy to manage a single patch using the standard `diff` and `patch` programs (see "Understanding Patches" on page 186 for a discussion of these tools). Once the number of changes grows, it starts to make sense to maintain patches as discrete "chunks of work," so that for example a single patch will contain only one bug fix (the patch might modify several files, but it's doing "only one thing"), and you may have a number of such patches for different bugs you need fixed and local changes you require. In this situation, if you submit a bug fix patch to the upstream maintainers of a package and they include your fix in a subsequent release, you can simply drop that single patch when you're updating to the newer release.

Maintaining a single patch against an upstream tree is a little tedious and error-prone, but not difficult. However, the complexity of the problem grows rapidly as the number of patches you have to maintain increases. With more than a tiny number of patches in hand, understanding which ones you have applied and maintaining them moves from messy to overwhelming.

Fortunately, Mercurial includes a powerful extension, Mercurial Queues (or simply "MQ"), that massively simplifies the patch management problem.

The Prehistory of Mercurial Queues

During the late 1990s, several Linux kernel developers started to maintain "patch series" that modified the behavior of the Linux kernel. Some of these series were focused on stability, some on feature coverage, and some were more speculative.

The sizes of these patch series grew rapidly. In 2002, Andrew Morton published some shell scripts he had been using to automate the task of managing his patch queues. Andrew was successfully using these scripts to manage hundreds (sometimes thousands) of patches on top of the Linux kernel.

A Patchwork Quilt

In early 2003, Andreas Gruenbacher and Martin Quinson borrowed the approach of Andrew's scripts and published a tool called "patchwork quilt", or simply "quilt" (*http://savannah.nongnu.org/projects/quilt/*). Because quilt substantially automated patch management, it rapidly gained a large following among open source software developers.

Quilt manages a *stack of patches* on top of a directory tree. To begin, you tell quilt to manage a directory tree, and tell it which files you want to manage; it stores away the names and contents of those files. To fix a bug, you create a new patch (using a single command), edit the files you need to fix, then "refresh" the patch.

The refresh step causes quilt to scan the directory tree; it updates the patch with all of the changes you have made. You can create another patch on top of the first, which will track the changes required to modify the tree from "tree with one patch applied" to "tree with two patches applied."

You can *change* which patches are applied to the tree. If you "pop" a patch, the changes made by that patch will vanish from the directory tree. Quilt remembers which patches you have popped, though, so you can "push" a popped patch again, and the directory tree will be restored to contain the modifications in the patch. Most importantly, you can run the "refresh" command at any time, and the topmost applied patch will be updated. This means that you can, at any time, change both which patches are applied and what modifications those patches make.

Quilt knows nothing about revision control tools, so it works equally well on top of an unpacked tarball or a Subversion working copy.

From Patchwork Quilt to Mercurial Queues

In mid-2005, Chris Mason took the features of quilt and wrote an extension that he called Mercurial Queues, which added quilt-like behavior to Mercurial.

The key difference between quilt and MQ is that quilt knows nothing about revision control systems, while MQ is *integrated* into Mercurial. Each patch that you push is represented as a Mercurial changeset. Pop a patch, and the changeset goes away.

Because quilt does not care about revision control tools, it is still a tremendously useful piece of software to know about for situations where you cannot use Mercurial and MQ.

The Huge Advantage of MQ

I cannot overstate the value that MQ offers through the unification of patches and revision control.

A major reason that patches have persisted in the free software and open source world—in spite of the availability of increasingly capable revision control tools over the years—is the *agility* they offer.

Traditional revision control tools make a permanent, irreversible record of everything that you do. While this has great value, it's also somewhat stifling. If you want to perform a wild-eyed experiment, you have to be careful in how you go about it, or you risk leaving unnecessary—or worse, misleading or destabilizing—traces of your missteps and errors in the permanent revision record.

By contrast, MQ's marriage of distributed revision control with patches makes it much easier to isolate your work. Your patches live on top of normal revision history, and you can make them disappear or reappear at will. If you don't like a patch, you can drop it. If a patch isn't quite as you want it to be, simply fix it—as many times as you need to, until you have refined it into the form you desire.

As an example, the integration of patches with revision control makes understanding patches and debugging their effects—and their interplay with the code they're based on—*enormously* easier. Since every applied patch has an associated changeset, you can give `hg log` a filename to see which changesets and patches affected the file. You can use the `hg bisect` command to binary-search through all changesets and applied patches to see where a bug got introduced or fixed. You can use the `hg annotate` command to see which changeset or patch modified a particular line of a source file. And so on.

Understanding Patches

Because MQ doesn't hide its patch-oriented nature, it is helpful to understand what patches are, and a little about the tools that work with them.

The traditional Unix diff command compares two files, and prints a list of differences between them. The patch command understands these differences as *modifications* to make to a file. Here is a simple example of these commands in action.

```
$ echo 'this is my original thought' > oldfile
$ echo 'i have changed my mind' > newfile
$ diff -u oldfile newfile > tiny.patch
$ cat tiny.patch
--- oldfile     2009-05-05 06:44:39.554480179 +0000
+++ newfile     2009-05-05 06:44:39.554480179 +0000
@@ -1 +1 @@
-this is my original thought
+i have changed my mind
$ patch < tiny.patch
patching file oldfile
$ cat oldfile
i have changed my mind
```

The type of file that diff generates (and patch takes as input) is called a "patch" or a "diff"; there is no difference between a patch and a diff. (We'll use the term "patch" since it's more commonly used.)

A patch file can start with arbitrary text; the patch command ignores this text, but MQ uses it as the commit message when creating changesets. To find the beginning of the patch content, patch searches for the first line that starts with the string diff -.

MQ works with *unified* diffs (patch can accept several other diff formats, but MQ doesn't). A unified diff contains two kinds of header. The *file header* describes the file being modified; it contains the name of the file to modify. When patch sees a new file header, it looks for a file with that name to start modifying.

After the file header comes a series of *hunks*. Each hunk starts with a header; this identifies the range of line numbers within the file that the hunk should modify. Following the header, a hunk starts and ends with a few (usually three) lines of text from the unmodified file; these are called the *context* for the hunk. If there's only a small amount of context between successive hunks, diff doesn't print a new hunk header; it just runs the hunks together, with a few lines of context between modifications.

Each line of context begins with a space character. Within the hunk, a line that begins with - means "remove this line," while a line that begins with + means "insert this line." For example, a line that is modified is represented by one deletion and one insertion.

We will return to some of the more subtle aspects of patches later (in "More About Patches" on page 192), but you should have enough information now to use MQ.

Getting Started with Mercurial Queues

Because MQ is implemented as an extension, you must explicitly enable it before you can use it. (You don't need to download anything; MQ ships with the standard Mercurial distribution.) To enable MQ, edit your *~/.hgrc* file, and add the lines below.

```
[extensions]
hgext.mq =
```

Once the extension is enabled, it will make a number of new commands available. To verify that the extension is working, you can use `hg help` to see if the `qinit` command is now available.

```
$ hg help qinit
hg qinit [-c]

init a new queue repository

    The queue repository is unversioned by default. If -c is
    specified, qinit will create a separate nested repository
    for patches (qinit -c may also be run later to convert
    an unversioned patch repository into a versioned one).
    You can use qcommit to commit changes to this queue repository.

options:

 -c --create-repo  create queue repository

use "hg -v help qinit" to show global options
```

You can use MQ with *any* Mercurial repository, and its commands only operate within that repository. To get started, simply prepare the repository using the `qinit` command.

```
$ hg init mq-sandbox
$ cd mq-sandbox
$ echo 'line 1' > file1
$ echo 'another line 1' > file2
$ hg add file1 file2
$ hg commit -m'first change'
$ hg qinit
```

This command creates an empty directory called *.hg/patches*, where MQ will keep its metadata. As with many Mercurial commands, the `qinit` command prints nothing if it succeeds.

Creating a New Patch

To begin work on a new patch, use the `qnew` command. This command takes one argument, the name of the patch to create.

MQ will use this as the name of an actual file in the *.hg/patches* directory, as you can see below.

```
$ hg tip
changeset:   0:aaa568b23a06
tag:         tip
user:        Bryan O'Sullivan <bos@serpentine.com>
date:        Tue May 05 06:44:42 2009 +0000
summary:     first change

$ hg qnew first.patch
$ hg tip
changeset:   1:ca4853f45c6e
tag:         qtip
tag:         first.patch
tag:         tip
tag:         qbase
user:        Bryan O'Sullivan <bos@serpentine.com>
date:        Tue May 05 06:44:42 2009 +0000
summary:     [mq]: first.patch

$ ls .hg/patches
first.patch  series  status
```

Also newly present in the *.hg/patches* directory are two other files, *series* and *status*. The *series* file lists all of the patches that MQ knows about for this repository, with one patch per line. Mercurial uses the *status* file for internal bookkeeping; it tracks all of the patches that MQ has applied in this repository.

 You may sometimes want to edit the *series* file by hand; for example, to change the sequence in which some patches are applied. However, manually editing the *status* file is almost always a bad idea, as it's easy to corrupt MQ's idea of what is happening.

Once you have created your new patch, you can edit files in the working directory as you usually would. All of the normal Mercurial commands, such as `hg diff` and `hg annotate`, work exactly as they did before.

Refreshing a Patch

When you reach a point where you want to save your work, use the `qrefresh` command to update the patch you are working on.

```
$ echo 'line 2' >> file1
$ hg diff
diff -r ca4853f45c6e file1
--- a/file1     Tue May 05 06:44:42 2009 +0000
+++ b/file1     Tue May 05 06:44:42 2009 +0000
@@ -1,1 +1,2 @@
 line 1
+line 2
$ hg qrefresh
$ hg diff
$ hg tip --style=compact --patch
```

```
1[qtip,first.patch,tip,qbase]   a560bf0a5cff   2009-05-05 06:44 +0000   bos
  [mq]: first.patch

diff -r aaa568b23a06 -r a560bf0a5cff file1
--- a/file1     Tue May 05 06:44:42 2009 +0000
+++ b/file1     Tue May 05 06:44:42 2009 +0000
@@ -1,1 +1,2 @@
 line 1
+line 2
```

This command folds the changes you have made in the working directory into your patch, and updates its corresponding changeset to contain those changes.

You can run qrefresh as often as you like, so it's a good way to "checkpoint" your work. Refresh your patch at an opportune time, try an experiment, and if the experiment doesn't work out, hg revert your modifications back to the last time you refreshed.

```
$ echo 'line 3' >> file1
$ hg status
M file1
$ hg qrefresh
$ hg tip --style=compact --patch
1[qtip,first.patch,tip,qbase]   8c986ab3b0da   2009-05-05 06:44 +0000   bos
  [mq]: first.patch

diff -r aaa568b23a06 -r 8c986ab3b0da file1
--- a/file1     Tue May 05 06:44:42 2009 +0000
+++ b/file1     Tue May 05 06:44:42 2009 +0000
@@ -1,1 +1,3 @@
 line 1
+line 2
+line 3
```

Stacking and Tracking Patches

Once you have finished working on a patch, or need to work on another, you can use the qnew command again to create a new patch. Mercurial will apply this patch on top of your existing patch.

```
$ hg qnew second.patch
$ hg log --style=compact --limit=2
2[qtip,second.patch,tip]   10e2b1e61af7   2009-05-05 06:44 +0000   bos
  [mq]: second.patch

1[first.patch,qbase]   8c986ab3b0da   2009-05-05 06:44 +0000   bos
  [mq]: first.patch

$ echo 'line 4' >> file1
$ hg qrefresh
$ hg tip --style=compact --patch
2[qtip,second.patch,tip]   fd12637a8b18   2009-05-05 06:44 +0000   bos
  [mq]: second.patch

diff -r 8c986ab3b0da -r fd12637a8b18 file1
```

```
--- a/file1     Tue May 05 06:44:42 2009 +0000
+++ b/file1     Tue May 05 06:44:43 2009 +0000
@@ -1,3 +1,4 @@
 line 1
 line 2
 line 3
+line 4

$ hg annotate file1
0: line 1
1: line 2
1: line 3
2: line 4
```

Notice that the patch contains the changes in our prior patch as part of its context (you can see this more clearly in the output of hg annotate).

So far, with the exception of qnew and qrefresh, we've been careful to only use regular Mercurial commands. However, MQ provides many commands that are easier to use when you are thinking about patches, as illustrated below.

```
$ hg qseries
first.patch
second.patch
$ hg qapplied
first.patch
second.patch
```

- The qseries command lists every patch that MQ knows about in this repository, from oldest to newest (most recently *created*).

- The qapplied command lists every patch that MQ has applied in this repository, again from oldest to newest (most recently *applied*).

Manipulating the Patch Stack

The previous discussion implied that there must be a difference between "known" and "applied" patches, and there is. MQ can manage a patch without it being applied in the repository.

An *applied* patch has a corresponding changeset in the repository, and the effects of the patch and changeset are visible in the working directory. You can undo the application of a patch using the qpop command. MQ still *knows about*, or manages, a popped patch, but the patch no longer has a corresponding changeset in the repository, and the working directory does not contain the changes made by the patch. Figure 12-1 illustrates the difference between applied and tracked patches.

You can reapply an unapplied, or popped, patch using the qpush command. This creates a new changeset to correspond to the patch, and the patch's changes once again become present in the working directory. See below for examples of qpop and qpush in action.

```
$ hg qapplied
first.patch
```

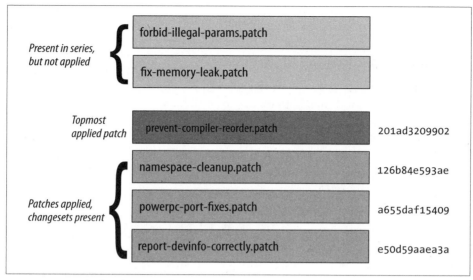

Figure 12-1. Applied and unapplied patches in the MQ patch stack

```
second.patch
$ hg qpop
now at: first.patch
$ hg qseries
first.patch
second.patch
$ hg qapplied
first.patch
$ cat file1
line 1
line 2
line 3
```

Notice that once we have popped a patch or two patches, the output of qseries remains the same, while that of qapplied has changed.

Pushing and Popping Many Patches

While qpush and qpop each operate on a single patch at a time by default, you can push and pop many patches in one go. The hg -a option to qpush causes it to push all un-applied patches, while the -a option to qpop causes it to pop all applied patches. (For some more ways to push and pop many patches, see "Getting the Best Performance Out of MQ" on page 197.)

```
$ hg qpush -a
applying second.patch
now at: second.patch
$ cat file1
line 1
line 2
```

```
line 3
line 4
```

Safety Checks, and Overriding Them

Several MQ commands check the working directory before they do anything, and fail if they find any modifications. They do this to ensure that you won't lose any changes that you have made but not yet incorporated into a patch. The example below illustrates this; the qnew command will not create a new patch if there are outstanding changes, caused in this case by the hg add of *file3*.

```
$ echo 'file 3, line 1' >> file3
$ hg qnew add-file3.patch
$ hg qnew -f add-file3.patch
abort: patch "add-file3.patch" already exists
```

Commands that check the working directory all take an "I know what I'm doing" option, which is always named -f. The exact meaning of -f depends on the command. For example, hg qnew hg -f will incorporate any outstanding changes into the new patch it creates, but hg qpop hg -f will revert modifications to any files affected by the patch that it is popping. Be sure to read the documentation for a command's -f option before you use it!

Working on Several Patches at Once

The qrefresh command always refreshes the *topmost* applied patch. This means that you can suspend work on one patch (by refreshing it), pop or push to make a different patch the top, and work on *that* patch for a while.

Here's an example that illustrates how you can use this ability. Let's say you're developing a new feature as two patches. The first is a change to the core of your software, and the second—layered on top of the first—changes the user interface to use the code you just added to the core. If you notice a bug in the core while you're working on the UI patch, it's easy to fix the core. Simply qrefresh the UI patch to save your in-progress changes, and qpop down to the core patch. Fix the core bug, qrefresh the core patch, and qpush back to the UI patch to continue where you left off.

More About Patches

MQ uses the GNU patch command to apply patches, so it's helpful to know a few more detailed aspects of how patch works, and about patches themselves.

The Strip Count

If you look at the file headers in a patch, you will notice that the pathnames usually have an extra component on the front that isn't present in the actual pathname. This is a holdover from the way that people used to generate patches (people still do this, but it's somewhat rare with modern revision control tools).

Alice would unpack a tarball, edit her files, then decide that she wanted to create a patch. So she'd rename her working directory, unpack the tarball again (hence the need for the rename), and use the -r and -N options to diff to recursively generate a patch between the unmodified directory and the modified one. The result would be that the name of the unmodified directory would be at the front of the left-hand path in every file header, and the name of the modified directory would be at the front of the right-hand path.

Since someone receiving a patch from the Alices of the Net would be unlikely to have unmodified and modified directories with exactly the same names, the patch command has a -p option that indicates the number of leading pathname components to strip when trying to apply a patch. This number is called the *strip count*.

An option of -p1 means "use a strip count of one." If patch sees a filename *foo/bar/baz* in a file header, it will strip *foo* and try to patch a file named *bar/baz*. (Strictly speaking, the strip count refers to the number of *path separators* [and the components that go with them] to strip. A strip count of one will turn *foo/bar* into *bar*, but */foo/bar* [notice the extra leading slash] into *foo/bar*.)

The "standard" strip count for patches is one; almost all patches contain one leading pathname component that needs to be stripped. Mercurial's hg diff command generates pathnames in this form, and the hg import command and MQ expect patches to have a strip count of one.

If you receive a patch from someone that you want to add to your patch queue, and the patch needs a strip count other than one, you cannot just qimport the patch, because qimport does not yet have a -p option; see issue 311 (*http://www.selenic.com/mercurial/bts/issue311*). Your best bet is to qnew a patch of your own, then use patch -pN to apply their patch, followed by hg addremove to pick up any files added or removed by the patch, followed by hg qrefresh. This complexity may become unnecessary; see issue 311 for details.

Strategies for Applying a Patch

When patch applies a hunk, it tries a handful of successively less accurate strategies to try to make the hunk apply. This falling-back technique often makes it possible to take a patch that was generated against an old version of a file and apply it against a newer version of that file.

First, patch tries an exact match, where the line numbers, the context, and the text to be modified must match exactly. If it cannot make an exact match, it tries to find an exact match for the context, without honoring the line numbering information. If this succeeds, it prints a line of output saying that the hunk was applied, but at some *offset* from the original line number.

If a context-only match fails, `patch` removes the first and last lines of the context, and tries a *reduced* context-only match. If the hunk with reduced context succeeds, patch prints a message saying that it applied the hunk with a *fuzz factor* (the number after the fuzz factor indicates how many lines of context `patch` had to trim before the patch applied).

When neither of these techniques works, `patch` prints a message saying that the hunk in question was rejected. It saves rejected hunks (also simply called "rejects") to a file with the same name and an added *.rej* extension. It also saves an unmodified copy of the file with a *.orig* extension; the copy of the file without any extensions will contain any changes made by hunks that *did* apply cleanly. If you have a patch that modifies *foo* with six hunks, and one of them fails to apply, you will have: an unmodified *foo.orig*, a *foo.rej* containing one hunk, and *foo*, containing the changes made by the five successful hunks.

Some Quirks of Patch Representation

There are a few useful things to know about how `patch` works with files:

- This should already be obvious, but `patch` cannot handle binary files.
- Neither does it care about the executable bit; it creates new files as readable, but not executable.
- `patch` treats the removal of a file as a diff between the file to be removed and the empty file. So your idea of "I deleted this file" looks like "every line of this file was deleted" in a patch.
- It treats the addition of a file as a diff between the empty file and the file to be added. So in a patch, your idea of "I added this file" looks like "every line of this file was added."
- It treats a renamed file as the removal of the old name and the addition of the new name. This means that renamed files have a big footprint in patches. (Note also that Mercurial does not currently try to infer when files have been renamed or copied in a patch.)
- `patch` cannot represent empty files, so you cannot use a patch to represent the notion "I added this empty file to the tree."

Beware the Fuzz

Although applying a hunk at an offset, or with a fuzz factor, will often be completely successful, these inexact techniques naturally leave open the possibility of corrupting the patched file. The most common cases typically involve applying a patch twice, or at an incorrect location in the file. If `patch` or `qpush` ever mentions an offset or fuzz factor, you should make sure that the modified files are correct afterwards.

It's often a good idea to refresh a patch that has applied with an offset or fuzz factor; refreshing the patch generates new context information that will make it apply cleanly. I say "often," not "always," because sometimes refreshing a patch will make it fail to apply against a different revision of the underlying files. In some cases, such as when you're maintaining a patch that must sit on top of multiple versions of a source tree, it's acceptable to have a patch apply with some fuzz, provided you've verified the results of the patching process in such cases.

Handling Rejection

If `qpush` fails to apply a patch, it will print an error message and exit. If it has left *.rej* files behind, it is usually best to fix up the rejected hunks before you push more patches or do any further work.

If your patch *used to* apply cleanly, and no longer does because you've changed the underlying code that your patches are based on, Mercurial Queues can help; see "Updating Your Patches When the Underlying Code Changes" on page 197 for details.

Unfortunately, there aren't any great techniques for dealing with rejected hunks. Most often, you'll need to view the *.rej* file and edit the target file, applying the rejected hunks by hand.

A Linux kernel hacker, Chris Mason (the author of Mercurial Queues), wrote a tool called `mpatch` (*http://oss.oracle.com/~mason/mpatch/*), which takes a simple approach to automating the application of hunks rejected by `patch`. The `mpatch` command can help with four common reasons that a hunk may be rejected:

- The context in the middle of a hunk has changed.
- A hunk is missing some context at the beginning or end.
- A large hunk might apply better—either entirely or in part—if it was broken up into smaller hunks.
- A hunk removes lines with slightly different content than those currently present in the file.

If you use `mpatch`, you should be doubly careful to check your results when you're done. In fact, `mpatch` enforces this method of double-checking the tool's output, by automatically dropping you into a merge program when it has done its job so that you can verify its work and finish off any remaining merges.

More on Patch Management

As you grow familiar with MQ, you will find yourself wanting to perform other kinds of patch management operations.

Deleting Unwanted Patches

If you want to get rid of a patch, use the `hg qdelete` command to delete the patch file and remove its entry from the patch series. If you try to delete a patch that is still applied, hg qdelete will refuse.

```
$ hg init myrepo
$ cd myrepo
$ hg qinit
$ hg qnew bad.patch
$ echo a > a
$ hg add a
$ hg qrefresh
$ hg qdelete bad.patch
abort: cannot delete applied patch bad.patch
$ hg qpop
patch queue now empty
$ hg qdelete bad.patch
```

Converting to and from Permanent Revisions

Once you're done working on a patch and want to turn it into a permanent changeset, use the `hg qfinish` command. Pass a revision to the command to identify the patch that you want to turn into a regular changeset; this patch must already be applied.

```
$ hg qnew good.patch
$ echo a > a
$ hg add a
$ hg qrefresh -m 'Good change'
$ hg qfinish tip
$ hg qapplied
$ hg tip --style=compact
0[tip]   3c8b7fe3998b   2009-05-05 06:44 +0000   bos
  Good change
```

The `hg qfinish` command accepts an `--all` or `-a` option, which turns all applied patches into regular changesets.

It is also possible to turn an existing changeset into a patch, by passing the `-r` option to `hg qimport`.

```
$ hg qimport -r tip
$ hg qapplied
0.diff
```

Note that it only makes sense to convert a changeset into a patch if you have not propagated that changeset into any other repositories. The imported changeset's ID will change every time you refresh the patch, which will make Mercurial treat it as unrelated to the original changeset if you have pushed it somewhere else.

Getting the Best Performance Out of MQ

MQ is very efficient at handling a large number of patches. I ran some performance experiments in mid-2006 for a talk that I gave at the 2006 EuroPython conference (on modern hardware, you should expect better performance than you'll see below). I used as my data set the Linux 2.6.17-mm1 patch series, which consists of 1,738 patches. I applied these on top of a Linux kernel repository containing all 27,472 revisions between Linux 2.6.12-rc2 and Linux 2.6.17.

On my old, slow laptop, I was able to hg qpush hg -a all 1,738 patches in 3.5 minutes, and hg qpop hg -a them all in 30 seconds. (On a newer laptop, the time to push all patches dropped to two minutes.) I could qrefresh one of the biggest patches (which made 22,779 lines of changes to 287 files) in 6.6 seconds.

Clearly, MQ is well suited to working in large trees, but there are a few tricks you can use to get the best performance out of it.

First of all, try to "batch" operations together. Every time you run qpush or qpop, these commands scan the working directory once to make sure you haven't made some changes and then forgotten to run qrefresh. On a small tree, the time that this scan takes is unnoticeable. However, on a medium-sized tree (containing tens of thousands of files), it can take a second or more.

The qpush and qpop commands allow you to push and pop multiple patches at a time. You can identify the "destination patch" that you want to end up at. When you qpush with a destination specified, it will push patches until that patch is at the top of the applied stack. When you qpop to a destination, MQ will pop patches until the destination patch is at the top.

You can identify a destination patch using either the name of the patch, or by number. If you use numeric addressing, patches are counted from zero; this means that the first patch is zero, the second is one, and so on.

Updating Your Patches When the Underlying Code Changes

It's common to have a stack of patches on top of an underlying repository that you don't modify directly. If you're working on changes to third-party code, or on a feature that is taking longer to develop than the rate of change of the code beneath, you will often need to sync up with the underlying code, and fix up any hunks in your patches that no longer apply. This is called *rebasing* your patch series.

The simplest way to do this is to hg qpop hg -a your patches, then hg pull changes into the underlying repository, and finally hg qpush hg -a your patches again. MQ will stop pushing any time it runs across a patch that fails to apply during conflicts, allowing you to fix your conflicts, qrefresh the affected patch, and continue pushing until you have fixed your entire stack.

This approach is easy to use and works well if you don't expect changes to the underlying code to affect how well your patches apply. If your patch stack touches code that is modified frequently or invasively in the underlying repository, however, fixing up rejected hunks by hand quickly becomes tiresome.

It's possible to partially automate the rebasing process. If your patches apply cleanly against some revision of the underlying repo, MQ can use this information to help you to resolve conflicts between your patches and a different revision.

The process is a little involved:

1. To begin, `hg qpush -a` all of your patches on top of the revision where you know that they apply cleanly.

2. Save a backup copy of your patch directory using `hg qsave hg -e hg -c`. This prints the name of the directory that it has saved the patches in. It will save the patches to a directory called *.hg/patches.N*, where `N` is a small integer. It also commits a "save changeset" on top of your applied patches; this is for internal bookkeeping, and records the states of the *series* and *status* files.

3. Use `hg pull` to bring new changes into the underlying repository. (Don't run `hg pull -u`; see below for why.)

4. Update to the new tip revision, using `hg update -C` to override the patches you have pushed.

5. Merge all patches using `hg qpush -m -a`. The `-m` option to `qpush` tells MQ to perform a three-way merge if the patch fails to apply.

During the `hg qpush hg -m`, each patch in the *series* file is applied normally. If a patch applies with fuzz or rejects, MQ looks at the queue you `qsave`d, and performs a three-way merge with the corresponding changeset. This merge uses Mercurial's normal merge machinery, so it may pop up a GUI merge tool to help you to resolve problems.

When you finish resolving the effects of a patch, MQ refreshes your patch based on the result of the merge.

At the end of this process, your repository will have one extra head from the old patch queue, and a copy of the old patch queue will be in *.hg/patches.N*. You can remove the extra head using `hg qpop -a -n patches.N` or `hg strip`. You can delete *.hg/patches.N* once you are sure that you no longer need it as a backup.

Identifying Patches

MQ commands that work with patches let you refer to a patch either by using its name or by a number. By name is obvious enough; pass the name *foo.patch* to `qpush`, for example, and it will push patches until *foo.patch* is applied.

As a shortcut, you can refer to a patch using both a name and a numeric offset; `foo.patch-2` means "two patches before `foo.patch`", while `bar.patch+4` means "four patches after `bar.patch`".

Referring to a patch by index isn't much different. The first patch printed in the output of `qseries` is patch zero (yes, it's one of those start-at-zero counting systems); the second is patch one; and so on.

MQ also makes it easy to work with patches when you are using normal Mercurial commands. Every command that accepts a changeset ID will also accept the name of an applied patch. MQ augments the tags normally in the repository with an eponymous one for each applied patch. In addition, the special tags `qbase` and `qtip` identify the bottom-most and topmost applied patches, respectively.

These additions to Mercurial's normal tagging capabilities make dealing with patches even more of a breeze.

- Want to patchbomb a mailing list with your latest series of changes?

      hg email qbase:qtip

  (Don't know what "patchbombing" is? See "Sending Changes via Email with the patchbomb Extension" on page 223.)

- Need to see all of the patches since `foo.patch` that have touched files in a subdirectory of your tree?

      hg log -r foo.patch:qtip subdir

Because MQ makes the names of patches available to the rest of Mercurial through its normal internal tag machinery, you don't need to type in the entire name of a patch when you want to identify it by name.

Another nice consequence of representing patch names as tags is that when you run the `hg log` command, it will display a patch's name as a tag, simply as part of its normal output. This makes it easy to visually distinguish applied patches from underlying "normal" revisions. The following example shows a few normal Mercurial commands in use with applied patches.

```
$ hg qapplied
first.patch
second.patch
$ hg log -r qbase:qtip
changeset:   1:c88942a2377a
tag:         first.patch
tag:         qbase
user:        Bryan O'Sullivan <bos@serpentine.com>
date:        Tue May 05 06:44:40 2009 +0000
summary:     [mq]: first.patch

changeset:   2:1934c63ed3c5
tag:         qtip
tag:         second.patch
```

```
tag:        tip
user:       Bryan O'Sullivan <bos@serpentine.com>
date:       Tue May 05 06:44:41 2009 +0000
summary:    [mq]: second.patch

$ hg export second.patch
# HG changeset patch
# User Bryan O'Sullivan <bos@serpentine.com>
# Date 1241505881 0
# Node ID 1934c63ed3c5ddf96f80bd5b965a15edbb2251a9
# Parent  c88942a2377a5d6d177ace3bea3e74cf653de8a3
[mq]: second.patch

diff -r c88942a2377a -r 1934c63ed3c5 other.c
--- /dev/null     Thu Jan 01 00:00:00 1970 +0000
+++ b/other.c     Tue May 05 06:44:41 2009 +0000
@@ -0,0 +1,1 @@
+double u;
```

Useful Things to Know About

There are a number of aspects of MQ usage that don't fit tidily into sections of their own, but that are good to know. Here they are, in one place.

- Normally, when you qpop a patch and qpush it again, the changeset that represents the patch after the pop/push will have a *different identity* from the changeset that represented the hash beforehand. See "qpush—Push Patches onto the Stack" on page 236 for information as to why this is.

- It's not a good idea to hg merge changes from another branch with a patch changeset, at least if you want to maintain the "patchiness" of that changeset and changesets below it on the patch stack. If you try to do this, it will appear to succeed, but MQ will become confused.

Managing Patches in a Repository

Because MQ's *.hg/patches* directory resides outside a Mercurial repository's working directory, the "underlying" Mercurial repository knows nothing about the management or presence of patches.

This presents the interesting possibility of managing the contents of the patch directory as a Mercurial repository in its own right. This can be a useful way to work. For example, you can work on a patch for a while, qrefresh it, then hg commit the current state of the patch. This lets you "roll back" to that version of the patch later on.

You can then share different versions of the same patch stack among multiple underlying repositories. I use this when I am developing a Linux kernel feature. I have a pristine copy of my kernel sources for each of several CPU architectures, and a cloned repository under each that contains the patches I am working on. When I want to test a change on a different architecture, I push my current patches to the patch repository associated with that kernel tree, pop and push all of my patches, and build and test that kernel.

Managing patches in a repository makes it possible for multiple developers to work on the same patch series without colliding with each other, all on top of an underlying source base that they may or may not control.

MQ Support for Patch Repositories

MQ helps you to work with the *.hg/patches* directory as a repository; when you prepare a repository for working with patches using `qinit`, you can pass the `hg -c` option to create the *.hg/patches* directory as a Mercurial repository.

 If you forget to use the `hg -c` option, you can simply go into the *.hg/patches* directory at any time and run `hg init`. Don't forget to add an entry for the *status* file to the *.hgignore* file, though (`hg qinit hg -c` does this for you automatically); you *really* don't want to manage the *status* file.

As a convenience, if MQ notices that the *.hg/patches* directory is a repository, it will automatically `hg add` every patch that you create and import.

MQ provides a shortcut command, `qcommit`, that runs `hg commit` in the *.hg/patches* directory. This saves some bothersome typing.

Finally, as a convenience to manage the patch directory, you can define the alias `mq` on Unix systems. For example, on Linux systems using the `bash` shell, you can include the following snippet in your *~/.bashrc*.

```
alias mq=`hg -R $(hg root)/.hg/patches'
```

You can then issue commands of the form `mq pull` from the main repository.

A Few Things to Watch Out For

MQ's support for working with a repository full of patches is limited in a few small respects.

MQ cannot automatically detect changes that you make to the patch directory. If you `hg pull`, manually edit, or `hg update` changes to patches or the *series* file, you will have to `hg qpop hg -a` and then `hg qpush hg -a` in the underlying repository to see those changes show up there. If you forget to do this, you can confuse MQ's idea of which patches are applied.

Third-Party Tools for Working with Patches

Once you've been working with patches for a while, you'll find yourself hungry for tools that will help you to understand and manipulate the patches you're dealing with.

The diffstat command (*http://linux.die.net/man/1/diffstat*) generates a histogram of the modifications made to each file in a patch. It provides a good way to "get a sense of" a patch—which files it affects, and how much change it introduces to each file and as a whole. (I find that it's a good idea to use diffstat's -p option as a matter of course, as otherwise it will try to do clever things with prefixes of filenames that inevitably confuse at least me.)

```
$ diffstat -p1 remove-redundant-null-checks.patch
 drivers/char/agp/sgi-agp.c          |   5 ++---
 drivers/char/hvcs.c                 |  11 +++++------
 drivers/message/fusion/mptfc.c      |   6 ++----
 drivers/message/fusion/mptsas.c     |   3 +--
 drivers/net/fs_enet/fs_enet-mii.c   |   3 +--
 drivers/net/wireless/ipw2200.c      |  22 ++++++----------------
 drivers/scsi/libata-scsi.c          |   4 +---
 drivers/video/au1100fb.c            |   3 +--
 8 files changed, 19 insertions(+), 38 deletions(-)
$ filterdiff -i '*/video/*' remove-redundant-null-checks.patch
--- a/drivers/video/au1100fb.c~remove-redundant-null-checks-before-free-in-drivers
+++ a/drivers/video/au1100fb.c
@@ -743,8 +743,7 @@ void __exit au1100fb_cleanup(void)
 {
        driver_unregister(&au1100fb_driver);

-       if (drv_info.opt_mode)
-               kfree(drv_info.opt_mode);
+       kfree(drv_info.opt_mode);
 }

        module_init(au1100fb_init);
```

The patchutils package (*http://cyberelk.net/tim/software/patchutils/*) is invaluable. It provides a set of small utilities that follow the "Unix philosophy": each does one useful thing with a patch. The patchutils command I use most is filterdiff, which extracts subsets from a patch file. For example, given a patch that modifies hundreds of files across dozens of directories, a single invocation of filterdiff can generate a smaller patch that only touches files whose names match a particular glob pattern. See "Viewing the History of a Patch" on page 214 for another example.

Good Ways to Work with Patches

Whether you are working on a patch series to submit to a free software or open source project, or a series that you intend to treat as a sequence of regular changesets when you're done, you can use some simple techniques to keep your work well organized.

Give your patches descriptive names. A good name for a patch might be *rework-device-alloc.patch*, because it will immediately give you a hint of the purpose of the patch. Long names shouldn't be a problem; you won't be typing the names often, but you *will* be running commands like qapplied and qtop over and over. Good naming becomes especially important when you have a number of patches to work with, or if you are juggling a number of different tasks and your patches only get a fraction of your attention.

Be aware of what patch you're working on. Use the qtop command and skim over the text of your patches frequently—for example, using hg tip -p—to be sure of where you stand. I have several times worked on and qrefreshed a patch other than the one I intended, and it's often tricky to migrate changes into the right patch after making them in the wrong one.

For this reason, it is very much worth investing a little time to learn how to use some of the third-party tools I described in "Third-Party Tools for Working with Patches" on page 202, particularly diffstat and filterdiff. The former will give you a quick idea of what changes your patch is making, while the latter makes it easy to splice hunks selectively out of one patch and into another.

MQ Cookbook

Managing "Trivial" Patches

Because the overhead of dropping files into a new Mercurial repository is so low, it makes a lot of sense to manage patches this way even if you simply want to make a few changes to a source tarball that you downloaded.

Begin by downloading and unpacking the source tarball, and turning it into a Mercurial repository.

```
$ download netplug-1.2.5.tar.bz2
$ tar jxf netplug-1.2.5.tar.bz2
$ cd netplug-1.2.5
$ hg init
$ hg commit -q --addremove --message netplug-1.2.5
$ cd ..
$ hg clone netplug-1.2.5 netplug
updating working directory
18 files updated, 0 files merged, 0 files removed, 0 files unresolved
```

Continue by creating a patch stack and making your changes.

```
$ cd netplug
$ hg qinit
$ hg qnew -m 'fix build problem with gcc 4' build-fix.patch
$ perl -pi -e 's/int addr_len/socklen_t addr_len/' netlink.c
$ hg qrefresh
$ hg tip -p
```

```
changeset:   1:3174f1d41d77
tag:         qtip
tag:         build-fix.patch
tag:         tip
tag:         qbase
user:        Bryan O'Sullivan <bos@serpentine.com>
date:        Tue May 05 06:44:41 2009 +0000
summary:     fix build problem with gcc 4

diff -r 566cfe2faac9 -r 3174f1d41d77 netlink.c
--- a/netlink.c    Tue May 05 06:44:41 2009 +0000
+++ b/netlink.c    Tue May 05 06:44:41 2009 +0000
@@ -275,7 +275,7 @@
        exit(1);
    }

-    int addr_len = sizeof(addr);
+    socklen_t addr_len = sizeof(addr);

    if (getsockname(fd, (struct sockaddr *) &addr, &addr_len) == -1) {
        do_log(LOG_ERR, "Could not get socket details: %m");
```

Let's say a few weeks or months pass, and your package author releases a new version. First, bring their changes into the repository.

```
$ hg qpop -a
patch queue now empty
$ cd ..
$ download netplug-1.2.8.tar.bz2
$ hg clone netplug-1.2.5 netplug-1.2.8
updating working directory
18 files updated, 0 files merged, 0 files removed, 0 files unresolved
$ cd netplug-1.2.8
$ hg locate -0 | xargs -0 rm
$ cd ..
$ tar jxf netplug-1.2.8.tar.bz2
$ cd netplug-1.2.8
$ hg commit --addremove --message netplug-1.2.8
```

The pipeline starting with hg locate above deletes all files in the working directory, so that hg commit's --addremove option can actually tell which files have really been removed in the newer version of the source.

Finally, you can apply your patches on top of the new tree.

```
$ cd ../netplug
$ hg pull ../netplug-1.2.8
pulling from ../netplug-1.2.8
searching for changes
adding changesets
adding manifests
adding file changes
added 1 changesets with 12 changes to 12 files
(run 'hg update' to get a working copy)
$ hg qpush -a
(working directory not at tip)
```

```
applying build-fix.patch
now at: build-fix.patch
```

Combining Entire Patches

MQ provides a command qfold that lets you combine entire patches. This "folds" the patches you name, in the order you name them, into the topmost applied patch, and concatenates their descriptions onto the end of its description. The patches that you fold must be unapplied before you fold them.

The order in which you fold patches matters. If your topmost applied patch is foo, and you qfold bar and quux into it, you will end up with a patch that has the same effect as if you applied first foo, then bar, followed by quux.

Merging Part of One Patch into Another

Merging *part* of one patch into another is more difficult than combining entire patches. If you want to move changes to entire files, you can use filterdiff's -i and -x options to choose the modifications to snip out of one patch, concatenating its output onto the end of the patch you want to merge into. You usually won't need to modify the patch you've merged the changes from. Instead, MQ will report some rejected hunks when you qpush it (from the hunks you moved into the other patch), and you can simply qrefresh the patch to drop the duplicate hunks.

If you have a patch that has multiple hunks modifying a file, and you only want to move a few of those hunks, the job becomes more messy, but you can still partly automate it. Use lsdiff -nvv to print some metadata about the patch.

```
$ lsdiff -nvv remove-redundant-null-checks.patch
 22    File #1        a/drivers/char/agp/sgi-agp.c
    24    Hunk #1      static int __devinit agp_sgi_init(void)
 37    File #2        a/drivers/char/hvcs.c
    39    Hunk #1      static struct tty_operations hvcs_ops =
    53    Hunk #2      static int hvcs_alloc_index_list(int n)
 69    File #3        a/drivers/message/fusion/mptfc.c
    71    Hunk #1      mptfc_GetFcDevPage0(MPT_ADAPTER *ioc, in
 85    File #4        a/drivers/message/fusion/mptsas.c
    87    Hunk #1      mptsas_probe_hba_phys(MPT_ADAPTER *ioc)
 98    File #5        a/drivers/net/fs_enet/fs_enet-mii.c
    100   Hunk #1       static struct fs_enet_mii_bus *create_bu
 111   File #6        a/drivers/net/wireless/ipw2200.c
    113   Hunk #1       static struct ipw_fw_error *ipw_alloc_er
    126   Hunk #2       static ssize_t clear_error(struct device
    140   Hunk #3       static void ipw_irq_tasklet(struct ipw_p
    150   Hunk #4       static void ipw_pci_remove(struct pci_de
 164   File #7        a/drivers/scsi/libata-scsi.c
    166   Hunk #1       int ata_cmd_ioctl(struct scsi_device *sc
 178   File #8        a/drivers/video/au1100fb.c
    180   Hunk #1      void __exit au1100fb_cleanup(void)
```

This command prints three different kinds of number:

- (in the first column) a *file number* to identify each file modified in the patch
- (on the next line, indented) the line number within a modified file where a hunk starts
- (on the same line) a *hunk number* to identify that hunk

You'll have to use some visual inspection, and reading of the patch, to identify the file and hunk numbers you'll want, but you can then pass them to `filterdiff`'s `--files` and `--hunks` options, to select exactly the file and hunk you want to extract.

Once you have this hunk, you can concatenate it onto the end of your destination patch and continue with the remainder of "Combining Entire Patches" on page 205.

Differences Between Quilt and MQ

If you are already familiar with quilt, MQ provides a similar command set. There are a few differences in the way that it works.

You will already have noticed that most quilt commands have MQ counterparts that simply begin with a q. The exceptions are quilt's `add` and `remove` commands, the counterparts for which are the normal Mercurial `hg add` and `hg remove` commands. There is no MQ equivalent to quilt's `edit` command.

## CHAPTER 13

Advanced Uses of Mercurial Queues

While it's easy to pick up straightforward uses of Mercurial Queues, the use of a little discipline and some of MQ's less frequently used capabilities makes it possible to work in complicated development environments.

In this chapter, I will use as an example a technique I have used to manage the development of an Infiniband device driver for the Linux kernel. The driver in question is large (at least as drivers go), with 25,000 lines of code spread across 35 source files. It is maintained by a small team of developers.

While much of the material in this chapter is specific to Linux, the same principles apply to any code base for which you're not the primary owner, and upon which you need to do a lot of development.

The Problem of Many Targets

The Linux kernel changes rapidly and has never been internally stable; developers frequently make drastic changes between releases. This means that a version of the driver that works well with a particular released version of the kernel will typically not even *compile* correctly against any other version.

To maintain a driver, we have to keep a number of distinct versions of Linux in mind:

- One target is the main Linux kernel development tree. Maintenance of the code is in this case partly shared by other developers in the kernel community, who make "drive-by" modifications to the driver as they develop and refine kernel subsystems.

- We also maintain a number of "backports" to older versions of the Linux kernel, to support the needs of customers who are running older Linux distributions that do not incorporate our drivers. (To *backport* a piece of code is to modify it to work in an older version of its target environment than the version it was developed for.)

- Finally, we make software releases on a schedule that is necessarily not aligned with those used by Linux distributors and kernel developers, so that we can deliver new features to customers without forcing them to upgrade their entire kernels or distributions.

Tempting Approaches That Don't Work Well

There are two "standard" ways to maintain a piece of software that has to target many different environments.

The first is to maintain a number of branches, each intended for a single target. The trouble with this approach is that you must maintain iron discipline in the flow of changes between repositories. A new feature or bug fix must start life in a "pristine" repository, then percolate out to every backport repository. Backport changes are more limited in the branches they should propagate to; a backport change that is applied to a branch where it doesn't belong will probably stop the driver from compiling.

The second is to maintain a single source tree filled with conditional statements that turn chunks of code on or off depending on the intended target. Because these "if-defs" are not allowed in the Linux kernel tree, a manual or automatic process must be followed to strip them out and yield a clean tree. A code base maintained in this fashion rapidly becomes a rat's nest of conditional blocks that are difficult to understand and maintain.

Neither of these approaches is well suited to a situation where you don't "own" the canonical copy of a source tree. In the case of a Linux driver that is distributed with the standard kernel, Linus's tree contains the copy of the code that will be treated by the world as canonical. The upstream version of "my" driver can be modified by people I don't know, without me even finding out about it until after the changes show up in Linus's tree.

These approaches have the added weakness of making it difficult to generate well-formed patches to submit upstream.

In principle, Mercurial Queues seems like a good candidate to manage a development scenario such as the above. While this is indeed the case, MQ contains a few added features that make the job more pleasant.

Conditionally Applying Patches with Guards

Perhaps the best way to maintain sanity with so many targets is to be able to choose specific patches to apply for a given situation. MQ provides a feature called "guards" (which originated from quilt's `guards` command) that does just this. To start off, let's create a simple repository for experimenting in.

```
$ hg qinit
$ hg qnew hello.patch
$ echo hello > hello
$ hg add hello
$ hg qrefresh
```

```
$ hg qnew goodbye.patch
$ echo goodbye > goodbye
$ hg add goodbye
$ hg qrefresh
```

This gives us a tiny repository that contains two patches that don't have any dependencies on each other, because they touch different files.

The idea behind conditional application is that you can "tag" a patch with a *guard*, which is simply a text string of your choosing, then tell MQ to select specific guards to use when applying patches. MQ will then either apply, or skip over, a guarded patch, depending on the guards that you have selected.

A patch can have an arbitrary number of guards; each one is *positive* ("apply this patch if this guard is selected") or *negative* ("skip this patch if this guard is selected"). A patch with no guards is always applied.

Controlling the Guards on a Patch

The `qguard` command lets you determine which guards should apply to a patch, or display the guards that are already in effect. Without any arguments, it displays the guards on the current topmost patch.

```
$ hg qguard
goodbye.patch: unguarded
```

To set a positive guard on a patch, prefix the name of the guard with +.

```
$ hg qguard +foo
$ hg qguard
goodbye.patch: +foo
```

To set a negative guard on a patch, prefix the name of the guard with -.

```
$ hg qguard -- hello.patch -quux
$ hg qguard hello.patch
hello.patch: -quux
```

Notice that we prefixed the arguments to the `hg + qguard` command with a -- here, so that Mercurial would not interpret the text -quux as an option.

Setting versus modifying

The `qguard` command *sets* the guards on a patch; it doesn't *modify* them. What this means is that if you run `hg qguard +a +b` on a patch, then `hg qguard +c` on the same patch, the *only* guard that will be set on it afterwards is +c.

Mercurial stores guards in the *series* file; the form in which they are stored is easy both to understand and to edit by hand. (In other words, you don't have to use the `qguard` command if you don't want to; it's okay to simply edit the *series* file.)

```
$ cat .hg/patches/series
hello.patch #-quux
goodbye.patch #+foo
```

Selecting the Guards to Use

The qselect command determines which guards are active at a given time. The effect of this is to determine which patches MQ will apply the next time you run qpush. It has no other effect; in particular, it doesn't do anything to patches that are already applied.

With no arguments, the qselect command lists the guards currently in effect, one per line of output. Each argument is treated as the name of a guard to apply.

```
$ hg qpop -a
patch queue now empty
$ hg qselect
no active guards
$ hg qselect foo
number of unguarded, unapplied patches has changed from 1 to 2
$ hg qselect
foo
```

In case you're interested, the currently selected guards are stored in the *guards* file.

```
$ cat .hg/patches/guards
foo
```

We can see the effect the selected guards have when we run qpush.

```
$ hg qpush -a
applying hello.patch
applying goodbye.patch
now at: goodbye.patch
```

A guard cannot start with a + or - character. The name of a guard must not contain whitespace, but most other characters are acceptable. If you try to use a guard with an invalid name, MQ will complain:

```
$ hg qselect +foo
abort: guard '+foo' starts with invalid character: '+'
```

Changing the selected guards changes the patches that are applied.

```
$ hg qselect quux
number of guarded, applied patches has changed from 0 to 2
$ hg qpop -a
patch queue now empty
$ hg qpush -a
patch series already fully applied
```

You can see in the example below that negative guards take precedence over positive guards.

```
$ hg qselect foo bar
number of unguarded, unapplied patches has changed from 0 to 2
$ hg qpop -a
```

```
no patches applied
$ hg qpush -a
applying hello.patch
applying goodbye.patch
now at: goodbye.patch
```

MQ's Rules for Applying Patches

The rules that MQ uses when deciding whether to apply a patch are as follows:

- A patch that has no guards is always applied.
- If the patch has any negative guard that matches any currently selected guard, the patch is skipped.
- If the patch has any positive guard that matches any currently selected guard, the patch is applied.
- If the patch has positive or negative guards, but none matches any currently selected guard, the patch is skipped.

Trimming the Work Environment

In working on the device driver I mentioned earlier, I don't apply the patches to a normal Linux kernel tree. Instead, I use a repository that contains only a snapshot of the source files and headers that are relevant to Infiniband development. This repository is 1% of the size of a kernel repository, so it's easier to work with.

I then choose a "base" version on top of which the patches are applied. This is a snapshot of the Linux kernel tree as of a revision of my choosing. When I take the snapshot, I record the changeset ID from the kernel repository in the commit message. Since the snapshot preserves the "shape" and content of the relevant parts of the kernel tree, I can apply my patches on top of either my tiny repository or a normal kernel tree.

Normally, the base tree atop which the patches apply should be a snapshot of a very recent upstream tree. This best facilitates the development of patches that can easily be submitted upstream with few or no modifications.

Dividing Up the Series File

I categorize the patches in the *series* file into a number of logical groups. Each section of like patches begins with a block of comments that describes the purpose of the patches that follow.

The sequence of patch groups that I maintain follows. The ordering of these groups is important; I'll describe why after I introduce the groups.

- The "accepted" group. Patches that the development team has submitted to the maintainer of the Infiniband subsystem and that he has accepted, but that are not present in the snapshot that the tiny repository is based on. These are "read only" patches, present only to transform the tree into a similar state as it is in the upstream maintainer's repository.

- The "rework" group. Patches that I have submitted, but that the upstream maintainer has requested modifications to before he will accept them.

- The "pending" group. Patches that I have not yet submitted to the upstream maintainer, but that we have finished working on. These will be "read only" for a while. If the upstream maintainer accepts them upon submission, I'll move them to the end of the "accepted" group. If he requests that I modify any, I'll move them to the beginning of the "rework" group.

- The "in progress" group. Patches that are actively being developed, and should not be submitted anywhere yet.

- The "backport" group. Patches that adapt the source tree to older versions of the kernel tree.

- The "do not ship" group. Patches that for some reason should never be submitted upstream. For example, one such patch might change embedded driver identification strings to make it easier to distinguish, in the field, between an out-of-tree version of the driver and a version shipped by a distribution vendor.

Now to discuss the reasons for ordering groups of patches in this way. We would like the lowest patches in the stack to be as stable as possible, so that we will not need to rework higher patches due to changes in context. Putting patches that will never be changed first in the *series* file serves this purpose.

We would also like the patches that we know we'll need to modify to be applied on top of a source tree that resembles the upstream tree as closely as possible. This is why we keep accepted patches around for a while.

The "backport" and "do not ship" patches float at the end of the *series* file. The backport patches must be applied on top of all other patches, and the "do not ship" patches might as well stay out of harm's way.

Maintaining the Patch Series

In my work, I use a number of guards to control which patches are to be applied:

- "Accepted" patches are guarded with `accepted`. I enable this guard most of the time. When I'm applying the patches on top of a tree where the patches are already present, I can turn this patch off, and the patches that follow it will apply cleanly.

- Patches that are "finished," but not yet submitted, have no guards. If I'm applying the patch stack to a copy of the upstream tree, I don't need to enable any guards in order to get a reasonably safe source tree.

- Those patches that need reworking before being resubmitted are guarded with `rework`.
- For those patches that are still under development, I use `devel`.
- A backport patch may have several guards, one for each version of the kernel to which it applies. For example, a patch that backports a piece of code to 2.6.9 will have a `2.6.9` guard.

This variety of guards gives me considerable flexibility in determining what kind of source tree I want to end up with. For most situations, the selection of appropriate guards is automated during the build process, but I can manually tune the guards to use for less common circumstances.

The Art of Writing Backport Patches

Using MQ, writing a backport patch is a simple process. All such a patch has to do is modify a piece of code that uses a kernel feature not present in the older version of the kernel, so that the driver continues to work correctly under that older version.

A useful goal when writing a good backport patch is to make your code look as if it were written for the older version of the kernel you're targeting. The less obtrusive the patch, the easier it will be to understand and maintain. If you're writing a collection of backport patches to avoid the "rat's nest" effect of multilple `#ifdef`s (hunks of source code that are only used conditionally) in your code, don't introduce version-dependent `#ifdef`s into the patches. Instead, write several patches, each of which makes unconditional changes, and control their application using guards.

There are two reasons to divide backport patches into a distinct group, away from the "regular" patches whose effects they modify. The first is that intermingling the two makes it more difficult to use a tool like the `patchbomb` extension to automate the process of submitting the patches to an upstream maintainer. The second is that a backport patch could disturb the context in which a subsequent regular patch is applied, making it impossible to apply the regular patch cleanly *without* the earlier backport patch already being applied.

Useful Tips for Developing with MQ

Organizing Patches in Directories

If you're working on a substantial project with MQ, it's not difficult to accumulate a large number of patches. For example, I have one patch repository that contains over 250 patches.

If you can group these patches into separate logical categories, you can store them in different directories if you like; MQ has no problems with patch names that contain path separators.

Viewing the History of a Patch

If you're developing a set of patches over a long time, it's a good idea to maintain them in a repository, as discussed in "Managing Patches in a Repository" on page 200. If you do so, you'll quickly discover that using the `hg diff` command to look at the history of changes to a patch is unworkable. This is in part because you're looking at the second derivative of the real code (a diff of a diff), but also because MQ adds noise to the process by modifying timestamps and directory names when it updates a patch.

However, you can use the `extdiff` extension, which is bundled with Mercurial, to turn a diff of two versions of a patch into something readable. To do this, you will need a third-party package called `patchutils` (*http://cyberelk.net/tim/software/patchutils/*). This provides a command named `interdiff`, which shows the differences between two diffs as a diff. Used on two versions of the same diff, it generates a diff that represents the diff from the first to the second version.

You can enable the `extdiff` extension in the usual way, by adding a line to the `exten sions` section of your *~/.hgrc*.

```
[extensions]
extdiff =
```

The `interdiff` command expects to be passed the names of two files, but the `extdiff` extension passes the program it runs a pair of directories, each of which can contain an arbitrary number of files. We thus need a small program that will run `interdiff` on each pair of files in these two directories. This program is available as *hg-interdiff* in the *examples* directory of the source code repository that accompanies this book.

With the *hg-interdiff* program in your shell's search path, you can run it as follows, from inside an MQ patch directory:

```
hg extdiff -p hg-interdiff -r A:B my-change.patch
```

Since you'll probably want to use this long-winded command a lot, you can get `hgext` to make it available as a normal Mercurial command, again by editing your *~/.hgrc*.

```
[extdiff]
cmd.interdiff = hg-interdiff
```

This directs `hgext` to make an `interdiff` command available, so you can now shorten the previous invocation of `extdiff` to something a little more wieldy.

```
hg interdiff -r A:B my-change.patch
```

The `interdiff` command works well only if the underlying files against which versions of a patch are generated remain the same. If you create a patch, modify the underlying files, and then regenerate the patch, `interdiff` may not produce useful output.

The `extdiff` extension is useful for more than merely improving the presentation of MQ patches. To read more about it, go to "Flexible Diff Support with the extdiff Extension" on page 220.

## CHAPTER 14

Adding Functionality with Extensions

While the core of Mercurial is quite complete from a functionality standpoint, it's deliberately shorn of fancy features. This approach of preserving simplicity keeps the software easy to deal with for both maintainers and users.

However, Mercurial doesn't box you in with an inflexible command set: you can add features to it as *extensions* (sometimes known as *plug-ins*). We've already discussed a few of these extensions in earlier chapters.

- "Simplifying the Pull-Merge-Commit Sequence" on page 42 covers the `fetch` extension; this combines pulling new changes and merging them with local changes into a single command, `fetch`.

- In Chapter 10, we covered several extensions that are useful for hook-related functionality: `acl` adds access control lists; `bugzilla` adds integration with the Bugzilla bug tracking system; and `notify` sends notification emails on new changes.

- The Mercurial Queues patch management extension is so invaluable that it merits two chapters and an appendix all to itself. Chapter 12 covers the basics; Chapter 13 discusses advanced topics; and Appendix B goes into detail on each command.

In this chapter, we'll cover some of the other extensions that are available for Mercurial, and briefly touch on some of the machinery you'll need to know about if you want to write an extension of your own.

In "Improve Performance with the inotify Extension" on page 217, we'll discuss the possibility of *huge* performance improvements using the `inotify` extension.

Improve Performance with the inotify Extension

Are you interested in having some of the most common Mercurial operations run as much as a hundred times faster? Read on!

Mercurial has great performance under normal circumstances. For example, when you run the `hg status` command, Mercurial has to scan almost every directory and file in your repository so that it can display file status. Many other Mercurial commands need to do the same work behind the scenes; for example, the hg diff command uses the status machinery to avoid doing an expensive comparison operation on files that obviously haven't changed.

Because obtaining file status is crucial to good performance, the authors of Mercurial have optimized this code to within an inch of its life. However, there's no avoiding the fact that when you run hg status, Mercurial is going to have to perform at least one expensive system call for each managed file to determine whether it's changed since the last time Mercurial checked. For a sufficiently large repository, this can take a long time.

To put a number on the magnitude of this effect, I created a repository containing 150,000 managed files. I timed hg status as taking ten seconds to run, even when *none* of those files had been modified.

Many modern operating systems contain a file notification facility. If a program signs up to an appropriate service, the operating system will notify it every time a file of interest is created, modified, or deleted. On Linux systems, the kernel component that does this is called inotify.

Mercurial's inotify extension talks to the kernel's inotify component to optimize hg status commands. The extension has two components. A daemon sits in the background and receives notifications from the inotify subsystem. It also listens for connections from a regular Mercurial command. The extension modifies Mercurial's behavior so that instead of scanning the filesystem, it queries the daemon. Since the daemon has perfect information about the state of the repository, it can respond with a result instantaneously, avoiding the need to scan every directory and file in the repository.

Recall that I measured plain Mercurial as taking ten seconds to run hg status on a 150,000 file repository. With the inotify extension enabled, the time dropped to 0.1 seconds, a factor of *one hundred* faster.

Before we continue, please pay attention to some caveats:

- The inotify extension is Linux-specific. Because it interfaces directly to the Linux kernel's inotify subsystem, it does not work on other operating systems.
- It should work on any Linux distribution that was released after early 2005. Older distributions are likely to have a kernel that lacks inotify, or a version of glibc that does not have the necessary interfacing support.
- Not all filesystems are suitable for use with the inotify extension. Network filesystems such as NFS are a non-starter, for example, particularly if you're running Mercurial on several systems, all mounting the same network filesystem. The kernel's inotify system has no way of knowing about changes made on another system. Most local filesystems (e.g., ext3, XFS, ReiserFS) should work fine.

The inotify extension is not yet shipped with Mercurial as of May 2009, so it's a little more involved to set up than other extensions. But the performance improvement is worth it!

The extension currently comes in two parts: a set of patches to the Mercurial source code, and a library of Python bindings to the inotify subsystem.

There are in fact two Python inotify binding libraries. One of them is called pyinotify, and is packaged by some Linux distributions as python-inotify. This is *not* the one you'll need, as it is too buggy and inefficient to be practical.

To get going, it's best to already have a functioning copy of Mercurial installed.

If you follow the instructions below, you'll be *replacing and overwriting* any existing installation of Mercurial that you might already have, using the latest "bleeding edge" Mercurial code. Don't say you weren't warned!

1. Clone the Python inotify binding repository. Build and install it.

   ```
   hg clone http://hg.kublai.com/python/inotify
   cd inotify
   python setup.py build --force
   sudo python setup.py install --skip-build
   ```

2. Clone the *crew* Mercurial repository. Clone the inotify patch repository so that Mercurial Queues will be able to apply patches to your copy of the *crew* repository.

   ```
   hg clone http://hg.intevation.org/mercurial/crew
   hg clone crew inotify
   hg clone http://hg.kublai.com/mercurial/patches/inotify inotify/.hg/patches
   ```

3. Make sure that you have the Mercurial Queues extension, mq, enabled. If you've never used MQ, read "Getting Started with Mercurial Queues" on page 187 to get started quickly.

4. Go into the *inotify* repo, and apply all of the inotify patches using the hg -a option to the qpush command.

   ```
   cd inotify
   hg qpush -a
   ```

5. If you get an error message from qpush, you should not continue. Instead, ask for help.

6. Build and install the patched version of Mercurial.

   ```
   python setup.py build --force
   sudo python setup.py install --skip-build
   ```

Once you've built a suitably patched version of Mercurial, all you need to do to enable the `inotify` extension is add an entry to your *~/.hgrc*.

```
[extensions] inotify =
```

When the `inotify` extension is enabled, Mercurial will automatically and transparently start the status daemon the first time you run a command that needs status in a repository. It runs one status daemon per repository.

The status daemon is started silently, and runs in the background. If you look at a list of running processes after you've enabled the `inotify` extension and run a few commands in different repositories, you'll thus see a few `hg` processes sitting around, waiting for updates from the kernel and queries from Mercurial.

The first time you run a Mercurial command in a repository when you have the `inotify` extension enabled, it will run with about the same performance as a normal Mercurial command. This is because the status daemon needs to perform a normal status scan so that it has a baseline against which to apply later updates from the kernel. However, *every* subsequent command that does any kind of status check should be noticeably faster on repositories of even fairly modest size. Better yet, the bigger your repository is, the greater performance advantage you'll see. The `inotify` daemon makes status operations almost instantaneous on repositories of all sizes!

If you like, you can manually start a status daemon using the `inserve` command. This gives you slightly finer control over how the daemon ought to run. This command will of course only be available when the `inotify` extension is enabled.

When you're using the `inotify` extension, you should notice *no difference at all* in Mercurial's behavior, with the sole exception of status-related commands running a whole lot faster than they used to. You should specifically expect that commands will *not* print different output, neither should they give different results. If either of these situations occurs, please report a bug.

Flexible Diff Support with the extdiff Extension

Mercurial's built-in `hg diff` command outputs plain text unified diffs.

```
$ hg diff
diff -r a6ba002523c0 myfile
--- a/myfile    Tue May 05 06:44:37 2009 +0000
+++ b/myfile    Tue May 05 06:44:37 2009 +0000
@@ -1,1 +1,2 @@
 The first line.
+The second line.
```

If you would like to use an external tool to display modifications, you'll want to use the `extdiff` extension. This will let you use, for example, a graphical diff tool.

The `extdiff` extension is bundled with Mercurial, so it's easy to set up. In the `extensions` section of your *~/.hgrc*, simply add a one-line entry to enable the extension.

```
[extensions]
extdiff =
```

This introduces a command named `extdiff`, which by default uses your system's `diff` command to generate a unified diff in the same form as the built-in `hg diff` command.

```
$ hg extdiff
--- a.a6ba002523c0/myfile     2009-05-05 06:44:37.769474821 +0000
+++ /tmp/extdiffXbMAOx/a/myfile     2009-05-05 06:44:37.677474721 +0000
@@ -1 +1,2 @@
 The first line.
+The second line.
```

The result won't be exactly the same as with the built-in `hg diff` variations, because the output of `diff` varies from one system to another, even when passed the same options.

As the "`making snapshot`" lines of output above imply, the `extdiff` command works by creating two snapshots of your source tree. The first snapshot is of the source revision; the second, of the target revision or working directory. The `extdiff` command generates these snapshots in a temporary directory, passes the name of each directory to an external diff viewer, then deletes the temporary directory. For efficiency, it only snapshots the directories and files that have changed between the two revisions.

Snapshot directory names have the same base name as your repository. If your repository path is */quux/bar/foo*, then *foo* will be the name of each snapshot directory. Each snapshot directory name has its changeset ID appended, if appropriate. If a snapshot is of revision `a631aca1083f`, the directory will be named *foo.a631aca1083f*. A snapshot of the working directory won't have a changeset ID appended, so it would just be *foo* in this example. To see what this looks like in practice, look again at the `extdiff` example above. Notice that the diff has the snapshot directory names embedded in its header.

The `extdiff` command accepts two important options. The `hg -p` option lets you choose a program to view differences with, instead of `diff`. With the `hg -o` option, you can change the options that `extdiff` passes to the program (by default, these options are `-Npru`, which only make sense if you're running `diff`). In other respects, the `extdiff` command acts similarly to the built-in `hg diff` command: you use the same option names, syntax, and arguments to specify the revisions you want, the files you want, and so on.

As an example, here's how to run the normal system `diff` command, getting it to generate context diffs (using the `-c` option) instead of unified diffs, and five lines of context instead of the default three (passing `5` as the argument to the `-C` option).

```
$ hg extdiff -o -NprcC5
*** a.a6ba002523c0/myfile     Tue May  5 06:44:37 2009
--- /tmp/extdiffXbMAOx/a/myfile     Tue May  5 06:44:37 2009
***************
*** 1 ****
```

```
--- 1,2 ----
  The first line.
+ The second line.
```

Launching a visual diff tool is just as easy. Here's how to launch the `kdiff3` viewer.

```
hg extdiff -p kdiff3 -o
```

If your diff viewing command can't deal with directories, you can easily work around this with a little scripting. For an example of such scripting in action with the `mq` extension and the `interdiff` command, see "Viewing the History of a Patch" on page 214.

Defining Command Aliases

It can be cumbersome to remember the options to both the `extdiff` command and the diff viewer you want to use, so the `extdiff` extension lets you define *new* commands that will invoke your diff viewer with exactly the right options.

All you need to do is edit your *~/.hgrc*, and add a section named `extdiff`. Inside this section, you can define multiple commands. Here's how to add a `kdiff3` command. Once you've defined this, you can type `hg kdiff3` and the `extdiff` extension will run `kdiff3` for you.

```
[extdiff]
cmd.kdiff3 =
```

If you leave the right-hand side of the definition empty, as above, the `extdiff` extension uses the name of the command you defined as the name of the external program to run. But these names don't have to be the same. Here, we define a command named hg wibble, which runs `kdiff3`.

```
[extdiff]
 cmd.wibble = kdiff3
```

You can also specify the default options that you want to invoke your diff viewing program with. The prefix to use is `opts.`, followed by the name of the command to which the options apply. This example defines a command hg vimdiff that runs the `vim` editor's `DirDiff` extension.

```
[extdiff]
 cmd.vimdiff = vim
opts.vimdiff = -f '+next' '+execute "DirDiff" argv(0) argv(1)'
```

Cherry-Picking Changes with the transplant Extension

Need to have a long chat with Brendan about this.

Sending Changes via Email with the patchbomb Extension

Many projects have a culture of "change review," in which people send their modifications to a mailing list for others to read and comment on before they commit the final version to a shared repository. Some projects have people who act as gatekeepers; they apply changes from other people to a repository to which those others don't have access.

Mercurial makes it easy to send changes over email for review or application, via its `patchbomb` extension. The extension is so named because changes are formatted as patches, and it's usual to send one changeset per email message. Sending a long series of changes by email is thus much like "bombing" the recipient's inbox, hence "patchbomb."

As usual, the basic configuration of the `patchbomb` extension takes just one or two lines in your */.hgrc*.

```
[extensions]
patchbomb =
```

Once you've enabled the extension, you will have a new command available, named `email`.

The safest and best way to invoke the `email` command is to *always* run it first with the `hg -n` option. This will show you what the command *would* send, without actually sending anything. Once you've had a quick glance over the changes and verified that you are sending the right ones, you can rerun the same command, with the `hg -n` option removed.

The `email` command accepts the same kind of revision syntax as every other Mercurial command. For example, this command will send every revision between 7 and `tip`, inclusive.

```
hg email -n 7:tip
```

You can also specify a *repository* to compare with. If you provide a repository but no revisions, the `email` command will send all revisions in the local repository that are not present in the remote repository. If you additionally specify revisions or a branch name (the latter using the `hg -b` option), this will constrain the revisions sent.

It's perfectly safe to run the `email` command without the names of the people you want to send to: if you do this, it will just prompt you for those values interactively. (If you're using a Linux or Unix-like system, you should have enhanced `readline`-style editing capabilities when entering those headers, too, which is useful.)

When you are sending just one revision, the `email` command will by default use the first line of the changeset description as the subject of the single email message it sends.

If you send multiple revisions, the `email` command will usually send one message per changeset. It will preface the series with an introductory message, in which you should describe the purpose of the series of changes you're sending.

Changing the Behavior of Patchbombs

Not every project has exactly the same conventions for sending changes in email; the `patchbomb` extension tries to accommodate a number of variations through command-line options.

- You can write a subject for the introductory message on the command line using the `hg -s` option. This takes one argument, the text of the subject to use.

- To change the email address from which the messages originate, use the `hg -f` option. This takes one argument, the email address to use.

- The default behavior is to send unified diffs (see "Understanding Patches" on page 186 for a description of the format), one per message. You can send a binary bundle instead with the `hg -b` option.

- Unified diffs are normally prefaced with a metadata header. You can omit this and send unadorned diffs with the `hg --plain` option.

- Diffs are normally sent "inline," in the same body part as the description of a patch. This makes it easiest for the largest number of readers to quote and respond to parts of a diff, as some mail clients will only quote the first MIME body part in a message. If you'd prefer to send the description and the diff in separate body parts, use the `hg -a` option.

- Instead of sending mail messages, you can write them to an `mbox`-format mail folder using the `hg -m` option. That option takes one argument, the name of the file to write to.

- If you would like to add a `diffstat`-format summary to each patch, and one to the introductory message, use the `hg -d` option. The `diffstat` command displays a table containing the name of each file patched, the number of lines affected, and a histogram showing how much each file is modified. This gives readers a qualitative glance at how complex a patch is.

Migrating to Mercurial

A common way to test the waters with a new revision control tool is to experiment with switching over an existing project, rather than starting a new project from scratch.

In this appendix, we discuss how to import a project's history into Mercurial, and what to look out for if you are used to a different revision control system.

Importing History from Another System

Mercurial ships with an extension named **convert**, which can import project history from most popular revision control systems. At the time this book was written, Mercurial could import history from the following systems:

- Subversion
- CVS
- Git
- Darcs
- Bazaar
- Monotone
- GNU Arch
- Mercurial

(To see why Mercurial itself is supported as a source, see "Tidying Up the Tree" on page 227.)

You can enable the extension in the usual way, by editing your *~/.hgrc* file.

```
[extensions]
convert =
```

This will make an easy-to-use **hg convert** command available. For instance, the following command will import the Subversion history for the Nose unit testing framework into Mercurial.

```
$ hg convert http://python-nose.googlecode.com/svn/trunk
```

The convert extension operates incrementally. In other words, after you have run hg convert once, running it again will import any new revisions committed after the first run began. Incremental conversion will only work if you run hg convert in the same Mercurial repository that you originally used, because the convert extension saves some private metadata in a non-revision controlled file named *.hg/shamap* inside the target repository.

When you want to start making changes using Mercurial, it's best to clone the tree in which you are doing your conversions, and leave the original tree for future incremental conversions. This is the safest way to let you pull and merge future commits from the source revision control system into your newly active Mercurial project.

Converting Multiple Branches

The hg convert command given above converts only the history of the trunk branch of the Subversion repository. If we instead use the URL http://python-nose.google code.com/svn, Mercurial will automatically detect the trunk, tags, and branches layout that Subversion projects usually use, and it will import each as a separate Mercurial branch.

By default, each Subversion branch imported into Mercurial is given a branch name. After the conversion completes, you can get a list of the active branch names in the Mercurial repository using hg branches -a. If you would prefer to import the Subversion branches without names, pass the --config convert.hg.usebranchnames=false option to hg convert.

Once you have converted your tree, if you want to follow the usual Mercurial practice of working in a tree that contains a single branch, you can clone that single branch using hg clone -r mybranchname.

Mapping Usernames

Some revision control tools save only short usernames with commits, and these can be difficult to interpret. The norm with Mercurial is to save a committer's name and email address, which is much more useful for talking to them after the fact.

If you are converting a tree from a revision control system that uses short names, you can map those names to longer equivalents by passing the --authors option to hg convert. This option accepts a filename that should contain entries of the following form.

```
arist = Aristotle <aristotle@phil.example.gr>
soc = Socrates <socrates@phil.example.gr>
```

Whenever `convert` encounters a commit with the username `arist` in the source repository, it will use the name `Aristotle <aristotle@phil.example.gr>` in the converted Mercurial revision. If no match is found for a name, it is used verbatim.

Tidying Up the Tree

Not all projects have pristine history. There may be a directory that should never have been checked in, a file that is too big, or a whole hierarchy that needs to be refactored.

The `convert` extension supports the idea of a "file map" that can reorganize the files and directories in a project as it imports the project's history. This is useful not only when importing history from other revision control systems, but also to prune or refactor a Mercurial tree.

To specify a file map, use the `--filemap` option and supply a filename. A file map contains lines of the following forms.

```
# This is a comment.
# Empty lines are ignored.

include path/to/file

exclude path/to/file

rename from/some/path to/some/other/place
```

The `include` directive causes a file, or all files under a directory, to be included in the destination repository. This also excludes all other files and directories not explicitly included. The `exclude` directive causes files or directories to be omitted, and others not explicitly mentioned to be included.

To move a file or directory from one location to another, use the `rename` directive. If you need to move a file or directory from a subdirectory into the root of the repository, use . as the second argument to the `rename` directive.

Improving Subversion Conversion Performance

You will often need several attempts before you hit the perfect combination of user map, file map, and other conversion parameters. Converting a Subversion repository over an access protocol like ssh or http can proceed thousands of times slower than Mercurial is capable of operating due to network delays. This can make tuning that perfect conversion recipe very painful.

The `svnsync` (*http://svn.collab.net/repos/svn/trunk/notes/svnsync.txt*) command can greatly speed up the conversion of a Subversion repository. It is a read-only mirroring program for Subversion repositories. The idea is that you create a local mirror of your Subversion tree, then convert the mirror into a Mercurial repository.

Suppose we want to convert the Subversion repository for the popular Memcached project into a Mercurial tree. First, we create a local Subversion repository.

```
$ svnadmin create memcached-mirror
```

Next, we set up a Subversion hook that svnsync needs.

```
$ echo '#!/bin/sh' > memcached-mirror/hooks/pre-revprop-change
$ chmod +x memcached-mirror/hooks/pre-revprop-change
```

We then initialize svnsync in this repository.

```
$ svnsync --init file://`pwd`/memcached-mirror \
    http://code.sixapart.com/svn/memcached
```

Our next step is to begin the svnsync mirroring process.

```
$ svnsync sync file://`pwd`/memcached-mirror
```

Finally, we import the history of our local Subversion mirror into Mercurial.

```
$ hg convert memcached-mirror
```

We can use this process incrementally if the Subversion repository is still in use. We run svnsync to pull new changes into our mirror, then hg convert to import them into our Mercurial tree.

There are two advantages to doing a two-stage import with svnsync. The first is that it uses more efficient Subversion network syncing code than hg convert, so it transfers less data over the network. The second is that the import from a local Subversion tree is so fast that you can tweak your conversion setup repeatedly without having to sit through a painfully slow network-based conversion process each time.

Migrating from Subversion

Subversion is currently the most popular open source revision control system. Although there are many differences between Mercurial and Subversion, making the transition from Subversion to Mercurial is not particularly difficult. The two have similar command sets and generally uniform interfaces.

Philosophical Differences

The fundamental difference between Subversion and Mercurial is of course that Subversion is centralized, while Mercurial is distributed. Since Mercurial stores all of a project's history on your local drive, it only needs to perform a network access when you want to explicitly communicate with another repository. In contrast, Subversion stores very little information locally, and the client must thus contact its server for many common operations.

Subversion more or less gets away with not having a well-defined notion of a branch: which portion of a server's namespace qualifies as a branch is a matter of convention, with the software providing no enforcement. Mercurial treats a repository as the unit of branch management.

Scope of commands

Since Subversion doesn't know what parts of its namespace are really branches, it treats most commands as requests to operate at and below whatever directory you are currently visiting. For instance, if you run `svn log`, you'll get the history of whatever part of the tree you're looking at, not the tree as a whole.

Mercurial's commands behave differently, by defaulting to operating over an entire repository. Run `hg log` and it will tell you the history of the entire tree, no matter what part of the working directory you're visiting at the time. If you want the history of just a particular file or directory, simply supply it by name, e.g., `hg log src`.

From my own experience, this difference in default behaviors is probably the most likely to trip you up if you have to switch back and forth frequently between the two tools.

Multi-user operation and safety

With Subversion, it is normal (though slightly frowned upon) for multiple people to collaborate in a single branch. If Alice and Bob are working together, and Alice commits some changes to their shared branch, Bob must update his client's view of the branch before he can commit. Since at this time he has no permanent record of the changes he has made, he can corrupt or lose his modifications during and after his update.

Mercurial encourages a commit-then-merge model instead. Bob commits his changes locally before pulling changes from, or pushing them to, the server that he shares with Alice. If Alice pushed her changes before Bob tries to push his, he will not be able to push his changes until he pulls hers, merges with them, and commits the result of the merge. If he makes a mistake during the merge, he still has the option of reverting to the commit that recorded his changes.

It is worth emphasizing that these are the common ways of working with these tools. Subversion supports a safer work-in-your-own-branch model, but it is cumbersome enough in practice to not be widely used. Mercurial can support the less-safe mode of allowing changes to be pulled in and merged on top of uncommitted edits, but this is considered highly unusual.

Published versus local changes

A Subversion `svn commit` command immediately publishes changes to a server, where they can be seen by everyone who has read access.

With Mercurial, commits are always local, and must be published via a `hg push` command afterwards.

Each approach has its advantages and disadvantages. The Subversion model means that changes are published, and hence reviewable and usable, immediately. On the other hand, this means that a user must have commit access to a repository in order to use the software in a normal way, and commit access is not lightly given out by most open source projects.

The Mercurial approach allows anyone who can clone a repository to commit changes without the need for someone else's permission, and they can then publish their changes and continue to participate however they see fit. The distinction between committing and pushing does open up the possibility of someone committing changes to their laptop and walking away for a few days having forgotten to push them, which in rare cases might leave collaborators temporarily stuck.

Quick Reference

Table A-1. Subversion commands and Mercurial equivalents

Subversion	Mercurial	Notes
svn add	hg add	
svn blame	hg annotate	
svn cat	hg cat	
svn checkout	hg clone	
svn cleanup	n/a	No cleanup needed
svn commit	hg commit; hg push	hg push publishes after commit
svn copy	hg clone	To create a new branch
svn copy	hg copy	To copy files or directories
svn delete (svn remove)	hg remove	
svn diff	hg diff	
svn export	hg archive	
svn help	hg help	
svn import	hg addremove; hg commit	
svn info	hg parents	Shows what revision is checked out
svn info	hg showconfig paths.parent	Shows what URL is checked out
svn list	hg manifest	
svn log	hg log	
svn merge	hg merge	
svn mkdir	n/a	Mercurial does not track directories
svn move (svn rename)	hg rename	
svn resolved	hg resolve -m	
svn revert	hg revert	

Subversion	Mercurial	Notes
svn status	hg status	
svn update	hg pull -u	

Useful Tips for Newcomers

Under some revision control systems, printing a diff for a single committed revision can be painful. For instance, with Subversion, to see what changed in revision 104654, you must type `svn diff -r104653:104654`. Mercurial eliminates the need to type the revision ID twice in this common case. For a plain diff, type `hg export 104654`. For a log message followed by a diff, type `hg log -r104654 -p`.

When you run `hg status` without any arguments, it prints the status of the entire tree, with paths relative to the root of the repository. This makes it tricky to copy a filename from the output of `hg status` into the command line. If you supply a file or directory name to `hg status`, it will print paths relative to your current location instead. So to get tree-wide status from `hg status`, with paths that are relative to your current directory and not the root of the repository, feed the output of `hg root` into `hg status`. You can easily do this as follows on a Unix-like system:

```
$ hg status `hg root`
```

Mercurial Queues Reference

MQ Command Reference

For an overview of the commands provided by MQ, use the command `hg help mq`.

qapplied—Print Applied Patches

The `qapplied` command prints the current stack of applied patches. Patches are printed in oldest-to-newest order, so the last patch in the list is the "top" patch.

qcommit—Commit Changes in the Queue Repository

The `qcommit` command commits any outstanding changes in the *.hg/patches* repository. This command only works if the *.hg/patches* directory is a repository, i.e., you created the directory using `hg qinit -c` or ran `hg init` in the directory after running `qinit`.

This command is shorthand for `hg commit --cwd .hg/patches`.

qdelete—Delete a Patch from the Series File

The `qdelete` command removes the entry for a patch from the *series* file in the *.hg/patches* directory. It does not pop the patch if the patch is already applied. By default, it does not delete the patch file; use the `-f` option to do that.

Option:

- `-f`: Delete the patch file.

qdiff—Print a Diff of the Topmost Applied Patch

The `qdiff` command prints a diff of the topmost applied patch. It is equivalent to `hg diff -r -2:-1`.

qfold—Move Applied Patches into Repository History

The `hg qfinish` command converts the specified applied patches into permanent changes by moving them out of MQ's control so that they will be treated as normal repository history.

qfold—Merge (fold) Several Patches into One

The `qfold` command merges multiple patches into the topmost applied patch, so that the topmost applied patch makes the union of all the changes in the patches in question.

The patches to fold must not be applied; `qfold` will exit with an error if this is the case. The order in which patches are folded is significant: `hg qfold a b` means "apply the current topmost patch, followed by `a`, followed by `b`".

The comments from the folded patches are appended to the comments of the destination patch, with each block of comments separated by three asterisk (*) characters. Use the `-e` option to edit the commit message for the combined patch/changeset after the folding has completed.

Options:

- `-e`: Edit the commit message and patch description for the newly folded patch.
- `-l`: Use the contents of the given file as the new commit message and patch description for the folded patch.
- `-m`: Use the given text as the new commit message and patch description for the folded patch.

qheader—Display the Header/Description of a Patch

The `qheader` command prints the header, or description, of a patch. By default, it prints the header of the topmost applied patch. Given an argument, it prints the header of the named patch.

qimport—Import a Third-Party Patch into the Queue

The `qimport` command adds an entry for an external patch to the *series* file, and copies the patch into the *.hg/patches* directory. It adds the entry immediately after the topmost applied patch, but does not push the patch.

If the *.hg/patches* directory is a repository, `qimport` automatically does an `hg add` of the imported patch.

qinit—Prepare a Repository to Work with MQ

The `qinit` command prepares a repository to work with MQ. It creates a directory called *.hg/patches*.

Option:

- `-c`: Create *.hg/patches* as a repository in its own right. Also creates a *.hgignore* file that will ignore the *status* file.

When the *.hg/patches* directory is a repository, the `qimport` and `qnew` commands automatically `hg add` new patches.

qnew—Create a New Patch

The `qnew` command creates a new patch. It takes one mandatory argument, the name to use for the patch file. The newly created patch is created empty by default. It is added to the *series* file after the current topmost applied patch, and is immediately pushed on top of that patch.

If `qnew` finds modified files in the working directory, it will refuse to create a new patch unless the `-f` option is used (see below). This behavior allows you to `qrefresh` your topmost applied patch before you apply a new patch on top of it.

Options:

- `-f`: Create a new patch if the contents of the working directory are modified. Any outstanding modifications are added to the newly created patch, so after this command completes, the working directory will no longer be modified.
- `-m`: Use the given text as the commit message. This text will be stored at the beginning of the patch file, before the patch data.

qnext—Print the Name of the Next Patch

The `qnext` command prints the name of the next patch in the *series* file after the topmost applied patch. This patch will become the topmost applied patch if you run `qpush`.

qpop—Pop Patches Off the Stack

The `qpop` command removes applied patches from the top of the stack of applied patches. By default, it removes only one patch.

This command removes the changesets that represent the popped patches from the repository, and updates the working directory to undo the effects of the patches.

The qpop command takes an optional argument, which it uses as the name or index of the patch to pop to. If given a name, it will pop patches until the named patch is the topmost applied patch. If given a number, `qpop` treats the number as an index into the entries in the *series* file, counting from zero (empty lines and lines containing only comments do not count). It pops patches until the patch identified by the given index is the topmost applied patch.

The `qpop` command does not read or write patches or the *series* file. It is thus safe to `qpop` a patch that you have removed from the *series* file, or a patch that you have renamed or deleted entirely. In the latter two cases, use the name of the patch as it was when you applied it.

By default, the `qpop` command will not pop any patches if the working directory has been modified. You can override this behavior using the `-f` option, which reverts all modifications in the working directory.

Options:

- `-a`: Pop all applied patches. This returns the repository to its state before you applied any patches.
- `-f`: Forcibly revert any modifications to the working directory when popping.
- `-n`: Pop a patch from the named queue.

The `qpop` command removes one line from the end of the *status* file for each patch that it pops.

qprev—Print the Name of the Previous Patch

The `qprev` command prints the name of the patch in the *series* file that comes before the topmost applied patch. This will become the topmost applied patch if you run `qpop`.

qpush—Push Patches onto the Stack

The `qpush` command adds patches onto the applied stack. By default, it adds only one patch.

This command creates a new changeset to represent each applied patch, and updates the working directory to apply the effects of the patches.

The default data used when creating a changeset is as follows:

- The commit date and time zone are the current date and time zone. Because this data is used to compute the identity of a changeset, this means that if you `qpop` a patch and `qpush` it again, the changeset that you push will have a different identity from the changeset you popped.
- The author is the same as the default used by the `hg commit` command.
- The commit message is any text from the patch file that comes before the first diff header. If there is no such text, a default commit message is used that identifies the name of the patch.

If a patch contains a Mercurial patch header, the information in the patch header overrides these defaults.

Options:

- `-a`: Push all unapplied patches from the *series* file until there is none left to push.
- `-l`: Add the name of the patch to the end of the commit message.
- `-m`: If a patch fails to apply cleanly, use the entry for the patch in another saved queue to compute the parameters for a three-way merge, and perform a three-way merge using the normal Mercurial merge machinery. Use the resolution of the merge as the new patch content.
- `-n`: Use the named queue if merging while pushing.

The `qpush` command reads, but does not modify, the *series* file. It appends one line to the `hg status` file for each patch that it pushes.

qrefresh—Update the Topmost Applied Patch

The `qrefresh` command updates the topmost applied patch. It modifies the patch, removes the old changeset that represented the patch, and creates a new changeset to represent the modified patch.

The `qrefresh` command looks for the following modifications:

- Changes to the commit message, i.e., the text before the first diff header in the patch file, are reflected in the new changeset that represents the patch.
- Modifications to tracked files in the working directory are added to the patch.
- Changes to the files tracked using `hg add`, `hg copy`, `hg remove`, or `hg rename`.
- Added files and copy and rename destinations are added to the patch, while removed files and rename sources are removed.

Even if `qrefresh` detects no changes, it still recreates the changeset that represents the patch. This causes the identity of the changeset to differ from the previous changeset that identified the patch.

Options:

- `-e`: Modify the commit and patch description, using the preferred text editor.
- `-m`: Modify the commit message and patch description, using the given text.
- `-l`: Modify the commit message and patch description, using text from the given file.

qrename—Rename a Patch

The `qrename` command renames a patch, and changes the entry for the patch in the *series* file.

With a single argument, qrename renames the topmost applied patch. With two arguments, it renames its first argument to its second.

qseries—Print the Entire Patch Series

The qseries command prints the entire patch series from the *series* file. It prints only patch names, not empty lines or comments. It prints in order from first to be applied to last.

qtop—Print the Name of the Current Patch

The qtop command prints the name of the topmost currently applied patch.

qunapplied—Print Patches Not yet Applied

The qunapplied command prints the names of patches from the *series* file that are not yet applied. It prints them in order from the next patch that will be pushed to the last.

hg strip—Remove a Revision and Descendants

The hg strip command removes a revision, and all of its descendants, from the repository. It undoes the effects of the removed revisions from the repository, and updates the working directory to the first parent of the removed revision.

The hg strip command saves a backup of the removed changesets in a bundle, so that they can be reapplied if removed in error.

Options:

- -b: Save unrelated changesets that are intermixed with the stripped changesets in the backup bundle.
- -f: If a branch has multiple heads, remove all heads.
- -n: Do not save a backup bundle.

MQ File Reference

The Series File

The *series* file contains a list of the names of all patches that MQ can apply. It is represented as a list of names, with one name saved per line. Leading and trailing whitespace in each line is ignored.

Lines may contain comments. A comment begins with the # character, and extends to the end of the line. Empty lines, and lines that contain only comments, are ignored.

You will often need to edit the *series* file by hand, hence the support for comments and empty lines noted above. For example, you can comment out a patch temporarily, and `qpush` will skip over that patch when applying patches. You can also change the order in which patches are applied by reordering their entries in the *series* file.

Placing the *series* file under revision control is also supported; it is a good idea to place all of the patches that it refers to under revision control, as well. If you create a patch directory using the `-c` option to `qinit`, this will be done for you automatically.

The Status File

The *status* file contains the names and changeset hashes of all patches that MQ currently has applied. Unlike the *series* file, this file is not intended for editing. You should not place this file under revision control, or modify it in any way. It is used by MQ strictly for internal bookkeeping.

Installing Mercurial from Source

On a Unix-Like System

If you are using a Unix-like system that has a sufficiently recent version of Python (2.3 or newer) available, it is easy to install Mercurial from source. Here's how:

1. Download a recent source tarball from *http://www.selenic.com/mercurial/down load*.

2. Unpack the tarball:

   ```
   gzip -dc mercurial-MYVERSION.tar.gz | tar xf -
   ```

3. Go into the source directory and run the installer script. This will build Mercurial and install it in your home directory.

   ```
   cd mercurial-MYVERSION
   python setup.py install --force --home=$HOME
   ```

Once the install finishes, Mercurial will be in the *bin* subdirectory of your home directory. Don't forget to make sure that this directory is present in your shell's search path.

You will probably need to set the PYTHONPATH environment variable so that the Mercurial executable can find the rest of the Mercurial packages. For example, on my laptop, I have set it to */home/bos/lib/python*. The exact path that you will need to use depends on how Python was built for your system, but should be easy to figure out. If you're uncertain, look through the output of the installer script above, and see where the contents of the *mercurial* directory were installed to.

On Windows

Building and installing Mercurial on Windows requires a variety of tools, a fair amount of technical knowledge, and considerable patience. I very much do *not* recommend this route if you are a "casual user." Unless you intend to hack on Mercurial, I strongly suggest that you use a binary package instead.

If you are intent on building Mercurial from source on Windows, follow the "hard way" directions on the Mercurial wiki at *http://www.selenic.com/mercurial/wiki/index .cgi/WindowsInstall*, and expect the process to involve a lot of fiddly work.

Open Publication License

Version 1.0, 8 June 1999

Requirements on Both Unmodified and Modified Versions

The Open Publication works may be reproduced and distributed in whole or in part, in any medium physical or electronic, provided that the terms of this license are adhered to, and that this license or an incorporation of it by reference (with any options elected by the author(s) and/or publisher) is displayed in the reproduction.

Proper form for an incorporation by reference is as follows:

> Copyright (c) *year* by *author's name or designee*. This material may be distributed only subject to the terms and conditions set forth in the Open Publication License, v*x.y* or later (the latest version is presently available at *http://www.opencontent.org/openpub/*).

The reference must be immediately followed with any options elected by the author(s) and/or publisher of the document (see "License Options" on page 245).

Commercial redistribution of Open Publication-licensed material is permitted.

Any publication in standard (paper) book form shall require the citation of the original publisher and author. The publisher and author's names shall appear on all outer surfaces of the book. On all outer surfaces of the book the original publisher's name shall be as large as the title of the work and cited as possessive with respect to the title.

Copyright

The copyright to each Open Publication is owned by its author(s) or designee.

Scope of License

The following license terms apply to all Open Publication works, unless otherwise explicitly stated in the document.

Mere aggregation of Open Publication works or a portion of an Open Publication work with other works or programs on the same media shall not cause this license to apply to those other works. The aggregate work shall contain a notice specifying the inclusion of the Open Publication material and appropriate copyright notice.

Severability. If any part of this license is found to be unenforceable in any jurisdiction, the remaining portions of the license remain in force.

No warranty. Open Publication works are licensed and provided "as is" without warranty of any kind, express or implied, including, but not limited to, the implied warranties of merchantability and fitness for a particular purpose or a warranty of non-infringement.

Requirements on Modified Works

All modified versions of documents covered by this license, including translations, anthologies, compilations and partial documents, must meet the following requirements:

1. The modified version must be labeled as such.
2. The person making the modifications must be identified and the modifications dated.
3. Acknowledgment of the original author and publisher, if applicable, must be retained according to normal academic citation practices.
4. The location of the original unmodified document must be identified.
5. The original author's (or authors') name(s) may not be used to assert or imply endorsement of the resulting document without the original author's (or authors') permission.

Good-Practice Recommendations

In addition to the requirements of this license, it is requested from and strongly recommended of redistributors that:

1. If you are distributing Open Publication works on hardcopy or CD-ROM, you provide email notification to the author(s) of your intent to redistribute at least thirty days before your manuscript or media freeze, to give the author(s) time to provide updated documents. This notification should describe modifications, if any, made to the document.
2. All substantive modifications (including deletions) be either clearly marked up in the document or else described in an attachment to the document.
3. Finally, while it is not mandatory under this license, it is considered good form to offer a free copy of any hardcopy and CD-ROM expression of an Open Publication-licensed work to its author(s).

License Options

The author(s) and/or publisher of an Open Publication-licensed document may elect certain options by appending language to the reference to or copy of the license. These options are considered part of the license instance and must be included with the license (or its incorporation by reference) in derived works.

1. To prohibit distribution of substantively modified versions without the explicit permission of the author(s). "Substantive modification" is defined as a change to the semantic content of the document, and excludes mere changes in format or typographical corrections.

2. To accomplish this, add the phrase "Distribution of substantively modified versions of this document is prohibited without the explicit permission of the copyright holder." to the license reference or copy.

3. To prohibit any publication of this work or derivative works in whole or in part in standard (paper) book form for commercial purposes unless prior permission is obtained from the copyright holder.

4. To accomplish this, add the phrase "Distribution of the work or derivative of the work in any standard (paper) book form is prohibited unless prior permission is obtained from the copyright holder." to the license reference or copy.

Index

Symbols

* (asterisk) in pattern matching, 104
** (asterisks) in pattern matching, 104
\ (backslash) for escape sequences, 175
{ } (braces) in pattern matching, 104, 173
[ ] (brackets) in pattern matching, 104
! (exclamation point)
    in hg status output, 64
    in pattern matching, 104
- (hyphen)
    for negative guards, 209
    in unified diffs, 186
+ (plus sign)
    for negative guards, 209
    in unified diffs, 186
for comments in .hgrc files, 24
? (question mark)
    in hg status output, 61
    in pattern matching, 104

A

aborting commits, 26
accepted group (patches), 212
access control for repositories, 154–156
access privileges, hooks and, 146
accesslog option (hg serve), 98
acclaim-based collaboration models, 84
acl extension, 154–156, 217
[acl] section (.hgrc file)
    sources entry, 155
activity control (hooks), 145, 149, 150
addbreaks filter (templates), 175
adding files to repositories, 31, 61
    add-remove in one step, 64

adding files to repository
    entire directories of files, 62
    undoing add, 71, 121, 125
address option (hg serve), 98
age filter (templates), 175
aliases for commands, defining, 222
allow_archive web configuration option, 96
allowpull web configuration option, 97
anarchy (collaboration model), 79
Apache web server, 92
appending to revlog files, 47
applied vs. known patches, 190
* (asterisk) in pattern matching, 104
** (asterisks) in pattern matching, 104
Atom feeds of repository changes, 77
atomicity of Mercurial transactions, 48
atomicity of repositories, 57
authentication, hg serve and, 86
authentication agents for ssh, 88, 89
author keyword (templates), 173

B

backing out of changesets, 126–132
backing out of merges, 133
backport group (patches), 212, 213
\ (backslash) for escape sequences, 175
backups of repositories, 76
base repository, creating, 211
base version, 39
basename filter (templates), 175
benefits of revision control, 1–3
    distributed approach to, 4–6
Berliner, Brian, 11
big-picture branches, 113
binary files, tracking, 74

We'd like to hear your suggestions for improving our indexes. Send email to *index@oreilly.com*.

Blandy, Jim, 11
{ } (braces) in pattern matching, 104, 173
[ ] (brackets) in pattern matching, 104
branches, 50
    big-picture branches, 113
    creating new, 116
    hg bisect command and, 138
    for individual features, 82
    for isolated development directions, 80–82
    little-picture branches, 113
    managing, when collaborating, 85
    merging across, 66, 114
    migrating to Mercurial, 226
    naming, 115–117, 119
    with very many targets, 208
branches keyword (templates), 174
bugs, finding changesets with, 137–142
    tips for, 142–144
Bugzilla, integration with, 156–159
bugzilla extension, 156–159, 217
[bugzilla] section (.hgrc file), 157
built-in help for Mercurial, 14
bundle entry, [acl] section (.hgrc), 155
bundled hooks, 154–162
bundled styles, 171
Burrows-Wheeler compression algorithm, 56

C

Cantey, Lee, 13
capitalization sensitivity with file names, 107
case sensitivity of file names, 107
central repository (collaboration models), 79
    hosted repository, 80
    single (unhosted) repository, 80
CGI interface for Mercurial, 91–98
changegroup hook, 145, 164
changelog style (output), 172
changelogs, 46
changeset field (hg log output), 17
changeset IDs (identifiers), 17, 18, 35
    using tags for, 110
changesets, 17
    backing out of, 126–132
    with bugs, finding, 137–142
        tips for, 142–144
    displaying newest, 26
    email notification with, 160–162
    head changesets, 34
        multiple in repository, 118

head changesets, creating new, 53
    identifying current branch for, 115
    manifests, 46
    merge process, 54
    origin of, determining, 163
    propagating into other repositories, 26–31
    recording information in changelogs, 46
    removing completely from history
        (impossible), 136
    removing with descendants, 238
    viewing specific revisions, 18
character classes, 104
children of parent changesets, 34
chmod command, 92
choosing a revision control tool, 10
cloning repositories, 15, 21
    before making backups, 76
    tags and, 112
collaboration workflow, 77–99
    models for, 78–85
    not sharing hooks, 147
    problem of many targets, 207
    technical issues, 85–99
        information sharing with hg serve, 85–
           86
        system-wide configuration, 99
        using ssh protocol, 86–91
        web server configuration, 91–98
    web interface for Mercurial, 77–78
[collections] section (hgweb.config file), 95
combining patches, 205
commands
    defining aliases for, 222
    directories as arguments, 62
    getting help on, 14
    options for, about, 20
    running without file names, 101
comments in .hgrc files, 24
commercial projects, 6
commercial revision control tools, 10
commit hook, 145, 148, 152, 164
commit messages, 24
    writing meaningful, hook for, 152
committers, mapping to Bugzilla user names,
    158
committing changes, 23–26
    aborting process of, 26
    backing out of changesets, 126–132
    of merges, 37

sensitive information release, handling, 135

pushing patches, 184

   several patches at once, 191

Python functions, hooks as, 150, 151, 162

PYTHONPATH environment variable, 90, 241

Q

-q option (for several commands), 103

qapplied command (MQ), 190, 233

qcommit command (MQ), 201, 233

qdelete command (MQ), 196, 233

qdiff command (MQ), 233

qfinish command (MQ), 196, 234

qfold command (MQ), 205, 234

qguard command (MQ), 209

qheader command (MQ), 234

qimport command (MQ), 234

   hg -r option, 196

qinit command (MQ), 187, 235

   hg -c option, 201

qnew command (MQ), 187, 189, 235

qnext command (MQ), 235

qpop command

   effects of guards on, 210

qpop command (MQ), 190, 235

   batching operations with, 197

   hg -a option, 191

   hg -f option, 192

   updating patches when underlying code changes, 197

qprev command (MQ), 236

qpush command

   effects of guards on, 210

qpush command (MQ), 190, 236

   batching operations with, 197

   hg -a option, 191

   hg -f option, 192

   rejected patches, 194, 195

   updating patches when underlying code changes, 197

qrefresh command (MQ), 188, 192, 237

qrename command (MQ), 237

qselect command (MQ), 210

qseries command (MQ), 190, 238

qtop command (MQ), 203, 238

? (question mark)

   in hg status output, 61

in pattern matching, 104

quilt tool, 184, 206

Quinson, Martin, 184

qunapplied command (MQ), 238

R

R symbol (hg status output), 73

range notation, 19

RCS (Revision Control System), 11

re syntax (patterns), 103, 105

read/write ordering, 57

recompression of compressed data, 56

recovering deleted files, 64

recovering from mistakes, 71

   erasing local history, 121–123

   reverting mistaken changes, 124–125

redefining hooks, 147

refreshing patches, 188

regular expression (regexp) matching, 105

rejected hunks, in patch application, 194, 195

release management, 109–119

   merging across branches, 66

   persistent names for revisions, 109–112

     local tags (not revision controlled), 112

     tagging with guards, 208–211

   problem of many targets, 207

release train (collaboration model), 83

remote repositories, sharing with, 30

remote repository URLs, 163

removing files from repositories, 63–65

   add-remove in one step, 64

   undoing remove, 71, 121, 125

removing tags from changesets, 111

rename directive (convert extension), 227

renaming branches, 116

renaming files, 43, 56, 68–70

   handling divergent renames, 69

renaming patches, 237

repositories, 15–16

   access control for, 154–156

   adding new files to, 31, 61

     add-remove in one step, 64

   backups and mirrors, 76

   base trees, 211

   case-safe storage, 107

   concurrent access to, 57

   contents of, 16

   default location for, setting, 30

   empty directories in, 62

video compression techniques, 48

W

web interface for Mercurial, 77–78
    system-wide configuration, 99
[web] section (hgweb.config file), 96
web server collaboration, 91–98
    configuring, as really painful, 91
whitespace (trailing) in code, checking for,
        152
Windows, installing Mercurial on, 13, 241
working directory, 50
    case conflicts, detecting and fixing, 107–
        108
    operating on, 102
    parents of, 50
        when merging changes, 54
    removed files and, 64
    safety checks with MQ commands, 192
    undoing changes to, 71, 121
    updated when merging, 36
    updating, 28
    updating to different changeset, 53

X

-X (--exclude) option (for several commands),
        105

About the Author

Bryan O'Sullivan is an Irish writer and developer who works with distributed systems, open source software, and programming languages. He coauthored the award-winning O'Reilly title *Real World Haskell*. He has made significant contributions to the popular Mercurial revision control system, and to a number of other open source projects. He lives in San Francisco with his family. Whenever he can, he runs off to climb rocks.

Colophon

The animal on the cover of *Mercurial: The Definitive Guide* is a House Martin (*Delichon urbicum*), which is part of the swallow family. Originally cliff and cave dwellers, these noisy birds now prefer human structures and can be found nesting in bridges and houses throughout Europe, north Africa, and the more temperate regions of Asia. The name House Martin is derived from the bird's tendency to build its nests under the eaves of buildings. They build closed-cup nests, attached to both the vertical surface and the overhang of the structure, and reinforce them with mud, creating unusually strong dwellings.

Given the House Martin's wide range of habitation, if you are trying to avoid the eternal pit of peril and are presented with the immortal question, "Is that an African swallow or a European swallow?", you should answer, "Both."

The cover image is from *Cassell's Natural History*. The cover font is Adobe ITC Garamond. The text font is Linotype Birka; the heading font is Adobe Myriad Condensed; and the code font is LucasFont's TheSansMonoCondensed.

Related Titles from O'Reilly

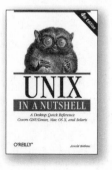

Unix Administration

Classic Shell Scripting

DNS and BIND, *5th Edition*

DNS & BIND Cookbook

Essential System
Administration, *3rd Edition*

Essential System Administration
Pocket Reference

Postfix: The Definitive Guide

qmail

sendmail, *4th Edition*

sendmail Cookbook

System Performance Tuning,
2nd Edition

Unix Basics

bash Cookbook

GNU Emacs Pocket Reference

Learning GNU Emacs,
3rd Edition

Learning the bash Shell,
3rd Edition

Learning the Korn Shell,
2nd Edition

Learning the Unix Operating
System, *5th Edition*

Learning the vi Editor,
6th Edition

sed & awk Pocket Reference,
2nd Edition

sed & awk, *2nd Edition*

Unix in a Nutshell, *4th Edition*

Using csh & tcsh

Unix Tools

BSD Hacks

CVS Pocket Reference,
2nd Edition

Effective awk Programming,
3rd Edition

Essential CVS, *2nd Edition*

GDB Pocket Reference

lex & yacc, *2nd Edition*

Managing Projects with GNU
make, *3rd Edition*

Practical PostgreSQL

The Complete FreeBSD,
4th Edition

Unix Power Tools, *3rd edition*

Version Control with
Subversion

O'REILLY®